# ˈER

# WITHOUT CONSTRAINT

## THE POST-9/11 PRESIDENCY AND
## NATIONAL SECURITY

CHRIS EDELSON

The University of Wisconsin Press

The University of Wisconsin Press
1930 Monroe Street, 3rd Floor
Madison, Wisconsin 53711-2059
uwpress.wisc.edu

3 Henrietta Street, Covent Garden
London WC2E 8LU, United Kingdom
eurospanbookstore.com

Printed in the United States of America

This book may be available in a digital edition

Library of Congress Cataloging-in-Publication Data
Names: Edelson, Chris, author.
Title: Power without constraint: the post-9/11 presidency and national security / Chris Edelson.
Description: Madison, Wisconsin : The University of Wisconsin Press, [2016] | ©2016 |
Includes bibliographical references and index.
Identifiers: LCCN 2015036812 | ISBN 9780299307400 (cloth: alk. paper)
Subjects: LCSH: Executive power—United States—History—21st century. | National security—
United States. | Bush, George W. (George Walker), 1946– | Obama, Barack.
Classification: LCC JK511 .E34 2016 | DDC 363.325/15610973—dc23
LC record available at http://lccn.loc.gov/2015036812

anticipated by grant from

## FIGURE FOUNDATION

truth be a killer solution

For
**ANNABELLE**
whose beauty, intelligence, and love energize me

For
**PETER**
whose smile and demeanor radiate love

For
**KITTY**
whose ferocious love makes it all possible

# Contents

# Acknowledgments

I am deeply grateful to have the opportunity to write about issues that I find engaging and essential. I appreciate the University of Wisconsin Press and in particular Gwen Walker for supporting this project.

My grateful thanks to Ly Le for her research assistance and to Joshua Kennedy for his comments on an earlier version of some of this material that I presented at the Southern Political Science Association annual meeting in 2015.

Michael Genovese and Mitch Sollenberger provided valuable comments on the manuscript that improved this book, and I am deeply grateful to them for their feedback. Both Michael and Mitch helped make this a significantly better book and were generous both with their time and with their advice.

It is my great fortune to have gotten to know Lou Fisher, a giant and a legend in the field of presidential power but also a very down-to-earth person who has always been incredibly generous to me with his time, comments, and advice. I first got to know Lou after I e-mailed him in the winter of 2009. He took the time to respond to me in detail, even though I had contacted him completely out of the blue, and he agreed to speak to my presidential power class at American University. Ever since then, he has been a mentor and a friend. I have benefited immeasurably from speaking to Lou, from reading his own work in this field, and from specific comments he made that substantially improved this book. Lou embodies the spirit of the Constitution in the sense that he is a person who rejects hierarchy and pretension. His work and his way of interacting with other people each give meaning to the best promises made by the framers of the Constitution.

My wife, Jen Stark, also offered valuable comments that significantly improved this book. Without her, none of this would have been possible.

That is quite literally true, as she was instrumental in finding a way for me to do this work in the first place.

Although they did not directly comment on this book, my children, Annabelle and Peter, both contributed to it by providing me with the energy and enthusiasm that made it much easier (and more fun) to write this book.

# POWER WITHOUT CONSTRAINT

# INTRODUCTION

In 2008, Harold Koh, then dean of Yale Law School and later to serve in the Obama administration as legal adviser to the State Department, declared that "the next eight years will determine whether the pendulum of American policy will swing back from where it has been pushed, or whether it will stay stuck in the direction in which it has been pushed since September 11th [, 2001]."[1] What Koh meant, as he had made clear in the years following the September 11 attacks, was that the George W. Bush administration had dangerously overextended presidential power in areas such as torture, warrantless surveillance, and "the process of deciding whether to go to war."[2] In Koh's view, the Bush administration had "assert[ed] a constitutional theory of unfettered power, based on extraordinarily broad interpretations of the Article II Commander in Chief Clause and the Supreme Court's decision in *United States v. Curtiss-Wright Export Corp.*, which famously called the president the 'sole organ of the federal government in the field of international relations.'"[3] Koh, like other critics of the Bush administration's approach to national security power, rejected the idea of a president unconstrained by meaningful constitutional and statutory limits.

Candidate Obama agreed with Koh's critique of unchecked power as exercised by the Bush administration. When Barack Obama first ran for the presidency, he criticized the unitary executive theory and inherent power while promising to restore the rule of law and limits on presidential power. However, as discussed in this book, the Obama administration, like the Bush administration, has failed to recognize meaningful limits on presidential national security power. It is essential to emphasize at the outset that the two approaches are not identical. The Obama administration has rejected some of the specific methods employed by the Bush administration, including torture and extraordinary rendition.[4] In addition, the Obama administration does not seem to rely on inherent power and does not invoke the sole organ doctrine or speak the language of the unitary executive theory, a doctrine that expressly claims unilateral presidential authority to set aside the law. Significantly, the Obama administration has not claimed the authority to set aside criminal laws in the course of carrying out national security powers; the Bush administration, in contrast, relied on the unitary executive theory to set aside criminal laws in the areas of torture[5] and warrantless surveillance.[6]

The Obama administration has, however, found different ways to reach essentially the same conclusion as the Bush administration in a number of substantive areas. Specifically, like the Bush administration, the Obama administration has concluded that when it comes to the use of military force, targeted killing, state secrets, and surveillance, the president can do what he (or, at some point, she) wants, regardless of statutory and constitutional constraints. The Obama administration purports to respect statutory and constitutional limits on presidential power but ultimately finds ways around these would-be limits, sometimes with the acquiescence of Congress and the courts.

Other books on the Obama administration have reached different conclusions than I do here. Jack Goldsmith's *Power and Constraint: The Accountable Presidency after 9/11* argues that President Obama is continuing the approach of the post-2003 President Bush but that each has been effectively constrained when it comes to national security power.[7] I fully agree that there are similarities between presidents Obama and Bush but disagree with Goldsmith that either has been effectively constrained. In *The Executive Unbound: After the Madisonian Republic*, Eric Posner and Adrian Vermeule argue that the modern president (including after 9/11) cannot and should not be restrained by the rule of law.[8] I disagree with them, arguing that (1) subjecting presidents to the rule of law should be the goal, (2) President Obama is making a dangerous mistake by continuing President Bush's approach, and (3) Congress and the courts are making a mistake by failing to rein in unrestrained presidential action.

Some scholars have been critical of the Obama administration's use of national security power, but none has taken precisely the same approach or covered the same material as my book does. For example, Lou Fisher has written "Military Operations in Libya: No War? No Hostilities?," arguing that President Obama illegitimately authorized the use of military force against Libya in 2011 without congressional approval.[9] Bob Spitzer has written "Comparing the Constitutional Presidencies of George W. Bush and Barack Obama: War Powers, Signing Statements, Vetoes,"[10] and Dick Pious has written "Prerogative Power in the Obama Administration: Continuity and Change in the War on Terrorism."[11] I agree with Fisher and Spitzer that President Obama's authorization of military action in

Libya was illegitimate, and I agree with Pious that, in some areas, "Obama has not yielded any grounds in his claims for prerogative power, and in some respects he has gone even farther in these claims than his predecessors [including George W. Bush]."[12] However, my book takes a more comprehensive approach than these important articles, exploring President Obama's actions in more detail (including significant actions taken or exposed after these articles were published, such as Edward Snowden's revelations regarding surveillance and the Obama administration's military action against ISIS). Also, my book compares the Obama and the Bush administrations more directly than any of these scholars did. Pious's article comes the closest, but he does not explore my specific hypothesis: President Obama has found new ways to reach the same conclusion as President Bush—that the president may exercise national security power without meaningful constitutional or statutory restraint.

Michael Glennon's penetrating book *National Security and Double Government* concludes, as I do, that "U.S. national security policy has scarcely changed from the Bush to the Obama administration."[13] Glennon argues, however, that the reason for this is not necessarily that President Obama, like President Bush, believes in unconstrained presidential power. Instead, it is that none of what Glennon refers to as the "Madisonian" institutions—the executive, legislative, and judicial branches—*really* make decisions about national security.[14] Instead, Glennon concludes, most national security decisions are made by "Trumanites"—a "network of several hundred high-level military, intelligence, diplomatic, and law enforcement officials within the executive branch who are responsible for national security policymaking."[15] This, in Glennon's view, explains the continuity between Bush and Obama—the reality that unelected national security bureaucrats working outside public view largely determine national security decisions.[16] The Madisonian institutions—including the presidency—defer to the national security experts and "go along with policymaking by the Trumanites so long as it is popular."[17]

The conclusions Glennon reaches in his well-reasoned, acutely observed book demand to be taken seriously. I intend to offer observations that I hope will supplement his analysis. Glennon's thesis suggests it is more important to focus on the Trumanites, the national security bureaucrats, than the president. In his model, it hardly matters who occupies the White House—the president is less a "decider" than a "presider" who confirms decisions made by others.[18] Glennon writes that, "[i]n a narrow sense, of course, Trumanite policies are the President's own; after all, he did formally approve them. But the policies ordinarily are formulated by Trumanites."[19] Parallel to the way in which I argue that President Obama has exercised presidential national security power without being limited by meaningful legal constraints, Glennon argues that "[t]he Trumanites are committed to the rule of law . . . but the rule of law to which they are committed . . . is largely devoid of meaningful constraints."[20]

However, even Glennon concedes that presidents are capable of making changes in national security policy—"[l]eadership does matter, or at least it can matter."[21] Glennon sees this, though, as the exception to the rule. I agree that, in many areas, there has not been much change from Bush to Obama, but the *possibility* of change is important. I also see 9/11 as a key turning point. The Bush administration implemented a new theory[22] of presidential power that produced new national security policy in the areas discussed in Section II of this book as a response to the threat of terrorism. These decisions were made and justified by President Bush, Vice President Dick Cheney, and lawyers in the executive branch. President Obama was capable of making changes to the Bush approach to national security and in fact did make some significant changes, as alluded to in this introduction and as discussed in more detail in Section III.

Moreover, even if Glennon's central point is correct—that presidents (along with other Madisonian actors) generally go along with policies shaped by unelected national security experts—it is still important to understand how those policies are justified by the president. Although Glennon is skeptical that checks and balances—the calling card of the Madisonian system—can effectively rein in his Trumanites,[23] he ultimately concludes that the key to maintaining American democracy is to ensure that national security power not be allowed "to escape the control of the people."[24] If this is correct, then it is important to understand how President Obama has justified his national security decisions and why his approach has followed Bush's if Americans hope to change this by setting meaningful limits on the exercise of national security power.

With this ideal as the starting point—that it is both essential and possible for presidential national security power to be meaningfully constrained by the rule of law—my book compares the George W. Bush and Obama administrations when it comes to the use—and justifications for the use—of presidential national security power. Ultimately, I conclude that the Obama administration has often used different rationales to reach the same result as the Bush administration. It is merely an illusion that the Obama administration did not *seem* to be doing the same thing as the Bush administration. The Obama administration avoided (for the most part) the language of the unitary executive theory and the sole organ doctrine[25] and claimed to respect legal limits on presidential power. But when the rhetoric is stripped away and the administration's actions and explanations are examined more closely, it is clear that the claimed limits are only an illusion.

Although Obama has not expressly endorsed the unitary executive theory,[26] he has failed to restore meaningful limits on presidential national security power. The story of how this has played out is not uniform—it varies from subject area to subject area, as discussed in Section III. In the use of military force, targeted killings, and surveillance, the Obama administration found ways to turn would-be statutory limits on presidential power into ineffective "faux law."[27] In the context of military detention and trials at Guantanamo, the story is more complicated, as the Obama administration did not always follow the Bush approach. However, it still reached some of the same conclusions as the Bush administration: most centrally, that at least some prisoners could be tried by military tribunals, while others could simply be held without trial in any venue. On torture, the Obama administration has the best case for claiming to have successfully broken with the Bush administration, but even in this area Obama's failure to hold anyone accountable for torture authorized and carried out during the Bush years marked a failure to set limits on presidential power. In its use of state secrets, the Obama administration's approach is essentially identical to that of the Bush administration.

The Obama administration's failure to recognize meaningful limits on presidential national security power is, of course, first and foremost President Obama's responsibility. But he is not solely at fault. An acquiescent Congress and court system, as well as executive branch lawyers who helped find ways to hide the reality of unrestrained presidential power behind a veneer of meretricious legal reasoning, also bear responsibility. Obama's presidency is a reminder that the Framers' understanding of human nature still applies today. People are not angels,[28] and it is a mistake to trust any president to fully deliver on promises to voluntarily relinquish or rein in power accumulated or arrogated by his or her predecessors. This is an important lesson to keep in mind as we consider the actions of future presidents.

Section I provides historical background necessary to understand and evaluate the use of presidential power since 9/11. Section II considers the justifications the Bush administration relied on to define the scope of presidential national security power in the areas of (1) military force, (2) surveillance, (3) military detention and trial, (4) torture, and (5) state secrets. Section III considers the Obama administration's approach to the same matters and explains how President Obama, like President Bush, has failed to recognize or set meaningful limits on presidential national security power. In the conclusion, I consider what this means both for future presidents and for those who would seek to hold them accountable to the rule of law.

# SECTION I

# 1

# THE CONSTITUTION AND PRESIDENTIAL NATIONAL SECURITY POWER

Although the Framers of the U.S. Constitution worried most about overreaching legislative power, Peter Shane points out that, in the twenty-first century, the president "poses the most profound threat to our checks and balances system."[1] This is the case, in part, because the president "has the greatest capacity to act in secret and without the assistance of the two other branches" and because Congress and the courts have not recently been up to the task of checking presidential power.[2] The result has been an "aggressive presidentialism breed[ing] an insularity, defensiveness, and even arrogance within the executive branch that undermines sound decisionmaking, discounts the rule of law and attenuates the role of authentic deliberation in shaping political outcomes."[3] Though many hoped that the Obama administration would rein in the Bush administration's extravagant claims to power, this is not a problem easily solved by a change in presidential administration.[4]

This book focuses on a particular kind of presidential power in a specific setting: the Obama administration's use of presidential power in the area of national security.[5] In order to evaluate Obama's actions, it is essential to provide context, beginning in this section with questions of constitutional interpretation and an overview of the ways in which presidents historically used power in the name of national security before 9/11. Since this book argues that, in many ways, Obama has followed George W. Bush in his use of presidential power, Section II provides background on the ways in which the Bush administration justified unconstrained presidential power in the area of national security. Section III compares the Obama administration's actions with the Bush administration's.

The Constitution is notoriously spare when it comes to defining presidential power regarding national security. The primary sources of presidential authority in this area are Article II's Commander in Chief and Vesting Clauses, though neither of these clauses provides much detail or clarity. Among scholars, there are primarily two competing schools of thought when it comes to defining presidential power under the Constitution.[6] On one side are those who argue that the president has plenary, essentially unchecked, power over foreign affairs and the military.[7] On the other side are those who emphasize checks and balances, the idea that, while presidents must have the ability to respond to emergencies that threaten the United States, presidential power must be limited by the rule of law.[8]

Advocates of plenary presidential power generally rely on the Commander in Chief Clause, the unitary executive theory, and/or the sole organ doctrine to support their position. I consider each point in turn. Article II makes the president "Commander in Chief of the Army and Navy of the United States, and the Militia of the several states, when called into the actual service of the United States." Some read this as a broad grant of substantive power, providing "support for any presidential action, internal or external, involving use of force, the idea being that it vests power [in the president] to do anything, anywhere, that can be done with an army or navy."[9] During the George W. Bush administration, John Yoo and other executive branch lawyers went even further. They claimed that, as commander in chief, the president can make any decision related to the conduct of a military campaign, including matters (such as surveillance or interrogation of prisoners) that do not directly involve the use of military force.[10] However, this broad interpretation cannot stand in the face of historical evidence and common sense. Alexander Hamilton, the strongest advocate of presidential power among the Framers, made clear in Federalist No. 69 that authority as commander in chief "would amount to nothing more than the supreme command and direction of the military and naval forces, as first General and admiral of the Confederacy."[11] It did not mean the president could use military force in any way he or she chooses, let alone that the president could absolutely control decisions about gathering intelligence and interrogating prisoners—there are limits on power under the Constitution and statute. For instance, unlike the eighteenth-century British monarch, the president has no power to declare war or (absent statutory authorization) to raise and regulate fleets and armies.

Additional historical evidence makes clear that the Framers did not intend to grant the president unchecked power when it came to the use of military force. They wanted the president to have "the power to repel sudden attacks"—an implied power, not expressly spelled out in the text of the Constitution, though discussed during the Constitutional Convention of 1787.[12] This is only logical: if the country is under attack and there is no time for the president to seek authorization from Congress, then of course the president must take unilateral action to defend the nation.[13] Accepting Yoo's view of the meaning of the Commander in Chief Clause, in contrast, would give the president unlimited power to take any action directly or indirectly related to the use of the military, including deciding whether to initiate hostilities.[14] Yoo's approach endorses unchecked power incompatible with a constitutional republic.[15] In drafting the Constitution, the Framers consciously rejected the British model, which concentrated power over the military and foreign affairs in the king.[16] As Hamilton suggested in Federalist No. 69, the Constitution divides such powers between the president and Congress, rather than assigning the president plenary power in either area.

Advocates of broad presidential power in the context of national security also point to Article II's Vesting Clause. Advocates of the unitary executive theory insist that this clause assigns the president all power that is inherently "executive," whether or not such power is expressly or implicitly assigned to the president by the Constitution, and that the president independently determines the scope and limits of executive power.[17] They emphasize that the Framers chose different language for the Vesting Clauses in Articles I and II—while Congress is limited under Article I to "[a]ll legislative powers herein granted," Article II simply states, without qualification, that "[t]he executive power shall be vested in a President of the United States." The difference, advocates of the unitary executive conclude, is telling: the Framers must have meant to assign *all* executive power to the president, without limitation.

Defenders of the unitary executive theory sometimes trace its origins to Alexander Hamilton and the Pacificus-Helvidius debate. It is true that Hamilton argued in *Pacificus* that Article II's Vesting Clause broadly assigns executive power to the president. But Hamilton made clear that the Constitution's grant of executive power is not unlimited. In his view, "the Executive Power of the Nation is vested in the President; subject only to the *exceptions* and *qualifications* which are expressed in the [Constitution]."[18] This essential caveat places Hamilton's views in direct conflict with the unitary executive theory. While the unitary executive theory, in its broadest form, claims the president possesses all power that can be described as executive, without limitation, Hamilton conceded in his *Pacificus* essay that the executive power assigned to the president is limited by the Constitution. For instance, Hamilton observed that Congress is assigned war powers, including the power to declare war, that limit the president's executive power.[19] Unitarians like John Yoo claim the president's war power is unlimited, that decisions involving the use of military force in response to terrorist threats "are for the President alone to make."[20] Supporters of the unitary executive theory who claim Hamilton as their archetype typically ignore Federalist No. 69, in which Hamilton made clear that presidential power, including war power and power over foreign affairs, is limited.[21]

In contrast with how Hamilton described executive power, the unitary executive, in its most extreme form,[22] is a theory designed to justify unilateral, unchecked presidential power unaccountable to the rule of law. In this view, what Mark Tushnet calls the "super-strong theory of the unitary executive," the president's "primary duty is to take care that the nation be preserved, to which the duty to take care that the laws, including the Constitution, be faithfully executed, is subordinate."[23] This view of the unitary executive theory has its origins in the Reagan administration and those who defended its actions in the Iran-Contra affair.[24] The unitary executive theory has been invoked to justify whatever actions a president may deem necessary to provide national security; power over foreign affairs and the military are seen by advocates of the unitary executive as quintessentially "executive."

The George W. Bush administration employed the most robust and far-reaching version of the unitary executive theory, invoking it (initially in secret Office of Legal Counsel memos) to justify (a) plenary presidential power to make any and all decisions regarding the use of military force, (b) unilateral presidential power to hold suspected terrorists in a military detention system without access to civilian courts and, at the president's discretion, to try them in military tribunals using rules designed by the president, (c) presidential power to order interrogation methods that amounted to torture, even if such methods are prohibited by criminal law, and (d) presidential power to order warrantless surveillance of Americans, even if such surveillance is prohibited by criminal law.[25]

Defenders of the virtues of unilateral presidential action often point to the energetic executive model—the idea that presidents are, within the U.S. system, uniquely capable of swift, decisive action.[26] These scholars see unilateral presidential action as something to be embraced rather than feared. For instance, Eric Posner and Adrian Vermeule argue that those who worry about presidential power unrestrained by legal limits are "tyrannophobes."[27] They argue that unrestrained executive power is both inevitable and beneficial. William G. Howell and Jon C. Pevehouse similarly argue that the president's ability to act unilaterally places him or her "in a unique position to lead."[28] Howell and Pevehouse claim that "[i]n foreign policy making generally, and on issues involving the use of force in particular, this feature of unilateral [presidential] powers [i.e., that the president is uniquely positioned to lead] reaps special rewards. If presidents had to build broad-based consensus behind every deployment before any military planning could be executed, most ventures would never get off the ground. . . . Because presidents, as a practical matter, can unilaterally launch ventures into distant locales without ever having to guide a proposal through a circuitous and uncertain legislative process, they can more effectively manage these responsibilities and take action when congressional deliberations often result in gridlock."[29] These observations are at odds with the historical record.[30] When prompt action in the name of national security has been necessary, Congress has not let gridlock get in the way of quick action. It declared war against Japan the day after Pearl Harbor; it declared war against Germany four days after President Wilson called for action to respond to the Zimmerman telegram and Germany's declaration of unrestrained submarine warfare.[31] More recently, Congress passed the Authorization for Use of Military Force against on September 14, 2001, just three days after al Qaeda's attacks against the United States. It took President Bush four days to sign the AUMF into law—longer than it took Congress to act.[32]

The assumption that Congress is incapable of prompt action when national security demands it is not supported by the historical record.[33] History also shows that unilateral presidential action can be dangerous, even disastrous. Consider Franklin D. Roosevelt's Executive Order 9066,[34] which paved the way for mass internment of Japanese Americans during World War II; Truman's decision to seize control of steel mills during the Korean War (as well as his decision to begin the war itself unilaterally); Nixon's domestic law-breaking operations and his secret war in Cambodia; or George W. Bush's decisions to authorize indefinite detention, torture, and warrantless surveillance, as discussed in Section II.

Those who praise unilateral presidential action face a problem in the historical record, which shows that unilateral presidential action in the name of national security is rarely either wise or necessary. The bigger problem for the unitary executive theory is that it sets forth a presidential model fundamentally at odds with a republican system of government because it utterly disregards the need to set limits on executive power.[35] Bizarrely, some advocates of unchecked presidential power argue that this is a virtue, that presidential power should not be and in fact cannot be limited by the rule of law.[36] If this is the case, then Americans can no longer hope to live in a constitutional republic and must grow accustomed to something else, something like the kind of "constitutional dictatorship" Clinton Rossiter envisioned during open-ended crisis.[37] If, instead, our goal is to maintain the constitutional system of checks and balances established by the Constitution, then we must judge any theory of presidential power by two criteria: (1) does it acknowledge meaningful constitutional and statutory limits on presidential power and (2) does it give presidents the power they need to carry out their responsibilities?

The unitary executive theory easily satisfies and surpasses the second criterion of the test I propose: it gives presidents whatever power they deem necessary to carry out their duties. However, it completely fails to satisfy the first criterion: the model places no real limits on presidential power, other than those the president chooses to acknowledge. In this view, presidents can decide, as a matter of unreviewable presidential discretion, to set aside statutory limits on their authority. All power—executive, legislative, and judicial—is concentrated in the hands of the president. This is, of course, what James Madison aptly described as "the very definition of tyranny."[38] As Peter Shane observes, "it is inconceivable that the revolutionary generation . . . would have unreservedly re-embraced the full power of a monarchy."[39]

In addition to citing the Commander in Chief Clause or the unitary executive theory, advocates of plenary presidential power frequently invoke the sole organ doctrine to justify presidential control of foreign affairs. However, this idea depends on an utter misreading of a speech John Marshall gave in 1800.[40] Marshall, then a member of the U.S. House of Representatives, was speaking in defense of President John Adams's controversial decision to extradite a man charged with murder in Great Britain. Marshall pointed out that Adams was simply carrying out U.S. treaty obligations—a duty that Marshall said fell to the president as "the sole organ of the nation in its external relations, and its sole representative with foreign nations."[41] Marshall explained that, since the president had this responsibility to act on behalf of the nation, "[o]f consequence, the demand of a foreign nation can only be made on him. He possesses the whole executive power. He holds and directs the force of the nation. Of consequence, any act to be performed by the force of the nation is to be performed through him."[42] Marshall was not endorsing the idea of plenary power. He emphasized that Adams had simply carried out a law: "[the president] is charged to execute the laws. A treaty is declared to be a law. He must then execute a treaty, where he, and he alone, possesses the means of executing it."[43] As Louis Fisher explains, "Marshall's objective was to defend the authority of President John Adams to carry out an extradition treaty. The president was not the sole organ in formulating the treaty. He was the sole organ in *implementing* it."[44]

Unfortunately, more than one hundred years after Marshall made these remarks, dicta in a Supreme Court opinion mangled the meaning of Marshall's words, deceptively transforming Marshall's description of a president executing law approved by others into the suggestion that the president could act unilaterally in the field of foreign affairs, without consulting or even considering Congress. In the 1936 *U.S. v. Curtiss-Wright* decision, Justice George Sutherland suggested that Marshall's speech was meant to refer to "the very delicate, plenary and exclusive power of the President as the sole organ of the federal government in the field of international relations—a power which does not require as a basis for its exercise an act of Congress, but which, of course, like every other governmental power, must be exercised in subordination to the applicable provisions of the Constitution."[45] Sutherland was simply wrong to suggest that Marshall's sole organ speech stood for a principle of plenary presidential power in the field of foreign affairs. Marshall said no such thing. He clearly understood that the president acted pursuant to law—in the case he addressed, a treaty enacted by both the president and the Senate. In fact, this was the essential point of Marshall's sole organ speech in 1800: that the president should not be blamed for extraditing a criminal suspect to Great Britain because Adams was not making this decision independently but was simply carrying out U.S. treaty obligations entered into "jointly by the President and the Senate."[46]

In addition, Sutherland's dicta, when examined more closely, is not internally consistent. Sutherland first claims that the president possesses plenary power in the area of foreign affairs to act without congressional authorization, but he then concedes that this power, "like every other governmental power, must be exercised in subordination to the applicable provisions of the Constitution."[47] But that makes no sense. The "applicable provisions of the Constitution" in the area of foreign affairs make clear that the president *cannot* always act unilaterally. Presidential action in this area normally requires congressional approval—for instance, the Senate approves treaties and confirms ambassadors nominated by the president, and Congress as a whole declares war, regulates commerce with foreign nations, and defines and punishes offenses against the law of nations.[48] If Sutherland acknowledges that presidential power in the area of foreign affairs is constrained by the Constitution, then how can such power be exclusive? Sutherland's claim of plenary power quickly dissolves when given a moment's thought. The Constitution expressly assigns significant power over foreign affairs to Congress, again indicating the Framers' intent to break with the existing British model that gave the executive broader control over foreign affairs.[49] There is no plenary presidential power in this area.

Although Sutherland's dicta in *Curtiss-Wright* has nothing to do with what Marshall actually said in 1800 or what the Constitution provides with regard to shared power over foreign affairs, some advocates of plenary presidential power continued to rely on Sutherland's misconceived notion of a president who has exclusive control over foreign affairs. For instance, John Yoo asserted in 2001 ( just two weeks after the 9/11 attacks) that "the Constitution vests the President with the plenary authority, as Commander in Chief and the sole organ of the Nation in its foreign relations, to use military force abroad."[50] Relying in part on an incorrect interpretation of Marshall's sole organ reference, Yoo declared that "the executive branch [has] consistently . . . assert[ed] the President's plenary authority in foreign affairs."[51] That is incorrect as a matter both of historical record and of constitutional interpretation.[52] Fortunately, a 2015 Supreme Court decision, *Zivotofsky v. Kerry*, rejected the idea that *Curtiss-Wright* supports plenary presidential authority over foreign affairs, observing that "[t]he Executive is not free from the ordinary controls and checks of Congress merely because foreign affairs are at issue."[53]

Advocates of plenary presidential power over national security have put forth a "theory that the Constitution envisions a Presidency answerable, in large measure, to no one."[54] They are forced to justify their position by relying on untenable interpretations of the Constitution. That is not surprising. In a nation founded as a constitutional republic, it is difficult to justify a theory of unchecked presidential power that sets aside the rule of law. In fact, two advocates of unchecked power, Eric Posner and Adrian Vermeule, have acknowledged as much and decided to argue that the rule of law simply cannot and should not limit presidential power.[55] This is revealing. As Peter Shane suggests, advocates of plenary presidential power who are not as aboveboard as Posner and Vermeule often create an illusion that the president is bound by the rule of law.[56] Presidents who exercise unchecked power "may develop [their] own legitimating documents, formal pieces of paper that sanction the President's expansive assertions of unilateral power."[57] In other words, legal justifications are used merely as window dressing. The real goal is for the president to do what he or she likes, with executive branch lawyers "generat[ing] what *looks like* legal authority for even utterly unprecedented claims."[58] The legal opinions put forth by executive branch lawyers "are citable. They are precedents of a sort. One is tempted, however, to say that they are faux law in just the same way creation science is faux science. Left unchallenged, they may still have the power to cow Congress and shape the behavior of executive underlings."[59] I argue in Sections II and III that this phenomenon aptly describes both the George W. Bush and the Obama administrations. The most significant difference between the definition of presidential power implemented by these presidential administrations and the definition put forth by Professors Posner and Vermeule is that Posner and Vermeule candidly reject the rule of law as a constraint on presidential power.

Critics of unchecked presidential power emphasize checks and balances, the need to place meaningful limits on presidential power and uphold the rule of law. Recognizing the need for checks on presidential power does not mean stripping the president of power to respond to national security emergencies. History shows us that presidents can defend the nation without discarding the rule of law. Fisher argues that presidents who need to act unilaterally in order to defend the nation when there is no time to consult with Congress must then seek retroactive approval for their actions, as Lincoln did at the beginning of the Civil War.[60] This approach permits presidents to take the kind of emergency action contemplated by the Framers—"to repel sudden attacks"—while preserving the constitutional framework and the rule of law. When a president seeks retroactive approval for unilateral action, Congress can decide whether to legitimize the president's actions.[61] The president, having taking extraconstitutional action by "[acting] illegally for the purpose of meeting an emergency" must then "assume the burden of explaining to the lawmaking body why his action was necessary and reasonable."[62]

James Pfiffner agrees with Fisher that it is essential to set limits on presidential power. Like Fisher, he emphasizes the Framers' decision to reject "the British model of royal power."[63] The Framers anticipated that Congress would have "primary control of public policy," including maintaining national security.[64] They correctly saw "the importance of a legislative check on executive power."[65] This was, in part, a lesson they had absorbed from British history as well as from their own recent experience, which "implanted in the colonists a profound distrust of executive power."[66] The Articles of Confederation did not provide for any executive: the American revolutionaries were wary of creating their own king. Although they maintained "a strong distrust of executive power" after the Revolution, the failures of the Articles of Confederation led the Framers to conclude it was necessary to create an executive—though a constrained one.[67] Under the Constitution, the president's power would be balanced by the other branches of the federal government. Pfiffner concludes that the Framers wisely created a constitutional republic that relied on the separation of powers to avoid "the concentration of power in any one branch of government."[68] Unless presidential power is checked, the rule of law cannot be maintained.[69]

Peter Shane agrees that the Framers "got [it] right" when they created a system of constitutional checks and balances designed to prevent the concentration of power in any one branch of government.[70] As presidents claim increasingly broad power, their successors are "tempted to embrace their predecessors' more audacious claims as sources of legal authority and strike out on their own."[71] Shane urges Congress and the courts to reassert themselves in order to produce a system in which "the scope of permissible presidential initiative depends very much on the actions of Congress and the courts."[72] It is also essential for executive branch lawyers, most centrally lawyers in the Office of Legal Counsel, to "play an objective, even quasi-adjudicative role."[73] As discussed in Sections II and III, executive branch lawyers in both the George W. Bush and the Obama administrations have, for the most part, failed to do this, serving instead to enable the exercise of unchecked presidential power. The Office of Legal Counsel must be restored to its traditional role as "a conscientious adviser to the President and to the Attorney General, not their [partisan] advocate."[74]

Scholars who emphasize the need to limit presidential power in the context of the rule of law and constitutional checks and balances make the stronger case, as a matter of both constitutional interpretation and common sense. The Framers clearly rejected the eighteenth-century British model, which concentrated most power over war and foreign affairs in the hands of the executive. In its place, they created a system that assigned the president important but clearly limited powers. Most notably, power over war and foreign affairs was divided between the executive and the legislative branches. As James Pfiffner aptly put it, advocates of unchecked presidential power who argue that they are simply carrying out the Framers' intent "stretch the text of the Constitution and the deliberations of the framers beyond reasonable interpretation."[75]

One might argue, however, that times have changed and that, whatever the Framers and ratifiers of the Constitution intended in the late eighteenth century, their design cannot provide twenty-first-century presidents with the necessary tools to confront modern threats. There are multiple problems, however, with this assertion. First, although the Framers lived in much different times than we do, "[t]hey knew what emergencies were, knew the pressures they engender for authoritative action, knew, too, how they afford a ready pretext for usurpation."[76] The Framers of the Constitution consciously and deliberately assigned the executive important but limited powers in a constitutional system designed to endure "for posterity."[77] Of course, the Framers also contemplated that the basic structure of the Constitution might change through the Article V amendment process.[78] However, if we were to accept the argument put forth by advocates of unchecked presidential power—that presidents are not restrained by constitutional or statutory limits—then we would no longer have a republican form of government based on the rule of law. A president unchecked by the other branches of government is a president above the law.

One way to test the argument put forth by advocates of unchecked presidential power is to consider the historical record. How have presidents exercised national security power in practice? When presidents have made claims to plenary power, what have the results been? The rest of Section I, as well as Section II, considers these questions, with particular emphasis on the Bush administration's claims of plenary power. As noted, this provides context for this book's central argument in Section III: that the Obama administration has continued the Bush administration's goal of exercising unrestrained power, although the Obama administration has camouflaged its actions behind rhetoric that purports to recognize limits on presidential power when it in fact simply provides cover for the president to act without constraint.

# 2

## PRESIDENTIAL NATIONAL SECURITY
## POWER BEFORE SEPTEMBER 11, 2001

When presidents have exercised plenary power, disregarding or finding ways around statutory and constitutional limits while rejecting the need to consult Congress in advance (or sometimes even at all), the results have often been troubling, dangerous, even disastrous. Infamous examples spring readily to mind—Franklin Roosevelt's internment of Japanese Americans during World War II,[1] Truman's decision to order military intervention in Korea and seize steel factories at home to support the war effort, the Huston plan and Nixon's secret bombing campaign in Cambodia, Reagan and the Iran-Contra affair, George W. Bush's decisions to authorize torture and illegal surveillance, Obama's authorization of the killing of U.S. citizens without due process. When presidents have obtained approval from Congress for actions taken in the name of national security, they frequently did so only after they had decided on a course of action and then used deception in order to secure Congress's blessing—for example, Polk seeking a declaration of war against Mexico, Lyndon Johnson and the Tonkin Gulf Resolution, George W. Bush and the authorization to use military force against Iraq.[2] Congressional approval given after a decision has already been made by the president can create the misimpression that presidential action is properly subject to checks and balances when, as is often the case, presidents take advantage of congressional acquiescence to expand their authority.

History teaches a clear lesson: presidents cannot be trusted with unilateral, unconstrained power. That is not an indictment of the specific people who have held the office; rather, it is confirmation of what James Madison recognized about human nature, borne out by the historical record.[3] It is far more difficult to find examples of unilateral presidential action leading to good results than it is to find examples of unilateral action that ended badly. Advocates of plenary presidential power frequently cite Lincoln, but this precedent fails to vindicate their position as he forthrightly sought and obtained congressional approval for unilateral actions he took at the beginning of the Civil War, in the process making clear that he respected the rule of law, understood he had exceeded the limits of his own power, and recognized he needed legislative approval for otherwise extraconstitutional actions.[4]

Advocates of plenary presidential national security power praise it in the abstract. They argue it is a positive force, something that is important, even necessary, in order for the United States to defend itself against threats that require an immediate response. But these claims can be tested against the historical record, and when we do this we find the claims do not describe reality. Unchecked presidential power has not proved its worth. Instead, it has proved to undermine constitutional checks and balances, produce poor decisions, and even threaten the republic. This has been true both before and after the September 11 terrorist attacks.[5]

## FRANKLIN D. ROOSEVELT AND PLENARY POWER DURING WORLD WAR II

The historical record before 9/11 reveals the bankruptcy of arguments for plenary presidential power. This has especially been true since World War II,[6] as presidents, beginning with Franklin Roosevelt, have consolidated power and often acted unilaterally.[7] In at least two significant ways, President Roosevelt asserted the authority to act unilaterally, each time producing troubling immediate consequences as well as creating dangerous precedent.

In June 1942, two teams of German saboteurs made separate landings at Long Island, New York, and Ponte Vedra, Florida.[8] The eight men, each of whom had previously lived in the United States, had received training in Germany "in the use of explosives, fuses, and detonators, all to be used against railroads, factories, bridges, and other strategic targets in the United States."[9] The saboteurs, however, proved unwilling or unable (or perhaps some of each) to carry out their assignment.[10] Shortly after entering the United States, the leader of the team that landed on Long Island contacted the FBI, helping agents locate the other saboteurs and take them into custody.[11]

Roosevelt believed it was important to avoid any civilian trial for the saboteurs and made clear to Attorney General Francis Biddle that he expected the men to be executed.[12] With a view to achieving this goal, Roosevelt issued a July 2, 1942, proclamation creating a military tribunal to try the saboteurs as well as "a military order appointing the members of the military commission, the prosecutors, and the defense counsel."[13] In issuing the July 2 proclamation, Roosevelt claimed to be acting "under a mix of constitutional authority accorded to the President and statutory authority granted by Congress."[14] The proclamation declared that enemies "enter[ing] upon the territory of the United States as part of an invasion . . . or who have entered in order to commit sabotage, espionage, or other hostile or warlike acts, should be promptly tried in accordance with the Laws of War."[15] That meant the saboteurs would be tried for crimes defined by "executive interpretations of the 'law of war'" instead of for offenses defined by Congress through duly enacted statute.[16] According to Roosevelt's proclamation, people covered by the proclamation, including the saboteurs, were also to be denied access to civilian courts.[17]

Although Roosevelt claimed to be acting pursuant to both constitutional and statutory authority, in reality he was not faithful to either. Roosevelt authorized the military tribunal to create its own procedural rules, rather than following procedures described in the Articles of War by Congress.[18] This contradicted the Articles of War, which required the president to personally create rules of procedure for any military tribunal and to describe such procedures in written regulations.[19] By delegating this responsibility to the tribunal itself and permitting the tribunal to make up procedural rules as it went along, Roosevelt was deviating from statutory authority.[20] The military order he issued "plainly departed from the Articles of War" in other ways, including "with regard to the votes needed for sentencing" and by directing that any appeal of the military trial would go directly to Roosevelt (the Articles of War provided for review of "any conviction or sentence by a military court . . . within the military system, including [by review of] the Judge Advocate General's office"),[21] There were also constitutional problems with Roosevelt's actions. Roosevelt had effectively suspended habeas corpus for the saboteurs, an emergency power left to Congress under Article I of the Constitution.[22] The president had issued the proclamation and order *after* the saboteurs had been captured, subjecting them to penalties and punishment, including the death penalty, that had not existed at the time they landed on U.S. shores—an apparent violation of the Constitution's Ex Post Facto Clause.[23] All in all, Roosevelt's actions "represented an unwise and ill-conceived concentration of power in the executive branch."[24]

Despite Roosevelt's efforts to bar judicial review for the saboteurs, military lawyers representing the saboteurs managed to bring the matter before the Supreme Court, which considered only the question of whether the saboteurs had the right of access to the civilian courts, not the question of guilt or innocence.[25] During oral argument before the Court, government lawyers (including Attorney General Biddle) claimed the president had plenary power to act, insisting that "[t]he President's power over enemies who enter this country in time of war, as armed invaders intending to commit hostile acts, must be absolute."[26] Although the Court, in deciding that the saboteurs had properly been tried[27] before the military tribunal as constituted and authorized by the president, did not expressly endorse the exercise of plenary presidential power, it effectively ratified Roosevelt's unilateral actions, relying on the fiction that the president had acted pursuant to congressional authorization.[28] Some members of the Court that decided the *Quirin* case in 1942 later expressed regret for their hasty decision, made without understanding the procedures the military tribunal had actually followed.[29] More recently, Justice Antonin Scalia has described *Quirin* as "not this Court's finest hour."[30]

The German saboteur episode was also not the finest hour for the presidency. Roosevelt established, on his own authority, a secret[31] military tribunal to try men for crimes that had not been defined until after they committed their offenses pursuant to procedures that were made up by the tribunal on the fly, without regard to statutory requirements. In the name of national security, Roosevelt had acted unilaterally to set aside the rule of law, ultimately creating a dangerous precedent. Six of the men were executed before the Supreme Court even issued its written opinion, even though it appeared that the saboteurs had abandoned their assignment and did not attempt to carry out any sabotage.[32] Kenneth Royall, one of the military lawyers assigned to defend the Germans, perhaps described the problem created by Roosevelt's actions most clearly when he admonished that the United States did not "want to win [the war] by throwing away everything we are fighting for, because we will have a mighty empty victory if we destroy the genuineness and truth of democratic government and fair administration of the law."[33]

A few months before President Roosevelt acted unilaterally to force the result he wanted for the German saboteurs, he issued an executive order paving the way for mass internment of more than 110,000 Japanese Americans living on the West Coast of the United States. On the surface, Executive Order 9066, issued on February 19, 1942, is not an example of unilateral presidential action.[34] Although Roosevelt initially acted unilaterally in issuing Executive Order 9066, authorizing the secretary of war or military commanders to designate "military areas" from which "any persons may be excluded," Roosevelt's actions were approved by Congress and the

Supreme Court. In this sense, one might conclude that Roosevelt's actions are not an example of a president exercising exclusive and plenary power. However, Roosevelt's executive order relied most centrally[35] on "the authority vested in [Roosevelt] as President of the United States, and Commander in Chief of the Army and Navy," suggesting that Roosevelt and his advisers believed congressional approval was not necessary.[36] Additional evidence makes clear that this was their belief.

Unlike Lincoln, Roosevelt never indicated that he believed congressional approval was needed to legitimize his unilateral actions. Some of his advisers raised objections to the February 1942 executive order, but "constitutional qualms fell before the military offensive that demanded evacuation [of Japanese Americans on the West Coast] as a mainland line of defense."[37] When the executive order was signed, Attorney General Biddle advised Roosevelt in a memorandum that no further action was needed: in Biddle's view, the president had acted under his "general war powers," and internment of Japanese Americans could move ahead "without further legislation."[38] Of course, Biddle's memo should have said "without *any* legislation" as the word "further" incorrectly suggested Congress had provided some advance approval for internment. However, other executive branch lawyers believed it would be important for Congress to pass enforcement legislation providing for criminal penalties in the event that Japanese Americans did not comply with military orders, including orders to leave their homes.[39] Accordingly, the War Department drafted legislation providing that any civilian who refused to obey a military order in a district described as a "military area" was committing a misdemeanor offense punishable by one year in prison and a fine.[40] The legislation would apply to Military Area No. 1, an area made up of "the western halves of California, Oregon, and Washington, and the southern half of Arizona."[41]

When Secretary of War Henry L. Stimson urged Congress to expedite passage of the enforcement legislation the War Department had drafted,[42] the House of Representatives passed the bill by voice vote after five members spoke on the floor for ten minutes each.[43] The bill had passed unanimously out of the House Committee on Military Affairs following a half-hour session during which a representative of the War Department told committee members that the legislation was needed in order "to enforce provisions of the Executive Order."[44] No one on the House committee raised any objections or questioned the president's authority for acting unilaterally: "the only suggestions offered were in favor of stiffening the [penalties provided for in the legislation]."[45] The Senate took similarly quick and deferential action: the Senate Military Affairs Committee unanimously approved the bill after a one-hour hearing.[46] As on the House side, there was just one witness—the same representative of the War Department who had testified before the House committee.[47] When the bill moved to the Senate floor, only a few senators were present to consider the bill, which, as on the House side, passed by voice vote.[48]

As enacted, Public Law No. 503 read as follows: "Be it enacted by the Senate and House of Representatives of the United States of America in Congress assembled. That whoever shall enter, remain in, leave, or commit any act in any military area or military zone prescribed, under the authority of an Executive order of the President, by the Secretary of War, or by any military commander designated by the Secretary of War, contrary to the restrictions applicable to any such area or zone or contrary to the order of the Secretary of War or any such military commander, shall, if it appears that he knew or should have known of the existence and extent of the restrictions or order and that his act was in violation thereof, be guilty of misdemeanor and upon conviction shall be liable to a fine of not to exceed $5,000 or to imprisonment for not more than one year, or both, for each offense."[49] The legislation did not comment on Roosevelt's authority to issue the executive order, as this power seems to have been taken for granted; the law simply provided penalties to apply to anyone who violated military orders issued pursuant to the executive order.

Just as Congress signed off on Roosevelt's actions without questioning whether he had the authority to issue the executive order in the first place, the Supreme Court's decisions in *Hirabayshi v. United States* and *Korematsu v. United States* pointedly avoided deciding the question of whether the president had authority to act alone in authorizing the military to subject Japanese Americans on the West Coast to curfew and internment.[50]

The Japanese American internment is an example of plenary presidential power. Roosevelt asserted the power to act unilaterally on the basis of constitutional authority assigned to the president. Although Congress passed legislation to enforce Roosevelt's executive order, congressional oversight was perfunctory at best. The executive branch made clear that it expected Congress to support Roosevelt's actions, while suggesting that Congress had no authority to contradict the executive order. Congress obliged by acquiescing to Roosevelt's fait accompli, as did the Supreme Court. Nothing in this painful episode gave any indication of meaningful constitutional and statutory limits on presidential power.

## TRUMAN:
## THE KOREAN WAR AND STEEL SEIZURE

In June 1950, the United States intervened in the Korean War when President Truman "ordered U.S. troops to Korea without first requesting or receiving congressional authority."[51] Instead of congressional authorization, Truman cited "treaty commitments reflected in resolutions passed by the [United Nations] Security Council as sufficient authority to use military force against North Korea."[52] But citation to UN resolutions could not legitimize Truman's actions: under the Constitution, only Congress can declare war.[53] Unless the president is authorizing the use of force to repel an attack against the United States—which was not the case in Korea— the president does not have constitutional "authority to take unilateral military actions."[54] Truman seemed to have recognized this five years earlier when the United Nations Charter came before the U.S. Senate for approval: he assured the Senate, as it considered approval of the Charter in 1945, that "[w]hen any such agreement or agreements [to use military force pursuant to a UN Security Council resolution] are negotiated it will be my purpose to ask the Congress for appropriate legislation to approve them."[55] After receiving Truman's reassurance, the Senate approved the UN Charter. Congress also passed the UN Participation Act of 1945, making clear that any agreements to provide military assistance pursuant to a Security Council resolution "shall be subject to the approval of the Congress by appropriate Act or joint resolution."[56]

In unilaterally sending troops to Korea, Truman ignored both statutory and constitutional limits on presidential power. In other words, he exercised plenary power. In addition to citing UN authorization,[57] the Truman administration defended the decision to act unilaterally by invoking the president's authority as commander in chief and the "traditional power of the President to use the armed forces of the United States without consulting Congress."[58] That is the language of unchecked presidential power. Truman might have attempted to place his actions under the rule of law by seeking retroactive congressional approval, as Lincoln had at the beginning of the Civil War. However, Truman did not seek any congressional approval, and "Congress's reaction to Truman's usurpation of the war power was largely passive."[59] Louis Fisher marks the Korean War as a crucial turning point in the history of presidential power, noting that "[n]o president in the past had taken the country to war without first receiving a declaration or authorization from Congress."[60] Fisher concludes that "Truman's decision to go to war against North Korea in 1950 represented a subversion of the Framers' design."[61] Presidents since Truman have claimed the Korean War as precedent for unilateral presidential action that is not in fact authorized by the Constitution.[62]

During the Korean War, President Truman also attempted to exercise plenary power at home in the name of national security, though here his actions met with resistance. In April 1952, as a labor dispute between the

United Steelworkers union and steel companies threatened to bring a stop to steel production that the Truman administration considered vital to the war effort, Truman ordered Secretary of Commerce Charles Sawyer to seize and operate the steel mills on behalf of the United States government in order to make sure production would continue unabated.[63] In an executive order, Truman justified his authority to issue these instructions to Secretary Sawyer "by virtue of the authority vested in me by the Constitution and laws of the United States, and as President of the United States and Commander in Chief of the armed forces of the United States."[64]

This was not necessarily an invocation of plenary power—Truman's executive order did make reference to unspecified "laws," which might suggest he was relying on statutory authority. However, statutory authority was not on Truman's side. While laws passed during World War II had expressly assigned the president authority to take possession of industry, the postwar Taft-Hartley Act did not provide for any presidential seizure authority. Instead, the Taft-Hartley Act allowed the president, in some circumstances, to seek an injunction from a court prohibiting strikes in defense-related industries for eighty days. There had been an attempt to include a provision in Taft-Hartley giving the president emergency seizure powers, but the effort failed, and no such provision was included in the law.[65] Recognizing that statutory authority was lacking, Truman sent a special message to Congress after issuing the executive order.[66] The president asked Congress to take action that would resolve the labor dispute, but he indicated that he did not see congressional action as "essential" and that, if Congress did not act, he would continue the course of action he had begun—steel companies would continue to operate under government order.[67] Truman did not expressly ask Congress to pass legislation authorizing seizure of the steel companies, and his message "seemed designed to show respect for Congress'[s] prerogative to pass legislation while at the same time discouraging any action."[68] As it turned out (and as the Truman administration seemed to hope), Congress took no action.[69]

Truman soon made clear that he did not believe congressional authorization was necessary. At an April 17, 1952, press conference designed "to explain his actions during the steel crisis," Truman asserted that he not only had the power to order seizure of the steel companies but also suggested that he could take control of the nation's newspapers and radio stations if that was "for the best of the country."[70] At another press conference a week later, Truman tried to reassure Americans that seizure of media companies was unlikely but emphasized his belief that unilateral presidential action was justified with regard to seizure of the steel companies, explaining that "the President of the United States has very great inherent authority to meet great national emergencies."[71] This is a clear reference to plenary power—extraconstitutional "inherent" power to do what is necessary to respond to crisis, or a kind of Lockean prerogative.[72]

When the steel companies sought a court order to halt Truman's actions, executive branch lawyers expanded on Truman's plenary power argument.[73] In federal district court, Assistant Attorney General Homer Baldridge argued that Article II's Vesting Clause, as well as the Commander in Chief and Take Care clauses, assigned the president whatever "power [is needed] to protect the country in times of national emergency by whatever means seem appropriate to achieve the end."[74] In response to a question from Judge Alexander Holtzoff, who was considering the steel companies' motions for a temporary restraining order, Baldridge declined to say whether there were any limits on this emergency power.[75] After the case moved to Judge David A. Pine for consideration of motions for a preliminary injunction and argument on the merits of the case,[76] Baldridge continued to invoke plenary presidential power, explaining that "[the government's] position is that there is no power in the Courts to restrain the President and . . . Secretary Sawyer is . . . not subject to injunctive order of the Court."[77] When Judge Pine asked Baldridge whether the president's emergency power was unlimited, Baldridge responded that the only limits were the electoral process and impeachment.[78] In other words, the president was not bound by the rule of law. Only political limits applied to presidential emergency action. When Judge Pine reminded Baldridge that government powers are limited by the Constitution, Baldridge responded that only legislative power was limited:

> JUDGE PINE: So, when the sovereign people adopted the Constitution, it enumerated the powers set up in the Constitution but limited the powers of the Congress and limited the powers of the judiciary, but it did not limit the powers of the Executive. Is that what you say?
>
> BALDRIDGE: That is the way we read Article II of the Constitution.[79]

Newspapers covering the case reasonably described Baldridge's argument as a description of unlimited presidential power.[80] Members of Congress, even Truman's supporters, sought to distance themselves from the position Baldridge had staked out.[81] Truman made an attempt at damage control by publicly responding to a letter he had received from a citizen who was concerned about the administration's actions.[82] In his April 27, 1952, letter, Truman backed away from Baldridge's claim that the courts had no role to play—Truman allowed that "[t]he legal problems that arise from the [steel seizure] are now being examined in the courts, as is proper."[83] However, Truman refused to retreat from the central position the administration had staked out regarding presidential power. In his April 27 letter, the president acknowledged that "the action I was taking in this case was very drastic" but insisted it was justified "as a matter of necessity to meet an extreme emergency."[84] Truman again suggested that affirmative congressional approval was not necessary by alluding to Congress's silence on the matter and implying that if Congress disagreed with his actions, it could have "prescribe[d] a course to be followed to achieve a solution of this case." The president argued that his actions were justified by "the duty of the President under the Constitution to act to preserve the safety of the Nation."[85] This was essentially a modified description of Lockean prerogative: Truman was asserting broad presidential emergency power that could be wielded unilaterally without the need for congressional approval and with only limited judicial review that would focus on the question of whether presidential action had infringed on individual rights.[86]

As it turned out, Judge Pine recognized that the Truman administration's actions depended on an unconstitutional assertion of emergency presidential power.[87] Judge Pine's April 29, 1952, ruling laid waste to the case for plenary presidential power and utterly eviscerated the government's position. Judge Pine declared that the administration's argument simply "did not comport with our recognized theory of government"; in fact, there was an "utter and complete lack of authoritative support for [the government's] position."[88] Pine rejected Baldridge's argument that plenary presidential power was justified by emergency and unlimited by legal checks. The executive power, like power assigned to the other branches of government, is limited under the Constitution.[89] "Inherent" power, Judge Pine concluded, is extraconstitutional power.[90] The Truman administration stood in an "untenable position" as its actions could not be supported by either "affirmative constitutional or statutory provision."[91] The administration had tried to justify its actions by "cit[ing] general language from the works of Alexander Hamilton," but Pine correctly observed that, "when read in context," Hamilton's writing does not endorse unlimited presidential power.[92] Pine concluded his ruling by declaring that allowing the steel seizure to stand would mean recognizing a "claim to unlimited and unrestrained Executive power" and "[s]uch recognition would undermine public confidence in the very edifice of government as it is known under the Constitution."[93] Judge Pine issued preliminary injunctions ordering the Truman administration to be restrained from continuing with its seizure of the steel companies.[94]

Judge Pine's opinion was praised by the press and by members of Congress as a steadfast defense of fundamental constitutional principles, and public opinion turned even further against the president's actions.[95]

However, the D.C. Circuit Court of Appeals issued a stay that prevented the ruling from going into effect until the Supreme Court weighed in, and the Truman administration had reason to hope for a favorable result there.[96] Both in briefing and in oral argument before the Supreme Court, government lawyers emphasized presidential emergency power.[97] In its brief the administration relied heavily on historical precedent, including the Emancipation Proclamation and seizure authority exercised by the Wilson and Roosevelt administrations during the world wars.[98] However, none of those examples was useful, as in each previous case the president had been able to rely, at least to some extent, on statutory authority. Although the Truman administration attempted to tone down the unrestrained language Baldridge had used before the district court, John W. Davis, arguing for the steel companies, charged that the administration's position still amounted to an assertion of "kingly prerogatives."[99] The government's brief referred to amorphous emergency powers related to provisions in Article II, including the Vesting, Commander in Chief, and Take Care Clauses.[100]

At oral argument, the government also emphasized an emergency context, insisting that pragmatic considerations—the realities of the Cold War—required presidential authority to act.[101] Solicitor General Philip Perlman claimed that the president could act without affirmative legislative approval—Congress's silence in the wake of the steel seizure was enough.[102] Perlman also argued that each branch of government had previously recognized presidential emergency power to seize private property and cited the historical precedents identified in the administration's brief.[103]

President Truman continued to stand by his previous claims regarding the nature of presidential emergency power. At a May 22, 1952, press conference held after oral argument had concluded, Truman declared that "[t]he President has the [emergency] power and [Congress and the courts] can't take it away from him."[104] Follow-up comments provided to the press by the White House press secretary emphasized that the administration was relying on a notion of inherent power. Press secretary Joseph Short explained that Truman had wanted to make clear that "neither the Congress nor the courts could deny the inherent powers of the presidency without tearing up the Constitution. . . . The Supreme Court, in the pending steel case, might properly decide that the conditions existing did not justify the use by the President of his inherent powers, but . . . such a decision would not deny the existence of the inherent powers."[105]

The Truman administration was essentially asking the Court to place its imprimatur on an idea of broad presidential emergency power to act in the name of national security. If it was successful, the administration would get a result similar to what the Roosevelt administration had received in *Quirin*, *Hirabayashi*, and *Korematsu*—a high court ruling legitimizing the exercise of plenary power.[106] Even if the administration lost its argument before the Court, Truman seemed committed to the idea of inherent power—perhaps to be wielded in other contexts.

In a 6-3 decision, the Court declined to endorse Truman's vision of inherent, extraconstitutional presidential power.[107] Instead, it "reaffirm[ed] . . . the proposition that the President is not above the law."[108] Justice Hugo Black wrote the majority opinion, although each of the five other justices voting with the majority also wrote separate opinions. Black's majority opinion rejected the idea of inherent power, concluding that presidential authority must be based, expressly or implicitly, in either the Constitution or statute.[109] In the case before the Court, the president could not rely on statutory authority—the Taft-Hartley Act had specifically "rejected an amendment which would have authorized such governmental seizures in cases of emergency."[110] The majority opinion concluded that there was no constitutional authority for Truman's decision: the Commander in Chief Clause could not justify the domestic seizure of private property in order to avoid a strike.[111] Taking what could be described as a formalistic[112] approach to separation of powers analysis, Black declared that the seizure order looked more like an act of lawmaking than an act of carrying out the law as enacted by Congress.[113] The executive order itself looked like a statute—"[t]he preamble of the order itself, like that of many statutes, sets out reasons why the President believes certain policies should be adopted, proclaims these policies as rules of conduct to be followed, and again, like a statute, authorizes a government official to promulgate additional rules and regulations consistent with the policy proclaimed and needed to carry that policy into execution."[114]

Justice Robert H. Jackson's concurring opinion in *Youngstown Sheet* has been more influential than Black's majority opinion, most centrally because of Jackson's well-known tripartite test for assessing the constitutionality of presidential action.[115] Jackson offered pragmatic flexibility as an alternative to Black's formalism. The tripartite test seems both to provide a way to ensure that the president has the ability to respond to national security crises and also to limit presidential power. The president is best advised to seek congressional support for action, since "[w]hen the President acts pursuant to an express or implied authorization of Congress, his authority is at its maximum, for it includes all that he possesses in his own right plus all that Congress can delegate. In these circumstances, and in these only, may he be said (for what it may be worth) to personify the federal sovereignty."[116] On the other hand, when the "President takes measures incompatible with the expressed or implied will of Congress, his power is at its lowest ebb, for then he can rely only upon his own constitutional powers minus any constitutional powers of Congress over the matter. Courts can sustain exclusive presidential control in such a case only by disabling the Congress from acting upon the subject."[117] For Jackson, this scenario described the steel seizure, as Truman was acting in the face of "statutory policies inconsistent with this seizure."[118] Truman could find support for his actions only by showing "that seizure of such strike-bound industries is within his domain and beyond control by Congress."[119] That would mean identifying constitutional authority for plenary presidential power in this area.

Jackson addressed each of the administration's arguments in support of plenary power and concluded that no such power existed. The administration cited Article II's Vesting Clause, stating in its brief that "[i]n our view, this clause constitutes a grant of all the executive powers of which the Government is capable."[120] Jackson pointed out that this argument failed to impose any meaningful limits on presidential power. If the Framers had meant to give the president *all* the executive power, "it is difficult to see why the forefathers bothered to add several specific items [describing executive power in Article II], including some trifling ones."[121] As Jackson aptly observed, it defies logic and the historical record to suggest that the Framers, who had just rid themselves of a monarch, desired to create a president with "unlimited executive power."[122] Even Alexander Hamilton did not go so far as the Truman administration dared. In his *Pacificus* essay, Hamilton acknowledged limits on executive power, conceding that the Constitution assigned some traditionally executive functions, such as declaring war, to Congress, while other powers, such as treaty interpretation, were concurrently possessed by both the president and Congress.[123]

Jackson noted that other clauses in Article II also failed to provide a basis for plenary presidential power. The Commander in Chief Clause did not give the president a "monopoly of 'war powers.'"[124] The text of the Constitution set limits on presidential power in this area by assigning some powers to Congress (e.g., to raise and support armies, provide and maintain a navy, and make rules for the "government and regulation of land and naval forces"), while the Bill of Rights made clear that the president could exercise some war powers (specifically, quartering troops in civilian homes) only pursuant to statutory authority.[125] The Commander in Chief Clause could not be read as broad "support for any presidential action, internal or external, involving use of force."[126] The president's power as commander in chief was not meant "to supersede representative government of internal [i.e. domestic] affairs."[127] The Take Care Clause could not be read as enabling the president to set aside constitutional or statutory limits on presidential power: to the contrary, the Take Care Clause was a reminder that the president was subject to the rule of law.[128]

Jackson was particularly emphatic in rejecting the administration's argument that "inherent" presidential power justified the steel seizure. Jackson criticized the "[l]oose and irresponsible use of adjectives" like "inherent," "plenary," and "emergency" to describe presidential power.[129] There was no way to clearly define or limit such powers, as the Framers understood—the only "emergency" power they included in the Constitution was Article I's Suspension Clause, providing Congress with authority to suspend habeas corpus during rebellion or invasion when required for the public safety.[130] It was reasonable to surmise that the Framers recognized that "emergency powers would tend to kindle emergencies."[131] Recent history, Jackson concluded, had confirmed the Framers' wisdom: Hitler had achieved dictatorial power by using emergency as a pretext.[132] As the tripartite framework suggested, presidents would be best advised to seek congressional authorization for emergency power.[133]

The problem, however, is that Jackson's tripartite test does not always provide clear answers. As noted, two of the three categories seem, at first glance, to provide clarity. On closer inspection, though, gaps and ambiguities appear. Jackson's test states that presidential authority is at its maximum when "the President acts pursuant to an express or implied authorization of Congress" (category one under the test) and "at its lowest ebb" when "the President takes measures incompatible with the expressed or implied will of Congress" (category three).[134] The problem, of course, is that it is not always clear which category best describes presidential action. How is "implied" congressional authorization to be determined? The Truman administration believed its actions fit into category one—the high ebb of presidential power—because congressional silence in response to Truman's message indicated that Congress had implicitly consented to the steel seizure.[135]

The Truman administration could have alternatively argued that its action fit into category two, with president acting "in absence of either a congressional grant or denial of authority."[136] In such circumstances, Jackson wrote, the president "can rely upon his own independent powers."[137] However, the Constitution may not clearly assign authority one way or the other, and there may be "a zone of twilight in which [the president] and Congress may have concurrent authority,[138] or in which its distribution is uncertain."[139] When this is the case, Jackson wrote, "congressional inertia, indifference or quiescence may sometimes, at least, as a practical matter, enable, if not invite, measures on independent presidential responsibility.

In this area, any actual test of power is likely to depend on the imperatives of events and contemporary imponderables, rather than on abstract theories of law."[140] This part of Jackson's test is the most ambiguous and, in fact, seems to leave no role for judicial review, leaving definition of the scope and limits of presidential power to the interbranch practice of Congress and the president.

Although Justice Jackson's opinion in *Youngstown* makes clear that he believed the Constitution limits presidential power, advocates of unchecked presidential power have been able to exploit gaps in the tripartite framework, as we will see in Sections II and III. It is to their advantage to seize on any plausible (or even, perhaps, any implausible) connection between presidential action and statutory authority so that they can claim presidential action falls under category one of Jackson's framework. This permits advocates of unchecked presidential power to claim they respect the rule of law when, in reality, they are relying on the illusion that presidential power is limited in this way.

## NIXON:
## A PRESIDENCY ABOVE THE LAW

The Truman administration advanced a claim of plenary power in defending its decision to seize the steel companies. The Truman administration's case depended on inherent power, especially in the context of emergency, to set aside constitutional checks and balances. That argument was rejected by the Supreme Court, though Justice Jackson's tripartite test left room for future presidents to stake claims to unchecked power. Also, the Cold War provided Truman's successors in the White House with an opportunity to expand their power free of effective congressional restraint.

Richard Nixon's presidency brought claims of unchecked power that in some ways echoed Truman's defense of the steel seizure but in other ways were different and went even further. For one thing, unlike Truman, Nixon did not, at first, make his case publicly. The Nixon administration carried out a secret campaign to spy on and "screw" its political opponents.[141] That, of course, initially prevented congressional and public oversight of presidential actions. Also, Nixon's vision of unchecked power encompassed his entire presidency and was not limited to responding to discrete crises. Nixon defined his political opponents as dangerous enemies who threatened to thwart the popular will. In Nixon's mind, he, as president, was the true representative of the people, and plenary presidential power was justified by the need to protect the president from political opponents.[142]

Nixon saw defending the presidency against political opposition as a national security matter and, accordingly, tried to enlist the national security apparatus of the federal government—the FBI, CIA, Defense Intelligence Agency, and National Security Agency—in carrying out the Huston Plan,[143] an intelligence-gathering campaign designed to carry out acts of espionage and burglary against Nixon's critics.[144] When the FBI refused to carry out the plan, Nixon secretly assigned a personal team of burglars and saboteurs known as the "plumbers" to carry out acts of political espionage.[145] Although the plumbers are most notorious for their attempt to wiretap and burglarize the Democratic National Committee's office at the Watergate Hotel and office complex in 1972, some also broke into the offices of Daniel Ellsberg's psychiatrist in an effort to find information that could be used to discredit Ellsberg.[146]

After the Watergate break-in and other acts of malfeasance[147] were publicly revealed, special prosecutors[148] issued subpoenas to the Nixon administration seeking production of secret tape recordings of conversations Nixon had had with administration officials in the Oval Office. Nixon refused to produce the tapes, and the matter came before the Supreme Court. The Nixon administration argued that the tapes were protected by executive privilege and that no court could force the president to produce the tapes, even if the tapes contained evidence relevant to an ongoing criminal investigation. The administration claimed that the president, not the courts, had the power to define the scope of privilege, arguing that "the separation of powers doctrine precludes judicial review of a President's claim of privilege" and that "the Constitution . . . provid[es] an absolute privilege of confidentiality for all Presidential communications."[149] This argument, if successful, would have effectively placed the president above the law, with the ability to foreclose judicial review of any conversation between the president and his advisers, even if the conversation was evidence of criminal wrongdoing.

In an 8-0 decision[150] handed down on July 24, 1974, the Supreme Court rejected Nixon's argument and required production of the tapes, a decision that led to Nixon's resignation from office two weeks later.[151] The Court reasoned that accepting the administration's argument would "be contrary to the basic concept of separation of powers and the checks and balances that flow from the scheme of a tripartite government."[152] However, the Court left an opening for future presidents, saying that "[a]bsent a claim of need to protect military, diplomatic, or sensitive national security secrets, we find it difficult to accept the argument that even the very important interest in confidentiality of Presidential communications is significantly diminished by production of such material for *in camera* inspection with all the protection that a district court will be obliged to provide."[153]

The implication, of course, was that presidents who claimed their conversations involved sensitive military, diplomatic, or national security secrets *could* prevent even *in camera* judicial review. This was an allusion to the "state secrets" doctrine described in the 1953 *U.S. v. Reynolds* decision,[154] a privilege successfully invoked by both the Bush and the Obama administrations after 9/11 and a powerful tool in the cause of unchecked presidential power, as discussed in Sections II and III.

## THE IRAN-CONTRA MINORITY REPORT AND THE MODERN UNITARY EXECUTIVE THEORY

In the years following Nixon's resignation, it seemed that arguments for unrestrained presidential power had been discredited. Nixon had resigned in disgrace, and Congress was taking action aimed at reining in presidential power through the War Powers Resolution (1973) and the Foreign Intelligence Surveillance Act (FISA) (1978). However, not everyone believed that the emphasis should be on limiting presidential power. Dick Cheney, who served as chief of staff for President Gerald Ford, complained that the reaction to Nixon's excesses had led to "the nadir of the modern presidency in terms of authority and legitimacy."[155] Cheney believed this was a dangerous mistake that was weakening the presidency.

As a member of Congress in the 1980s, Cheney had the opportunity to advance his views on presidential power while serving as a member of the House Select Committee investigating the Iran-Contra affair, which came to light after a U.S. plane carrying supplies to Contra forces in Nicaragua was shot down. It turned out the flight was part of a larger covert operation. The Reagan administration had secretly sold missiles to Iran as part of a plan to secure the release of U.S. hostages held in Lebanon. The administration then used money gained from those arms sales to support the Contras, an opposition force fighting against the leftist Sandinista regime governing Nicaragua.[156] These activities violated federal law.[157]

While the executive summary prepared by the congressional committees investigating Iran-Contra criticized "[Reagan] administration officials . . . [for] repeatedly evidenc[ing] disrespect for Congress' efforts to perform its [c]onstitutional oversight role in foreign policy,"[158] the minority report (which Cheney and seven other members of Congress signed) took a different view. The minority report argued that the Reagan administration's "actions toward Nicaragua and Iran were constitutionally protected exercises of *inherent* [p]residential powers."[159] The minority report suggested the president could not be limited by laws that encroached on "core presidential foreign power functions."[160] According to the minority report, the Framers of the Constitution had intended to allow presidents "some discretion to use military force without a declaration of war," and the extent of this discretion was something that "would have to be worked out in subsequent practice."[161] Of course, that subsequent practice included the unilateral war waged by the Truman administration in Korea.

The ideas expressed in the minority report suggest a president capable of operating outside the rule of law on the basis of inherent power that could trump statutory restrictions. The minority report described presidential power as especially broad in the areas of foreign policy and the use of military force. If historical practice was the touchstone for defining the scope of authority to use military force, as the minority report claimed, then presidential power included the unilateral ability to order the use of military force well beyond the limited self-defense context envisioned by the Framers.

Vice President Cheney later remarked that the views expressed in the Iran-Contra minority report "[were] very good in laying out a robust view of the President's prerogative with respect to the conduct of especially foreign policy and national security matters."[162] Ultimately, this vision of a president possessing inherent power that could not be limited by the other branches of government was implemented by the Bush administration, as discussed in the next section.

# SECTION II

# 3

# THE GEORGE W. BUSH
# ADMINISTRATION AND
# NATIONAL SECURITY POWER

When the George W. Bush administration considered how to define the scope of presidential power after the September 11 attacks, previous examples of presidents who exercised or sought to exercise unchecked power should have served as a cautionary tale. A number of Bush's predecessors had claimed the right to plenary power and acted unilaterally without congressional approval—Roosevelt with the Nazi saboteurs, Truman in Korea and with the steel seizure, Nixon in ordering surveillance and espionage against his political opponents, Reagan with the Iran-Contra affair—or else counted on congressional acquiescence to give their initially unilateral actions a veneer of legitimacy, as Roosevelt did in the course of interning Japanese Americans. By 2001, none of these should have been precedents the Bush administration would want to follow. However, the Bush administration believed it could find success in claiming plenary power where previous administrations had foundered. September 11, it insisted, had changed everything.[1] Bush, Vice President Dick Cheney, and other administration officials concluded that Americans wanted the president to have whatever power he needed in order to keep them safe.

In a position articulated mainly in secret Office of Legal Counsel (OLC) memos, the Bush administration "claimed powers once asserted by kings."[2] The administration made the decision to "go it alone . . . eschew[ing] genuine consultation with Congress."[3] Vice President Cheney; his counsel, David Addington; and an OLC lawyer, John Yoo, were the strongest proponents of plenary power. They initially relied on the unitary executive theory, most centrally in once-secret memos written by Yoo, to justify plenary executive power over national security.[4] Other executive branch lawyers, including James Comey and Jack Goldsmith, recognized that the unitary executive theory placed the president above the law.[5] Comey and Goldsmith challenged the Cheney/Addington/Yoo assertion of plenary power, most notably in the context of the secret warrantless surveillance program known as the President's Surveillance Program.[6]

Although Goldsmith ultimately concluded that the Bush administration was held accountable for its excesses and ultimately constrained by the rule of law,[7] the evidence does not support that conclusion. The administration consistently defended its unilateral authority to make decisions regarding the use of military force, detention and trial of prisoners, warrantless surveillance, and interrogation methods. At times, it grudgingly sought congressional approval, for example when forced to do so by a Supreme Court decision.[8] However, congressional approval was typically gained retroactively and functioned more as a matter of congressional acquiescence than as the product of meaningful consultation with Congress as an equal partner. For instance, Congress passed the Military Commissions Act of 2006 to effectively ratify the military tribunal system the Bush administration had implemented and the Supreme Court had struck down.[9]

Retroactive congressional approval of unilateral presidential actions not otherwise authorized under the Constitution can be justified only when an emergency made it impossible to consult Congress in advance. But no emergency had prevented Bush from seeking advance approval for his unilateral actions. When Bush sought congressional approval for his actions, he usually "went to Congress out of prudence, not principle."[10] He "did not relinquish or renounce his claims to constitutional authority [to do what he had already done]."[11] In fact, his administration continued to steadfastly defend presidential authority to act alone and never repudiated the idea of unchecked presidential power.[12] As a consequence, James Pfiffner predicted in 2008 that "[t]he precedents of [Bush's] constitutional claims [to plenary power], unless effectively challenged, will remain 'loaded weapons' that future presidents can use to justify their own unilateral assertions of executive power."[13] As discussed in Section III, Pfiffner's prophecy has essentially been fulfilled by the actions of the Obama administration.

When the Bush administration's claims of plenary power were challenged, it either held its ground or, at times, presented a new argument to justify unchecked power, an argument that seemed to be based on statutory authority but actually went beyond what Congress had authorized or the Constitution allowed. This is what Peter Shane describes as "faux law," arguments that "[look] like legal authority for even utterly unprecedented claims [of presidential power]" but are designed only to give the appearance that presidential power is limited by the rule of law.[14] As discussed in

Section III, the Obama administration has often taken a similar approach. It has not embraced the unitary executive theory, and it has not continued all of the Bush administration's policies. However, like the Bush administration, the Obama administration has found ways to justify what the president wants to do by creating "faux law"—the illusion that the president is respecting constitutional and statutory limits.

Although the Bush administration advanced dangerous arguments to support unchecked power, it is not solely to blame for the post-9/11 deterioration of the rule of law. Congress played a significant role as well, sometimes by acquiescing to what the administration wanted—for example, with the 2006 Military Commissions Act (MCA) and 2008 FISA Amendments Act (FAA), as discussed later in this section and in Section III.[15] When Congress did attempt to assert meaningful limits on presidential authority, the Bush administration displayed disdain for such efforts.[16] This, of course, is a position consistent with the unitary executive theory— congressional efforts to limit executive power are defined as illegitimate.

When Congress approves presidential action, as with the 2006 MCA and the 2008 FAA, it may appear that the president is constrained by checks and balances and subject to the rule of law. Under Jackson's tripartite framework in *Youngstown Sheet*, presidential action in such circumstances would be "at its maximum."[17] On closer examination, however, this demonstrates the limitations of the tripartite framework. Congressional approval of presidential action does not necessarily render such action legitimate— constitutional limits still apply, as Jackson acknowledged.[18] Moreover, when the president fails to consult with Congress prior to taking action and seeks congressional ratification after the fact, that approval may be less meaningful. If the president does not have time to seek congressional approval before acting, then retroactive congressional approval can be legitimate— as when Lincoln sought retroactive approval from Congress for actions he took at the beginning of the Civil War while Congress was not in session. For the Bush administration, however, there was time to consult Congress before acting. As Jack Goldsmith observes, the Bush administration often acted with "unnecessary unilateralism."[19] The administration did not take unilateral actions (e.g., with regard to torture, detention, military trials, or warrantless surveillance) because time was short; it acted unilaterally because it believed the president knew best how to defend the nation and did not need congressional approval.[20] Under such circumstances—when congressional approval could have been sought in advance but was not— congressional approval is better described as congressional acquiescence,[21] as Congress is not really acting to limit presidential power; it is acting to enable presidential power.

This section considers four areas in which the Bush administration claimed plenary power to set aside or find ways around constitutional and statutory limits, often thanks in part to congressional acquiescence: (1) the president's ability to use military force, (2) surveillance, (3) the military detention system at Guantanamo, and (4) interrogation of prisoners. It also considers how the Bush administration used the state secrets privilege in an effort to insulate its claims of plenary power from judicial review. In Section III, I argue that the Obama administration has continued the same approach in some of these areas, although it has not relied on the unitary executive theory. The starting point for understanding all of this is the Bush administration's justification of unchecked presidential power, which began in a then-classified Office of Legal Counsel memorandum written just two weeks after the 9/11 attacks.

# 4

# THE BUSH ADMINISTRATION
# AND THE USE OF MILITARY FORCE

As Jack Goldsmith aptly observes, "[a] September 25, 2001, memo-randum from [John] Yoo to the White House, entitled 'The President's Constitutional Authority to Conduct Military Operations Against Terrorists and Nations Supporting Them,' set the tone for all that was to come."[1] Yoo's memo described a president with complete, uncon-strained power over the use of military force.[2] Although Yoo noted that Congress had, a few days after the 9/11 attacks, passed an Authorization for Use of Military Force (AUMF), authorizing the president to "use all neces-sary and appropriate force against those nations, organizations, or persons he determines planned, authorized, committed, or aided the terrorist attacks that occurred on September 11, 2001, or harbored such organizations or persons,"[3] Yoo concluded that the AUMF was not necessary and that, to the extent the AUMF sought to limit presidential power, it was an irrele-vancy.[4] In Yoo's view, the president possessed "plenary constitutional power" over the use of military force, and Congress could not "place any limits on the President's determinations as to any terrorist threat, the amount of military force to be used in response, or the method, timing, and nature of the response." Yoo concluded that any and all decisions regarding the use of military force in this context "under our Constitution, are for the President alone to make."[5]

Yoo's conclusions defied the intention of the Constitution's Framers and described a president unconstrained by the rule of law. Yoo insisted that the Framers, revolutionaries who had taken up arms against a monarch they saw as tyrannical, intended to assign plenary control over the use of military force and the conduct of foreign affairs to the president they created under the Constitution.[6] In order to justify this upside-down view of presidential power, Yoo relied on implausible readings of the constitutional text, selective citation to the Federalist Papers, and manipulation of John Marshall's sole organ speech.

Yoo argued that the language of Article II's Vesting Clause was evidence of the Framers' intention to assign *all* executive power to the president: "[the] difference in language [between the vesting clauses of Articles I and II] indicates that Congress's legislative powers are limited to the list enumerated in Article I, section 8, while the President's powers include inherent executive powers that are unenumerated in the Constitution."[7] But Yoo's argument cannot withstand even casual scrutiny. As Louis Fisher has observed, the very idea of "inherent" power is extraconstitutional: such powers are not described by the Constitution and cannot be readily defined or limited.[8] The Framers clearly rejected the British model, which concentrated war power and power over foreign affairs in the executive.[9] They recognized the need to set limits on power, with Madison describing checks and balances as a way to make sure that no one branch of government would have unlimited power.[10] David Gray Adler observes that, since the Framers intended to create a president with "confined and defined" powers, the unitary executive view that the president possesses open-ended inherent powers cannot be sustained.[11]

Yoo's conclusion that the president possesses plenary authority over the use of military force also runs afoul of Article I's Declare War Clause, which plainly assigns significant war power to Congress, including most centrally the authority to initiate hostilities.[12] He attempts to dismiss the Declare War Clause as a mere formality that does not assign Congress substantive power "to decide whether to make war."[13] Yoo finds it significant that the drafters of the Constitution originally planned to give Congress the power to "make" war, but changed that to (in Yoo's view) the reduced power to "declare" war.[14] But Yoo's reading is implausible. Records from the Constitutional Convention show that the Framers changed Congress's power to "make" war to the power to "declare" war in order to "leav[e] to the Executive the power to repel sudden attacks."[15] Louis Fisher declares it was "never the understanding" that, "although Congress may "declare war," the president is at liberty to "make" war."[16] Fisher observes that the interpretation championed by Yoo "would defeat everything the framers said about Congress being the only political body authorized to take the country from a state of peace to a state of war."[17]

Other scholars agree with Fisher that the Framers intended to give Congress the power to initiate war, reserving to the president only the power to respond to sudden attacks—in other words, that Yoo's argument is unsupported by the historical record. Andrew Campanelli, Kai Draper, and Jack Stucker find that "John Yoo's arguments to the contrary notwithstanding, there is compelling evidence that most, if not all, [of the Framers and ratifiers of the Constitution] believed that, in virtue of its Declare War Clause, the Constitution vests the power to create war in Congress alone."[18] James Pfiffner concludes "Yoo's arguments that the framers intended to give the war powers to the executive stretch the text of the Constitution and the deliberations of the framers beyond reasonable interpretations."[19] Jack Rakove believes it is not absolutely clear what the Framers intended when they changed the verb "make" to "declare" in the context of war power, but he observes that it may have been intended to "preserve the capacity of the president to wage war [in the sense of directing military operations] with the essential attributes of energy and dispatch."[20] Rakove's interpretation is consistent with Fisher's, Pfiffner's, and Campanelli, Draper, and Stucker's views.

Fisher and Pfiffner also point to additional evidence of the Framers' concerns about entrusting war power to the executive, including in the writings of John Jay and James Madison.[21] In Federalist No. 4, Jay warned of "[a]bsolute monarchs [who] will often make war when their nations are to get nothing by it, but for purposes and objects merely personal, such as a thirst for military glory, revenge for personal affronts, ambition, or private compacts to aggrandize or support their particular families or partisans."[22] Madison warned against the danger of concentrating war power in the hands of the executive, declaring in *Helvidius No. 1* that "[t]hose who are to *conduct* war cannot, in the nature of things, be proper or safe judges, whether a war ought to be *commenced, continued,* or *concluded.*"[23]

Madison's observation in *Helvidius* is consistent with the Framers' decision to break with the British model, which concentrated power over war and foreign affairs in the monarch.[24] Madison and other Framers believed it would be wiser and safer to divide these powers between Congress and the President. This view was not an aberration; it "reflected a broad consensus among the framers."[25] During the ratification debate, James Wilson praised the Constitution for creating a "system [that] will not hurry us into war: it is calculated to guard against it. It will not be in the power of a single man, or a single body of men, to involve us in such distress; for the important power of declaring war is vested in the legislature at large."[26] Even Hamilton. Madison's opponent in the Pacificus-Helvidius debate, consistently "insisted that Congress possessed the sole and exclusive authority to commence hostilities on behalf of the American people."[27] For instance, in 1801, Hamilton acknowledged that "it is the peculiar and exclusive province of Congress, *when the nation is at peace* to change that state into a state of war . . . in other words, it belong to Congress only, *to go to War.*[28]

Yoo's argument that the Framers meant to give the president complete control over the use of military force flies in the face of this historical evidence, as does Yoo's unfortunate reliance on the intellectually bankrupt "sole organ doctrine." As suggested in Section I, this is better described as the sole organ myth. Yoo is simply wrong to claim that Marshall's sole organ reference helps justify "the president's plenary authority in foreign affairs."[29] John Marshall did not use the term "sole organ" to refer to plenary presidential power, and Justice Sutherland's dicta in *Curtiss-Wright* quoted Marshall's remarks completely out of context. Marshall did not mean to suggest that the president has plenary power over foreign affairs. As Marshall fully understood and as even a cursory reading of the Constitution makes clear, this power is divided between the president and Congress.[30]

Yoo also claims that Alexander Hamilton's *Pacificus* essay supports plenary presidential power in this area.[31] Again, Yoo is wrong. Hamilton did not claim the president had exclusive power to act in the area of foreign affairs. Hamilton argued that Article II's Vesting Clause assigned all executive power to the president—"subject only to the *exceptions* and *qualifications which* are expressed in the [Constitution]."[32] Those are important limitations, and Hamilton quite clearly acknowledged that the Constitution assigned Congress (one or both houses) significant powers in the area of foreign affairs, including the Senate's role in making treaties and Congress's power to declare war and issue letters of marque and reprisal.[33] Even on those matters of foreign policy that Hamilton argued were part of the "executive power" assigned to the president (e.g., the power to interpret treaties and declare neutrality), Hamilton conceded that the president "cannot control the exercise of . . . power [over foreign affairs]."[34] If Congress disagreed with the president's conclusions regarding the meaning of a treaty or the nation's duty to remain neutral, it could declare war. The president had no plenary control over such decisions. If Congress acted, the president could, at most, veto legislation it passed. Even then, Hamilton conceded, the president's veto could be overridden.[35] There is nothing in *Pacificus*[36] to support Yoo's conclusion that Hamilton believed in plenary presidential authority over foreign affairs.[37] Moreover, in other writing, Hamilton made clear that he recognized Congress was assigned power under the Constitution to initiate hostilities.[38]

Yoo's September 25, 2001, memo was unnecessary. Congress had already provided Bush with the authority needed to use military force against al Qaeda and the Taliban in Afghanistan, and it would again provide authorization for the Bush administration to use military force against Iraq.[39] The real point of the Yoo memo was to make clear that the Bush administration believed "Congress could do nothing to check the President's power to respond to the terrorist threat."[40] The administration never repudiated Yoo's views on presidential control over the use of military force and, in fact, Yoo's memo was cited with approval in a 2002 OLC memo that concluded the president had unilateral authority to decide whether to use military force in Iraq.[41]

# 5

## THE BUSH ADMINISTRATION
## AND SURVEILLANCE

During his time as head of OLC, Jack Goldsmith learned about a secret warrantless surveillance program "long after it had been integrated into the post-9/11 counterterrorism architecture."[1] The operation, known as the Presidential Surveillance Program or PSP,[2] was first authorized by President Bush on October 4, 2001, and was aimed at gathering intelligence through electronic surveillance, including surveillance of phone calls and e-mails sent by or to Americans.[3] The entire program (including the president's authorization) was originally classified, and few people, even within the administration, knew about it.[4] James Risen and Eric Lichtblau made some information about the program public when they reported on it in late 2005.[5] However, their reporting provided details only about the Terrorist Surveillance Program (TSP), itself only a portion of the larger PSP. Information about some other intelligence activities involved in the PSP, apart from the TSP, remain classified, although there has been reporting about bulk metadata collection that began as part of the PSP before it was authorized by secret FISA court orders beginning in 2006 and continuing during the Obama administration.[6]

Through the TSP, President Bush authorized the National Security Agency to "[intercept] . . . the content of communications into and out of the United States where there was a reasonable basis to conclude that one party to the communication was a member of [al-Qaeda] or related terrorist organizations." The executive branch could conclude whether such a "reasonable basis" existed without obtaining a warrant.[7] In short, "if the president concluded that Americans were [communicating with] someone outside the United States who the president reasonably believed was connected with al-Qaeda or an affiliated organization, the NSA could intercept those communications without obtaining a warrant."[8] Bush authorized the TSP and other intelligence activities under the PSP through "a single Presidential Authorization that was periodically reauthorized."[9] The program was reauthorized by the Department of Justice every thirty to sixty days. Before Goldsmith became head of OLC in 2003, the attorney general had always reauthorized the program on the basis of advice he received from John Yoo, the only lawyer in the Office of Legal Counsel who knew about the program at the time.[10]

The problem, as Goldsmith recognized when he learned of the program, was that the TSP violated FISA, the Foreign Intelligence Surveillance Act of 1978.[11] FISA was created to provide an "exclusive" framework for the executive branch to gather foreign intelligence through electronic surveillance and other means.[12] At the time the PSP was in effect, FISA required that, in most cases, the executive branch obtain a warrant from a special FISA court before conducting electronic surveillance.[13] A warrant was not required (a) if surveillance was aimed only at obtaining the contents of communications between "foreign powers" when there was no substantial likelihood the surveillance would acquire the contents of communications involving a U.S. citizen, a lawful U.S. resident, or a U.S. corporation or association; the surveillance was to continue for one year or less; and the attorney general certified its limited aims; (b) under "an emergency situation" as determined by the attorney general, in which case warrantless surveillance could be conducted for up to seventy-two hours, as long as the attorney general informed a FISA judge of the decision to authorize emergency warrantless surveillance; or (c) within fifteen days of a declaration of war by Congress.[14] If none of these circumstances applied, a warrant had to be obtained.

Under the TSP, however, the president was authorizing surveillance of U.S. persons—U.S. citizens, permanent residents, associations made up substantially of U.S. citizens or permanent residents, or corporations incorporated in the U.S.—without a warrant and in violation of FISA.[15] This was a serious matter—violations of FISA are criminal offenses, with each offense punishable by up to five years in prison and/or a fine of up to $10,000.[16]

The Bush administration saw FISA as a nuisance. David Addington, Vice President Cheney's counsel, sarcastically told Goldsmith that "[w]e're one bomb away from getting rid of that obnoxious [FISA] court." Addington apparently spoke for the vice president on this matter. Goldsmith writes that Cheney and Addington "had abhorred FISA's intrusion on presidential power since its enactment in 1978. After 9/11 they and other top officials in the administration dealt with FISA the way they dealt with other laws they didn't like; they blew through them in secret based on flimsy legal opinions that they guarded closely so no one could question the legal basis for their operations."[17]

One of these flimsy legal opinions was contained in yet another OLC memo written by John Yoo. In a November 2001 memo, Yoo concluded the president could authorize warrantless surveillance that was prohibited by FISA.[18] Yoo's memo was made available in March 2011 but is heavily redacted: only eight sentences in the memo have been publicly revealed.[19] However, those eight sentences make clear how Yoo justified his conclusions: once again, he relied on plenary presidential power, flatly asserting FISA could be set aside because "we do not believe that Congress may restrict the President's inherent constitutional powers, which allow him to gather intelligence necessary to defend the nation from direct attack." Somewhat oddly, Yoo's memo suggested that Congress might have been able "to restrict presidential authority to conduct warrantless searches in the national security area" if it had included "a clear statement in FISA" to this effect. This is hard to decipher, as Yoo seemed to conclude elsewhere in the memo that Congress simply had no authority to "restrict the President's inherent constitutional powers" in this area.[20] However, since Yoo concluded that FISA did not contain a clear statement of Congress's intent to restrict presidential power to conduct warrantless searches, he apparently did not have to resolve the problem of deciding whether Congress in fact possessed such authority.[21]

Before his resignation, in May 2003, Yoo was the only OLC lawyer who knew about the PSP, and he advised Attorney General John Ashcroft that it should be periodically reauthorized. After Yoo left OLC, Patrick Philbin (another OLC lawyer) and Jack Goldsmith were read into the program. Goldsmith and Philbin were "concerned about the factual and legal basis for Yoo's legal memoranda supporting the program." They recognized Yoo was wrong to claim that Congress included no clear statement in FISA indicating its intent to restrict presidential authority to order warrantless searches in the context of national security—FISA creates an exception allowing warrantless searches for fifteen days following a congressional declaration of war. Logically, this provision makes clear that Congress intended to prohibit the president from otherwise authorizing warrantless searches during wartime, unless some other exception to the warrant requirement under FISA applied. Goldsmith and Philbin believed that it was necessary to identify some congressional authorization for the PSP. They concluded that the September 2001 AUMF implicitly provided authorization for some but not all of the PSP. Although Goldsmith and Philbin did not believe that all of the intelligence activities authorized by the PSP were legal, they initially advised Attorney General Ashcroft to continue certifying the legality of the program as they continued to develop their legal analysis.[22]

In late January 2004, Deputy Attorney General James Comey was also read into the PSP. Comey shared Goldsmith's and Philbin's "concerns about Yoo's legal analysis." Comey, like Goldsmith, was "particular[ly] concern[ed] . . . that Yoo's legal analysis entailed ignoring an act of Congress, and doing so without full congressional authorization." Goldsmith had already informed David Addington and White House Counsel Alberto Gonzales about his concerns with the program. On March 6, 2004, "Goldsmith and Philbin, with Comey's concurrence, met with Addington and Gonzales . . . to convey their conclusions that certain activities in the PSP should cease." The forty-five-day authorization period was coming to an end, and reauthorization by the Attorney General was needed by March 11, but Ashcroft was hospitalized with an illness and Comey was acting as attorney general in his place.[23] Vice President Cheney met with Comey, Goldsmith, and Philbin and told Comey that he if he did not reauthorize the PSP, "thousands" of lives would be at risk. Comey, however, said that he could not reauthorize the program unless changes were made.[24]

Vice President Cheney would not agree to make changes to the PSP. Instead, he held an "emergency meeting" on March 10, 2004, with the "Gang of Eight," congressional leaders who had previously received some briefings about the PSP. There is a dispute as to what happened during this meeting. White House Counsel Gonzales, who attended the meeting, later testified before a Senate committee that there was a "consensus" among the Gang of Eight that the PSP should continue in place. However, some of the congressional leaders who were present at the meeting disagree with Gonzales's account. In any event, after the meeting between Cheney and the Gang of Eight, President Bush told Gonzales and Andrew Card, the president's chief of staff, to speak with Ashcroft, who was in the hospital recovering from surgery. Card, as well as President Bush, called the hospital and spoke with Ashcroft's wife, who said Ashcroft could not speak on the phone. At this point, Mrs. Ashcroft "was informed [by Card and/or Bush] that Gonzales and Card were coming to the hospital to see Ashcroft regarding a matter of national security." Ashcroft's chief of staff, David Ayres, called Comey to tell him what was happening, and Comey then tried to "get as many of my people as possible to the hospital immediately."[25] It was clear that Gonzales and Card were planning to try to get Ashcroft, who might not be in full command of his mental capacity, to sign a reauthorization of the PSP from his hospital bed.

What happened next bears an uncomfortable resemblance to the scene from the movie *The Godfather* in which the wounded Don Corleone lies in a hospital bed as his enemies are on their way to finish him off. His son (played by Al Pacino) races over and manages to scare the rival mobsters away. Although no one was trying to kill Ashcroft, Comey clearly believed the White House was attempting something untoward by sending Gonzales and Card to the hospital. After Comey learned of their plan, an incredible race to the hospital ensued, with Comey, Goldsmith, and Philbin arriving before Gonzales and Card. Comey, Goldsmith, and Philbin told Ashcroft that he should "not . . . sign anything." Comey believed Ashcroft, who was lying in his bed, was "pretty bad off" and unable to focus. When Gonzales and Card arrived, Gonzales was carrying a presidential authorization of the PSP for Ashcroft to sign. Gonzales told Ashcroft that reauthorization was necessary (the most recent authorization was to expire the next day). Ashcroft "told Gonzales and Comey 'in very strong terms' about his legal concerns with the PSP." But, Ashcroft added, that didn't matter, because Comey was the acting attorney general who would decide whether the program should be reauthorized. Gonzales and Card left, having failed to obtain a signature reauthorizing the PSP.[26]

The next day, March 11, 2004, with the authorization expiring, President Bush signed a new authorization certified by White House Counsel Gonzales. This deviated from standing practice, which had been for the attorney general to certify the program's legality. The reauthorization claimed that Bush was acting on the basis of his authority as commander in chief, which allowed him to "[displace] any contrary provisions of law, including FISA." When Bush reauthorized the PSP without certification from the attorney general or acting attorney general, a number of senior Department of Justice lawyers and FBI officials prepared to resign, including Comey, Goldsmith, and FBI director Robert Mueller.[27] However, after Bush agreed to modify the PSP, on March 17, 2004, the resignations were averted.[28]

The precise changes[29] Bush made to the PSP remain classified, so it is impossible to know exactly what the administration did to address Comey's and Goldsmith's concerns. However, Goldsmith wrote a memo in May 2004 after Bush agreed to modify the PSP that shows not much, if anything, changed when it came to the administration's assertion of plenary power.

As Jameel Jaffer puts it, "what's striking about the memo that Goldsmith wrote in May 2004 is how similar it is to the one that Yoo wrote in November 2001."[30] Goldsmith, in an analysis reminiscent of Yoo's, asserted that the president has "inherent constitutional authority . . . to conduct warrantless searches for foreign intelligence purposes." Goldsmith also claimed the president possesses "exclusive constitutional authority, derived from his dual roles as Commander in Chief and sole organ for the Nation in foreign affairs, to order warrantless foreign intelligence surveillance targeted at communications of the enemy that Congress cannot override by legislation." Accordingly, in Goldsmith's view, provisions in FISA that interfere with the president's authority in this area are unconstitutional. Unlike Yoo, Goldsmith acknowledged *Youngstown Sheet* and identified the September 2001 AUMF as providing implied statutory authorization that could put the president in the strongest *Youngstown* category—having acted pursuant to congressional authorization.[31] However, Goldsmith made clear this was merely a backup argument, as he did not believe *Youngstown* applied at all to the PSP and, therefore, "we do not think *Youngstown* provides any persuasive precedent suggesting that Congress may constitutionally prohibit the President from engaging in the activities contemplated in [the PSP]."[32] Goldsmith's point is clear: the president can authorize warrantless surveillance regardless of what Congress says, and provisions in FISA that infringe on the president's exclusive authority in this area are unconstitutional.[33]

As Jaffer observes, "Goldsmith may have disagreed with Yoo's November 2001 memo, but one wouldn't know that from reading Goldsmith's May 2004 memo . . . the unredacted portions of the memos are remarkably similar."[34] Goldsmith insists that his views on presidential power cannot be fully understood without access to the redacted portions of his May 2004 memo, as well as other classified documents.[35] However, it is hard to see what could change the central feature of Goldsmith's 2004 memo: by relying on inherent presidential powers and exclusive presidential authority based partly on the discredited sole organ doctrine, Goldsmith was staking out a defense of plenary presidential power. In addition, an unclassified 2006 Department of Justice white paper makes clear the Bush administration did not retreat from its position that the president has plenary power in the area of foreign surveillance; it continued to claim that "the NSA activities [involved in the TSP] are supported by the President's well-recognized inherent constitutional authority as Commander in Chief and sole organ for the Nation in foreign affairs to conduct warrantless surveillance of enemy forces for intelligence purposes to detect and disrupt armed attacks against the United States."[36]

Like Goldsmith's May 2004 memo, the unsigned 2006 white paper argued that the president was acting at the "zenith" of his power because Congress had implicitly authorized warrantless surveillance through the AUMF, which made the president's activities "fully consistent with FISA."[37] But, also like the May 2004 memo, the white paper concluded that, even if Congress *did* intend to prohibit the president from authorizing such surveillance, "FISA would be unconstitutional as applied to this narrow context."[38] The white paper relied in part on the notion that "the President has inherent constitutional authority to conduct warrantless searches and surveillance within the United States for foreign intelligence purposes."[39] This is the language of plenary power and echoes very similar language in Yoo's November 2001 memo and Goldsmith's May 2004 memo. The white paper concluded that the AUMF simply "confirm[ed] and supplement[ed] the President's inherent power to use warrantless surveillance against the enemy in the current armed conflict."[40]

A December 22, 2005, letter from Assistant Attorney General William Moschella to the chairs and ranking members of the Senate and House Select Committees on Intelligence took a similar position. Moschella claimed that the president possessed "constitutional authority . . . to order warrantless wiretapping" through the TSP. He also argued that the TSP had been authorized by Congress through the 2001 AUMF and that this authorization "supplemented" the president's constitutional authority to order warrantless surveillance.[41] The argument that the AUMF authorized warrantless surveillance, which was also made by Goldsmith and in the 2006 white paper, simply makes no sense. As noted, FISA contained an exception to the warrant requirement permitting warrantless surveillance for up to fifteen days following a congressional declaration of war. Logically, if Congress had intended to extend this limited window through the AUMF, it would have had to say so. Otherwise, the limited FISA exception would be meaningless, as any congressional declaration (or, here, authorization) of war or the use of military force would be implicitly understood as granting ongoing warrantless surveillance authority to the president.

In Yoo's November 2001 memo, Goldsmith's May 2004 memo, the unsigned January 2006 Department of Justice white paper, and the December 2005 letter to congressional leaders, the Bush administration claimed plenary power (purportedly "supplemented" by the AUMF) to authorize warrantless surveillance of Americans' overseas communications, including the authority to disregard FISA. Congressional approval was nice but certainly not necessary.

Critics argued that the administration could have and should have applied for warrants from the FISC to authorize NSA surveillance. In 2006, however, then-Attorney General Alberto Gonzales argued that the FISC's review process was too slow to respond to terrorist threats "since even a very short delay may make the difference between success and failure in preventing the next attack."[42] Assuming Gonzales was correct and the FISA warrant application process was too slow, the obvious next step would be to ask Congress to amend the law. In fact, as Goldsmith has observed, it seems odd that the administration did not seek explicit congressional approval for warrantless surveillance and other activities included in the PSP.[43] In the aftermath of the 9/11 attacks, it is hard to believe that Congress would have refused to make changes to the law (whether or not those changes were necessary or effective).

Indeed, after the TSP was made public, the Bush administration found it possible to gain explicit congressional approval for its surveillance program. Congress amended FISA in 2007 and 2008, granting the president "new legislative authority . . . to engage in many of the practices that he previously undertook against the law under his own claimed constitutional authority."[44] The 2008 FISA Amendments Act (FAA), as reauthorized by the 2012 FISA Amendments Act Reauthorization Act, "vastly increased the government's powers to conduct surveillance of [Americans'] international communications without individualized judicial review and severely limited the scope of review performed by the FISC when the court's approval is actually required."[45] These developments are discussed in more detail in Section III with regard to the PRISM program.

In ordering illegal warrantless surveillance the Bush administration was, once again, able to exercise plenary power with impunity. The administration simply set aside FISA, proceeding with a surveillance program that violated the law. When executive branch lawyers, including Jack Goldsmith, cried foul, their valid criticisms were first brushed aside, then somehow assuaged by way of classified modifications to the program. In the end, Goldsmith himself wrote a memo that vindicated plenary presidential power. When part of the program was publicly exposed, Congress deferentially granted the president statutory authority to accomplish much of what had previously been done illegally. No one was punished, and no one repudiated the Bush administration's vision of unchecked power. Instead, as James Pfiffner observed, the administration's actions threatened to become bogus precedent cited by Bush's successors, "'loaded weapons' that future presidents can use to justify their own unilateral assertions of executive power."[46] Although the Obama administration did not follow exactly the same model as the Bush administration, the lesson it learned was that presidents can do what they believe necessary for national security, regardless of statutory or constitutional limitations. It was only a matter of generating some theoretical justification that could be cited in support for whatever the president wanted to do. As discussed in Section III, the Obama administration found these justifications through creative misreadings of statutory law and by relying on congressional acquiescence.

# THE BUSH ADMINISTRATION
# AND MILITARY DETENTION

The Bush administration also applied the idea of plenary power to the context of military detention and trial. In a November 6, 2001, memo, Patrick Philbin (a colleague of Yoo's at the OLC) concluded that the president had "inherent powers as Commander in Chief . . . to establish military commissions[1] to prosecute and punish terrorists apprehended as part of the investigation into, or the military and intelligence operations in response to, the September 11 attacks."[2] Although the memo addressed the president's authority to authorize military trials, the primary significance of Philbin's memo was that it served as the springboard for President Bush to create a separate military detention system for suspected terrorists at Guantanamo Bay, Cuba, where hundreds of prisoners have been held for years without trial of any kind, military or civilian.

Philbin's memo concluded that the president has unilateral power to make decisions as to how (i.e., in what kind of court and according to what rules) to try suspected terrorists for war crimes. In Philbin's view, the president does not need authorization from Congress since the president, as commander in chief, possesses inherent authority to convene military tribunals.[3] Philbin's conclusions rested most centrally on faulty historical analysis. He traced a line back to General Washington and the Major Andre[4] trial in 1780 in an effort to show that American military commanders had always possessed independent authority "to convene military tribunals to punish offenses against the laws of war." Philbin reasoned that the drafters of the Constitution "surely intended to give the President the same authority that General Washington possessed during the Revolutionary War."[5] The problem, as Louis Fisher points out, is that General Washington possessed no unilateral authority to convene military tribunals. There was no executive branch of government during the Revolutionary War. There was, however, a Congress, and it had made rules for the military to follow in conducting the trial of accused enemy spies. Accordingly, when Washington ordered Andre's trial, he "acted on the basis of legislative authority, not some sort of 'inherent' executive authority."[6]

Despite the fact that the Philbin memo was based on an incorrect understanding of historical precedent as well as a flawed understanding of the Constitution,[7] it served as the basis for the military detention system created by the Bush administration at Guantanamo. On November 13, 2001, one week after Philbin's memo was completed, President Bush signed a military order that in some ways tracked the one Roosevelt issued in order to try the German saboteurs in 1942.[8] Although Bush's order referenced statutory authority (the September 2001 AUMF and the Uniform Code of Military Justice), it also relied on "authority vested in [the president] as President and as Commander in Chief of the Armed Forces of the United States by the Constitution."[9] Like Roosevelt, Bush asserted unilateral authority in creating the tribunals, declaring that he (Bush) would determine which individuals would be subject to military trial on the basis of his own determination that there was "reason to believe" a prisoner was a member of al Qaeda, was otherwise involved in terrorism, or had "knowingly harbored" a terrorist.[10] Bush's order gave the secretary of defense wide latitude to set rules for tribunals, just as Roosevelt had given the 1942 saboteur tribunal broad power to make its own rules of procedure.[11]

However, while Roosevelt's aim was to quickly try and then execute the saboteurs, Bush's goals were different. The November 2001 military order provided the secretary of defense with the authority to detain any individual subject to the order, without allowing access to civilian courts.[12] Detention proved to be the Bush administration's primary objective, as only a handful of prisoners were ever tried before military tribunals, while nearly eight hundred were ultimately detained (and interrogated).[13] Bush's military order reserved the claimed authority to try suspected terrorists in a forum using rules of the president's choosing but, more importantly, it asserted the power to simply hold suspected terrorists as prisoners without trial or hearing of any kind.[14] Although the military order's title referred to detention of noncitizens, the order also left room for U.S. citizens to be held in the military system without access to the courts.[15]

Pursuant to the November 13, 2001, military order, close to eight hundred men—mainly noncitizens, but some U.S. citizens as well—were imprisoned. Noncitizens were held at Guantanamo, while U.S. citizens (like Yaser Hamdi and Jose Padilla) were held in naval brigs in the United States.[16] Guantanamo was chosen as a site for noncitizen prisoners because it is not U.S. territory (although it is effectively controlled by the United States).[17] Some prisoners, noncitizens held at Guantanamo and a U.S. citizen (Hamdi) held in a naval brig, filed habeas corpus petitions in federal district court, seeking to challenge their detention.[18] On June 28, 2004, the Supreme Court issued decisions in two of these cases, *Rasul v. Bush* and *Hamdi v. Rumsfeld*.[19] In *Rasul*, a 6-3 majority of the Court rejected the administration's argument that it could deny statutory habeas access to noncitizens held at the Guantanamo prison. The administration had hoped it could rely on the 1950 Supreme Court *Eisentrager* decision denying habeas access to members of the German military who were captured in 1945 after Germany surrendered and tried by a U.S. military tribunal in China. The *Rasul* Court, however, distinguished *Eisentrager*, explaining that prisoners at Guantanamo were in a different position because their status as enemy combatants was disputed, they had received no trial of any kind, and Guantanamo (unlike China) was under the "complete jurisdiction and control" of the United States.[20]

In *Hamdi*, eight justices declined to endorse the Bush administration's position that "the Executive possesses plenary authority [to detain a U.S. citizen who it determines is an enemy combatant] pursuant to Article II of the Constitution."[21] However, those eight justices were divided on the question of whether there was some other way to justify Hamdi's detention. The plurality opinion, written by Justice O'Connor, avoided explicitly ruling on the administration's plenary power argument, concluding that "[w]e do not reach the question whether Article II provides such authority, however, because we agree with the Government's alternative position, that Congress has in fact authorized Hamdi's detention, through the [September 2001] AUMF."[22] But O'Connor's opinion, along with Souter's and Scalia's separate opinions, made clear that eight justices rejected the Bush administration's argument for unchecked presidential power.

Justice O'Connor's plurality opinion declared that "a state of war is not a blank check for the President when it comes to the rights of the Nation's citizens."[23] The Bush administration had argued that judicial review of its decisions regarding detention would improperly interfere with executive power, but O'Connor wrote that "we . . . reject the Government's assertion that separation of powers principles mandate a heavily circumscribed role for the courts in such circumstances."[24] It was clear that she was concerned about power concentrated in the hands of the executive. O'Connor pointed out that the administration's position would "turn our system of checks and balances on its head" by denying prisoners held as enemy combatants the opportunity to challenge their detention in court.[25]

Justices Scalia, Stevens, Souter, and Ginsburg shared the plurality's concern about power concentrated in the hands of the executive. Justice Scalia made this point most emphatically in his dissent, which was joined by Justice Stevens. In explaining why he and Stevens believed that, absent congressional suspension of the writ of habeas corpus, Hamdi was "entitled either to criminal trial or to a judicial decree requiring his release[,]" Scalia noted "the Founders' general distrust of military power permanently at the Executive's disposal."[26] Scalia cited Federalist No. 69 for the point that, under the Constitution, "the President's military authority would be 'much inferior' to that of the British king."[27] Souter's separate opinion ( joined by Ginsburg) emphasized the principle that the separation of powers is designed to prevent the concentration of power in any one branch of government, citing Madison's description of the function of checks and balances in Federalist No. 51.[28]

Faced with three opinions reflecting the views of eight Supreme Court justices who made clear that executive power must be constrained by the rule of law, the Bush administration did what any good believer in the unitary executive would: it reiterated its belief in plenary power. Unchastened by the result in *Hamdi*, an administration spokesperson triumphantly declared victory, claiming that "[t]he Justice Department is pleased that the U.S. Supreme Court . . . upheld the authority of the President as Commander in Chief of the armed forces to detain enemy combatants, including U.S. citizens. This power . . . is one of the most essential authorities the U.S. Constitution grants the President to defend America from our enemies."[29] The Supreme Court had actually upheld only the president's authority to detain citizens when authorized to do so by Congress, and even then a hearing had to be provided, but the logic of the unitary executive dictates that efforts by the other branches to rein in presidential power are viewed as a nullity.

As the Justice Department's reaction suggests, neither the *Rasul* nor the *Hamdi* decision effectively checked presidential power. Although both Hamdi and Rasul were released, the Bush administration continued to operate its system of military detention for other prisoners in much the same way as it had before the decisions. It appeared to make a concession to the *Hamdi* decision by creating Combatant Status Review Tribunals (CSRTs) to provide prisoners held as enemy combatants a chance to challenge their status designation. However, in practice, the CSRTs did not provide the "meaningful opportunity to contest the factual basis for . . . detention" that the *Hamdi* Court said was necessary.[30]

CSRTs were established by a July 7, 2004, order signed by Deputy Secretary of Defense Paul Wolfowitz.[31] The July 7 order described proceedings to be conducted in order to determine the status of foreign nationals held as enemy combatants at Guantanamo. The order provided that CSRTs be composed of three military officers, whose task was to determine whether the prisoner could properly be detained as an enemy combatant.[32] An "enemy combatant" was broadly defined as "an individual who was part of or supporting Taliban or al Qaeda forces, or associated forces that are engaged in hostilities against the United States or its coalition partners. This includes any person who has committed a belligerent act or has directly supported hostilities in aid of enemy armed forces."[33] Under the Court's decision in *Hamdi*, an enemy combatant could be held for "the duration of the relevant conflict[,]" which, as the Court conceded, might ultimately amount to lifetime imprisonment.[34] In determining whether the prisoner was an enemy combatant, the typical criminal justice standard that guilt must be proven beyond a reasonable doubt did not apply in CSRT proceedings. Instead, the CSRT would use a preponderance-of-the-evidence standard, which made it easier for the government to establish the prisoner's status as an enemy combatant.[35]

In addition, the CSRT was required to recognize "a rebuttable presumption in favor of the Government's evidence."[36] Prisoners had no right to counsel and were assigned only a "personal representative," a military officer who was required to tell members of the CSRT whatever the prisoner told them.[37] Ordinary rules of evidence and procedure did not apply: the tribunal was "free to consider any information it deems relevant and helpful to a resolution of the issue before it."[38] The order specified that such evidence could include hearsay evidence, and CSRTs also considered evidence obtained through coercion.[39] Prisoners had a limited right to call witnesses who were, in the tribunal's view, "reasonably available." Since witnesses were likely to be thousands of miles away, that could be a problem. CSRT decisions were reviewed only by a "convening authority" designated by the secretary of the navy.[40] Congress acquiesced to the CSRT system by including language in the 2005 Detainee Treatment Act providing for only very limited judicial review of the CSRT process.[41]

Instead of placing executive branch decisions under the rule of law, CSRTs served mainly "to validate a predetermined result[,]" effectively confirming the president's unchallenged authority to determine who could be held as an enemy combatant.[42] Between July 2004 and June 2007, 572 CSRT hearings were held. 534 prisoners were found to have been properly classified as enemy combatants, and just 38, or less than 1 percent, were found to not be enemy combatants.[43] A report prepared by Seton Hall Law School professors and students concluded that the CSRTs "afforded [prisoners] no meaningful opportunity to test the Government's evidence against them." The Seton Hall report, which reviewed CSRT records, found that "the large majority of [prisoners] never participated in any combat against the United States on a battlefield."[44] Under the vague definition provided to CSRTs by the July 7, 2004, order, prisoners could be held as enemy combatants if they had "directly supported" enemy armed forces, regardless of whether they did so willingly and regardless of whether that support involved hostile activity. CSRTs concluded that prisoners who were forced to join the Taliban could be held as enemy combatants, including one who was forced to serve as a cook.[45] The government argued that someone "associated with" al Qaeda or the Taliban could be held as an enemy combatant, and the Seton Hall report found that "this expansive definition of membership in al Qaeda could . . . be applied to anyone who the Government believed ever spoke to an al Qaeda member."[46] The Pentagon's own data conceded that "only a very few individuals [held as enemy combatants] were actively engaged in any activities for Al Qaeda or the Taliban."[47]

Many of the prisoners had come into U.S. custody after bounties were paid to their Afghan or Pakistani captors. In these cases, the government often relied on "information provided by the bounty hunters" as evidence. Bounty hunters, of course, had an incentive to hand over prisoners in exchange for payment whether or not the prisoners were actually associated with al Qaeda or the Taliban. The Seton Hall report found that "there is no doubt that bounties were paid for the capture and [imprisonment] of individuals who were not enemy combatants."[48] In fact, the government "publicly conceded" that some of these prisoners, notably a number of Chinese Uighurs, "were wrongly found to be enemy combatants." However, the Bush administration did not release these prisoners.[49]

Most of the prisoners who came before CSRTs and were found to be enemy combatants simply remained at Guantanamo without trial. However, a few, beginning with Salim Hamdan, were tried for war crimes before military tribunals. Hamdan, who was Osama Bin Laden's driver, appeared before a CSRT in October 2004; the CSRT determined that he was an enemy combatant. The government then charged Hamdan with war crimes, alleging that he had conspired with al Qaeda to carry out acts of terrorism. Proceedings began before a military tribunal, and Hamdan was assigned a military lawyer. Hamdan's lawyer filed a habeas corpus petition in federal court, initiating legal proceedings that ended up in the Supreme Court.

In *Hamdan v. Rumsfeld*, decided on June 29, 2006, the Court seemed to issue another rebuke to the Bush administration's theory of plenary power. However, as in *Rasul* and *Hamdi*, the decision did not have much effect in terms of checking presidential power. The Court ruled 5-3[50] that the military tribunal used to try Hamdan violated the Uniform Code of Military Justice as well as Common Article 3 of the Geneva Conventions.[51] However, Justices Breyer and Kennedy pointed a way forward for the Bush administration: it could seek congressional approval for its actions. When the Bush administration followed the justices' advice, it used congressional acquiescence to provide cover for what was really a continuation of unchecked presidential authority.

With the 2006 Military Commissions Act (MCA), enacted after the Supreme Court's decision in *Hamdan* temporarily rejected the Bush administration's military tribunal system, Congress "gave the Bush administration most of what it wanted in order to enable it to deal with [prisoners] in ways that had been invalidated by the *Hamdan* ruling."[52] The Court had rejected the administration's military tribunal system because the administration had unilaterally created rules for the tribunals without congressional authorization—much as Roosevelt had done in creating a tribunal to try German saboteurs in 1942.[53] But the 2006 MCA gave the administration ample leeway to continue to make its own rules for trial by tribunal, rather than simply following rules Congress had established for courts-martial. Coerced statements could be used as evidence in some circumstances, and classified information could be used as evidence without being disclosed to the prisoner on trial.[54]

In the 2006 MCA, Congress also assigned the president authority to "interpret the meaning and application of the Geneva Conventions."[55] In addition, the 2006 MCA strictly limited judicial review of military tribunal decisions, allowing the Court of Appeals for the District of Columbia Circuit to consider only whether military tribunals followed the procedures prescribed for them and, to the extent that the Constitution and statutory laws applied, whether such procedures complied with the law.[56] This meant that the reviewing court would be unable to correct factual errors or reverse a military tribunal decision on the merits. The court could not order the release of prisoner who had been wrongly convicted as long as the tribunal had followed the procedures set forth for it. Other than this limited review, prisoners tried before military tribunals or held at Guantanamo without trial had no access to the federal courts—the 2006 MCA barred habeas review.[57] The Bush administration had exploited congressional acquiescence to lend a patina of respectability to a military tribunal system that was slanted in favor of the executive. The administration largely succeeded in exercising unilateral power in this area, seeking (deferential) congressional approval only when necessary.

# 7

# THE BUSH ADMINISTRATION

# AND TORTURE

In August 2002, two Office of Legal Counsel memos authorized the use of torture on suspected terrorists held as prisoners outside the United States.[1] The OLC memos approved specific interrogation methods, including waterboarding, sleep deprivation, and confinement in a cramped box with an insect, for use on Abu Zubaydah, a prisoner believed to be an al Qaeda leader who might have information about possible terror plots planned to mark the first anniversary of the September 11 attacks.[2] CIA interrogators who wanted to use these methods were concerned that they could face prosecution under (1) the War Crimes Act, which applies to any "grave breach" of the Geneva Conventions, including torture and cruel or inhuman treatment, or (2) the federal anti-torture statute, which defines torture as "an act committed [outside the United States] by a person acting under the color of law specifically intended to inflict severe physical or mental pain or suffering (other than pain or suffering incidental to lawful sanctions) upon another person within his custody or physical control."[3] The OLC memos authorizing CIA interrogators to use the proposed methods served as a kind of "get-out-of-jail-free card," providing assurance that the interrogators would not face criminal prosecution by the Department of Justice.[4]

One of the OLC memos, commonly referred to as the Yoo-Bybee memo or the torture memo, bizarrely arrived at a definition of "torture" that was based on language in a health care statute describing when benefits could be paid to people experiencing an "emergency medical condition."[5] The federal anti-torture statute does not specifically define what it means to intend to cause "severe pain" sufficient to rise to the level of torture.

John Yoo reasoned that, since the health care statute used the words "severe pain" in describing an emergency medical condition, that same definition could be used to help understand what severe pain means in the context of the anti-torture law.[6] However, as Jack Goldsmith observes, "the health benefits statute's use of 'severe pain' had no relationship to the [anti] torture statute. And even if it did, the health benefits statute did not define 'severe pain.' Rather, it used the term 'severe pain' as a sign of an emergency medical condition that, if not treated, might cause organ failure [or impairment of bodily function or death]."[7]

After Jay Bybee left OLC, in 2003, John Yoo hoped to succeed him as head of OLC. When Yoo did not get the job, he recommended his friend Jack Goldsmith.[8] Goldsmith was named to the position, and several weeks after he took office, he began to review OLC opinions written by Yoo and Bybee, including the August 1, 2002, torture memo. Goldsmith was troubled by the memo, concluding that Yoo's definition of torture, as loosely based on a reference to "severe pain" in a health care statute, "didn't seem [to be] even in the ballpark." Goldsmith believed that the Yoo-Bybee memo was marked by an "unusual lack of care and sobriety in [its] legal analysis." In addition to the Yoo-Bybee memo's "errors of statutory interpretation," including the untenable definition of "severe pain," Goldsmith was concerned by the Yoo-Bybee memo's fallback position.[9] The memo concluded that, even if it had incorrectly interpreted the anti-torture statute and Congress actually had intended to prohibit waterboarding, sleep deprivation, or other planned interrogation methods, this made no difference because "[a]ny effort by Congress to regulate the interrogation of battlefield combatants would violate the Constitution's sole vesting of the Commander-in-Chief authority in the President."[10] This was a variant of the unitary executive theory, a claim that the president had authority to ignore any statutory efforts to limit his ability as commander in chief to order whatever interrogation methods he chose.[11] Goldsmith rightly denounced it as an "extreme conclusion [that] has no foundation in prior OLC opinions, or in judicial decisions, or in any other source of law." Goldsmith concluded in December 2003 that he would need to "withdraw and replace OLC's analysis [in the Yoo-Bybee memo]."[12]

In June 2004, Goldsmith finally withdrew the Yoo-Bybee memo.[13] On the same day, he resigned from OLC.[14] In December 2004, six months after Goldsmith left OLC, his interim successor, Daniel Levin, wrote a replacement memo. Levin's memo seemed to represent a sharp break from the Yoo-Bybee memo, beginning with the declaration that "[t]orture is abhorrent both to American law and values and to international norms." The Levin memo claimed to "[supersede] the [Yoo-Bybee] Memorandum in its entirety."[15] However, the Levin memo did not actually repudiate the Yoo-Bybee memo. Even after the Levin memo was published, the Bush administration continued to "[maintain] its basic position on the legality of various enhanced interrogation methods, including 'waterboarding.'"[16] Jeffrey Rosen reported that "Yoo says it is his understanding that no policies or interrogation techniques changed as a result of the withdrawal of the torture memo, [further] noting that all policies that were legal under the withdrawn opinions are also acknowledged as legal under the [December 2004 Levin] opinion that eventually replaced the withdrawn ones."[17] In fact, the Levin memo contained a footnote explaining that "[w]hile we have identified various disagreements with the [Yoo-Bybee] Memorandum, we have reviewed this Office's prior opinions addressing issues involving treatment of detainees and do not believe that any of their conclusions would be different under the standards set forth in this [December 2004 Levin] memorandum."[18] Yoo concluded that "the differences [between] the [Yoo-Bybee and Levin] opinions were for appearances' sake. In the real world of interrogation policy, nothing had changed."[19]

As Andrew Kaufman observes, "although the Levin memo did not affirm the [Yoo-]Bybee memo's extreme positions on presidential wartime-detention and interrogation power, it did not reject them either."[20] Levin concluded only that Yoo's argument that the president, as commander in chief, can brush aside statutory efforts to regulate interrogation methods was "unnecessary" and therefore was "eliminated from the analysis that follows [in the Levin memo]."[21] But calling something "unnecessary" is not the same thing as calling it wrong. Levin either missed or avoided the opportunity to reject Yoo's plenary power argument. Kaufman also points out that Yoo and Bybee were not punished for writing and signing the memo (other than perhaps suffering harm to their reputations). Although the Department of Justice's Office of Professional Responsibility concluded in 2009 that Yoo and Bybee had "committed professional misconduct," the Justice Department "ultimately chose not to adopt the misconduct finding, a decision criticized as letting Yoo and Bybee off the hook."[22]

The Yoo-Bybee torture memo episode shows that the Bush administration was able to advance arguments for plenary presidential power with impunity. In fact, even after the Levin memo was written, the Bush administration continued to assert its exclusive authority to decide what interrogation methods could be used with prisoners. In an initially secret May 10, 2005, memo, Steven Bradbury (by then head of the OLC) concluded that waterboarding, sleep deprivation for more than 48 hours but not to exceed 180 hours, cramped confinement, water dousing, and walling could be used by the CIA on a specific high-value al Qaeda detainee.[23] Unlike Yoo and Bybee, Bradbury did not rely on the unitary executive theory as part of his argument. This was "unnecessary," as Levin had suggested. Instead, Bradbury concluded that the U.S. anti-torture law simply did not prohibit these interrogation methods.

This conclusion, however, essentially renders the statutory limits on interrogation meaningless. The U.S. anti-torture law defines torture as "an act committed by a person acting under color of law specifically intended to inflict severe physical or mental pain (other than pain or suffering incidental to lawful sanctions) upon another person within his custody or physical control."[24] If waterboarding and sleep deprivation do not meet this definition, then the definition is devoid of practical meaning. According to Malcolm Nance, who helped train members of the U.S. military on methods of torture resistance, "[w]aterboarding is a controlled drowning . . . [during which] the lungs are actually filling with water. [In the American training model], [a] team doctor watches the quantity of water that is ingested and for the physiological signs which show when the drowning effect goes from painful psychological experience, to horrific suffocating punishment to the final death spiral. Waterboarding is slow motion suffocation with enough time to contemplate the inevitability of blackout and expiration—usually the person goes into hysterics on the board . . . When done right it is controlled death." Nance concludes that "[w]aterboarding is a torture technique. Period. There is no way to gloss over it or sugarcoat it. It has no justification outside of its limited role as a training demonstrator."[25] Waterboarding has been used since the fourteenth century, including during the Spanish Inquisition. U.S. courts have convicted members of the Japanese military for waterboarding Americans during World War II, as well as (decades later) a local law enforcement official in Texas who, along with his deputies, waterboarded suspected criminals.[26]

Sleep deprivation has a similarly long and sordid history. It has been used by Soviet interrogators, by the Japanese military during World War II, and by British officials who interrogated suspected members of the IRA. Menachem Begin, who, as a young man, was subject to sleep deprivation during interrogation by the Soviet KGB, remembered years later that "[i]n the head of the interrogated prisoner, a haze begins to form . . . he has one sole desire: to sleep. . . . Anyone who has experienced this desire knows that not even hunger and thirst are comparable with it. I came across prisoners who signed what they were ordered to sign, only to get what the interrogator promised [that is, the promise of sleep] . . . having signed, there was nothing in the world that could move them to risk again such [sleepless] nights and . . . days." John Schlapobersky, another man subjected to sleep deprivation, described the experience as being like "treating [a person] with medication that will make them psychotic. . . . I was kept without sleep for a week in all. I can remember the details of the experience, although it took place 35 years ago. . . . After two days without sleep, the hallucinations start. . . . By the week's end, people lose their orientation in place and time. . . . To deprive someone of sleep is to tamper with their equilibrium and their sanity."[27] In 1944, the U.S. Supreme Court observed that "[i]t has been known since 1500 at least that deprivation of sleep is the most effective torture and certain to produce any confession desired."[28]

Bradbury confronted none of this ghastly history in his May 2005 memo. Instead, he relied on a sanitized description of waterboarding and sleep deprivation provided to him by the CIA itself to reach the same conclusion contained in the Yoo-Bybee memo: that the methods simply were not torture.[29] In assessing the interrogation methods, Bradbury bizarrely cited information obtained from the CIA's own Office of Medical Service, rather than seeking neutral, objective sources.[30] On the basis of what CIA medical personnel told him, Bradbury concluded that "the authorized use of extended sleep deprivation by adequately trained interrogators would not be expected to cause and could not be reasonably considered [as] specifically intended to cause severe physical pain." He found, again citing CIA medical personnel, that sleep deprivation would not cause the kind of prolonged mental pain or suffering prohibited by the anti-torture law because "any hallucinatory effects of sleep deprivation would dissipate rapidly." Bradbury also claimed that controlled scientific experiments had concluded "little seemed to go wrong with the subjects physically" who were deprived of sleep.[31] One scientist whose work Bradbury cited said "to claim that 180 hours [of sleep deprivation] is safe is total nonsense." Another scientist whose work Bradbury cited noted that "[w]e were working with healthy volunteers and didn't deprive them of sleep for more than one day without allowing them to recover. . . . Even under these circumstances, certain changes can occur, such as hallucinations, depending on the individual's condition." The same scientist said that Bradbury's reliance on his research was like citing a study about "the transient reactions of a little schnapps" to support the conclusion that it was safe to force prisoners to "drink large amounts of alcohol." The researchers Bradbury cited had never studied the effects of 180 hours of sleep deprivation on a subject, as ethical considerations barred them from doing so.[32]

Although Bradbury acknowledged that "[t]here may be few more frightening experiences than feeling that one is unable to breathe[,]" he also concluded that waterboarding did not violate the U.S. anti-torture law. Bradbury noted that waterboarding had already been used by the CIA repeatedly on two prisoners and that "as far as can be determined, these [prisoners] did not experience physical pain [nor,] in the professional judgment of doctors, is there any medical reason to believe they would have done so." As with sleep deprivation, Bradbury relied on assurances from CIA medical personnel that "the waterboard technique is not physically painful."[33] The Senate Select Intelligence Committee's redacted report on CIA interrogation methods found that the information Bradbury received from the CIA was false, as, "[a]ccording to CIA records, Abu Zubaydah's waterboarding sessions 'resulted in immediate fluid intake and involuntary leg, chest, and arms spasms' and 'hysterical pleas.'" A CIA medical officer who observed Khalid Sheikh Mohammed (KSM) being waterboarded reported that waterboarding had gone beyond producing the "sensation of drowning" to a "series of near drownings." Both Abu Zubaydah and KSM vomited after being waterboarded.[34] However, Bradbury suggested that what CIA medical officials inaccurately told him about waterboarding not being painful "accords with the experience in SERE [Survival, Evasion, Resistance, and Escape] training, where the waterboard has been administered to several thousand members of the United States Armed Forces."[35]

SERE is the same U.S. military training program in which Malcolm Nance, quoted earlier, experienced and observed waterboarding. Nance's description of waterboarding closely tracks CIA records regarding waterboarding methods used on Abu Zubaydah and KSM. Nance explains SERE's purpose this way: "[t]housands of American POWs died and suffered resisting torture practices that we have always called the tools of the enemy. The SERE program was designed to help them grapple with this inhumanity and retain their dignity in the face of it." Nance charges that to use the SERE training methods as interrogation tools is to "embrace . . . tactics . . . taken from the Russians, the Communist Chinese, the North Koreans, the North Vietnamese, the Khmer Rouge—as our own." Finally, Nance challenged anyone who concludes waterboarding is not torture to undergo "just one hour of the CIA enhanced interrogation techniques that were authorized in the Bush Administration's OLC memos—including the CIA-approved variant of waterboarding. If at the end [they] still [believe] this is not torture, I'll respect [their] viewpoint. But not until then."[36]

Although Bradbury did not rely on the unitary executive theory to conclude that the president could simply ignore the anti-torture law, his reasoning produced essentially the same conclusion. It was unnecessary to invoke inherent power when, instead, Bradbury could simply reduce the criminal prohibitions in the anti-torture law to faux law that placed no meaningful restrictions on interrogation methods CIA interrogators wanted to use on prisoners.

After Congress passed the 2005 Detainee Treatment Act (DTA),[37] prohibiting "cruel, inhuman, or degrading treatment or punishment," of prisoners held anywhere by the U.S. government, President Bush included a signing statement when he signed the bill into law, providing that "[t]he executive branch shall construe [the DTA] in a manner consistent with the constitutional authority of the President to supervise the unitary executive branch and as Commander in Chief and consistent with the constitutional limitations on the judicial power."[38] As James Pfiffner observes, it is reasonable to conclude from this signing statement "[t]hat President Bush did not consider himself bound by [the DTA]."[39] Congress also passed the 2006 Military Commissions Act, which amended the War Crimes Act to define as criminal acts only specifically enumerated violations of Common Article 3 of the Geneva Convention (defined by the War Crimes Act as "grave breaches" of Common Article 3).[40] Although these changes to the War Crimes Act narrowed the area of liability by making it more difficult to prove a criminal violation, Congress had still stated that some violations of Common Article 3, including torture, would continue to be a war crime under U.S. law.

In a July 20, 2007, executive order, President Bush claimed that the CIA detention and interrogation program complied with the U.S. anti-torture law, the 2005 DTA, and the War Crimes Act.[41] However, it was immediately clear that the Bush administration would continue to "use . . . severe interrogation methods [that it believed did not rise to criminal violations of statute] for questioning terrorism suspects in secret [CIA black site] prisons overseas."[42] In addition, even as President Bush publicly claimed to respect statutory prohibitions against torture and other abuse, the administration continued to privately rely on secret OLC memoranda that laid waste to statutory limits. A case in point was another Bradbury OLC memo, this one dated July 20, 2007—the very day that President Bush publicly issued the executive order purporting to describe the CIA's compliance with statutory prohibitions against torture.[43] In that memo, Bradbury concluded sleep deprivation[44] is not prohibited by either the 2005 DTA, the U.S. War Crimes Act, or Common Article 3 of the Geneva Conventions (the Supreme Court's 2006 decision in *Hamdan* raised concerns about the application of the last two legal authorities to prisoners).[45]

Like his May 2005 memo, Bradbury's July 2007 memo again cited controlled medical studies not relevant to methods used on prisoners as well as the assurances of CIA medical staff to support his conclusion that sleep deprivation could be used. Bradbury also relied on false CIA representations that prisoners subjected to sleep deprivation would wear diapers for sanitary and hygienic reasons, not as part of an effort to humiliate or degrade prisoners. In fact, CIA records show that "in some cases, a central 'purpose' of diapers was 'to cause humiliation' and 'to induce a sense of helplessness.'"[46] Bradbury concluded statutory law prohibited interrogation methods that "shock the conscience."[47] Bradbury's memo cited CIA assurances that members of Congress who voted for the 2006 Military Commissions Act had "effectively endorsed . . . the continued use of the CIA's enhanced interrogation methods [including sleep deprivation]." Although Bradbury relied on these representations in part to support his conclusion that sleep deprivation did not shock the conscience, the CIA's representations were not correct. CIA records showed that Senator John McCain had told the CIA he believed both waterboarding and sleep deprivation constituted torture, and other senators had expressed concerns about the CIA's enhanced interrogation methods.[48]

Bradbury further concluded that extended sleep deprivation of up to 96 hours continuously or 180 hours over a thirty-day period would not shock the conscience because CIA interrogators "employ[ed] many safeguards to ensure that [prisoners subjected to sleep deprivation did] not endure significant pain or suffering." Those safeguards included making sure prisoners were not allowed to support their weight while hanging by their wrists in shackles and having CIA medical personnel monitor the prisoner "throughout the period of extended sleep deprivation."[49] Sleep deprivation would stop if the prisoner was hallucinating or experiencing "other abnormal psychological reactions" or "significant physical pain."[50]

It is surreal to write words like this—to explain that a lawyer in the Bush administration concluded it was a "safeguard" to make sure shackled prisoners subject to sleep deprivation were not hung in a position that would force them to support their weight. As Seth Kreimer has observed, "[t]orture is alien to our Constitution both because it impinges on bodily integrity, and because it assaults the autonomy and dignity of the victim."[51] As noted, prisoners subjected to sleep deprivation were shackled and forced to relieve themselves in diapers as they had no access to a toilet.[52] Kreimer wrote before these facts were reported, but this practice defines the assault on human dignity that he referred to in his 2003 article.

As with the use of military force and the detention of suspected terrorists, when it came to interrogation methods, the Bush administration demonstrated its belief in unrestrained executive power. The Yoo-Bybee memo made the breathtaking claim that the president can authorize any interrogation method he or she believes necessary, regardless of criminal laws enacted by Congress. This is a description of unbounded presidential power in an area with broad potential for abuse, as demonstrated by the more than two hundred waterboardings administered (in combination) to Abu Zubaydah and Khalid Sheikh Mohammed.[53] Although Jack Goldsmith and Daniel

Levin recognized that the Yoo-Bybee memo was dangerous, the Levin memo failed to expressly repudiate Yoo's flawed reasoning, and Bradbury's memos reduced statutory prohibitions on torture to faux law. Yoo was able to claim victory, both by managing to avoid reprisals for his role in writing the August 2002 memo and by noting that the Levin memo effectively changed nothing. The Bush administration never retreated from the position staked out by the Yoo-Bybee memo, and, when Congress attempted to reinforce limits on presidential power in the 2005 Detainee Treatment Act, Bush relied on a signing statement and yet another OLC memo to advance his belief that the president could ignore statutory limits.[54]

# 8

# THE BUSH ADMINISTRATION
# AND SECRECY

The George W. Bush administration's use of the state secrets privilege to block lawsuits seeking to hold it accountable to the rule of law helped make Bush known as "the secrecy President."[1] The state secrets privilege is a doctrine first created by the U.S. Supreme Court in 1953.[2] The Supreme Court made a mistake in the way it defined the state secrets privilege, and both the Bush and the Obama administrations have exploited that mistake to prevent effective review of executive branch decision making. For both administrations, use of the state secrets privilege has helped facilitate the assertion of unrestrained presidential power by preventing effective judicial review.

In the 1953 *Reynolds* case, the Supreme Court recognized the existence of a "privilege against revealing military secrets, a privilege which is well established in the law of evidence."[3] The Court concluded that this privilege allowed the executive branch to refuse to disclose military and state secrets in the course of litigation.[4] By itself, that is not a controversial point. In fact, one could reasonably conclude that the Constitution envisions the need for presidents to operate in secrecy under some circumstances, as Alexander Hamilton observed in Federalist No. 70.[5] The problem, however, is that the Court failed to set limits on the privilege, instead giving "[t]he executive branch an unreviewable power to withhold documents" it claimed were secret and privileged against disclosure.[6]

Chief Justice Vinson, writing for a majority of six justices in *Reynolds*, cautioned that, when evaluating a state secrets privilege claim asserted by the government, courts must take care not to "forc[e] a disclosure of the very thing the privilege is designed to protect." Again, that statement is not immediately problematic. However, the Court concluded that this principle precluded even *in camera* review. In other words, when a court reviews a state secrets claim, if it is "satisf[ied]" that requiring disclosure of the disputed materials would risk revealing state secrets, it may be able to accept the claim without even seeing the documents in question. Vinson wrote that "we will not go so far as to say that the court may automatically require a complete disclosure to the judge before the claim of privilege will be accepted in any case. It may be possible to satisfy the court, from all the circumstances of the case, that there is a reasonable danger that compulsion of the evidence will expose military matters which, in the interest of national security, should not be divulged. When this is the case, the occasion for the privilege is appropriate, and the court should not jeopardize the security which the privilege is meant to protect by insisting upon an examination of the evidence, *even by the judge alone, in chambers.*"[7]

The problem, of course, is that the Court's approach in *Reynolds* allows the executive branch, by invoking the state secrets privilege, to prevent courts from testing the legitimacy of the claim by actually reviewing the disputed documents. That allows the government to mislead the courts, which is precisely what happened in *Reynolds* itself. The *Reynolds* case involved an accident that killed nine men aboard a U.S. Air Force plane that was testing secret electronic equipment.[8] The widows of three of the men who were killed brought a lawsuit claiming that negligence by the government was responsible for their husbands' deaths.[9] The executive branch had refused to comply with a court order to produce the accident report and statements given by survivors of the crash: these were the documents to which the Supreme Court applied the state secrets privilege.[10] The Court did not order dismissal of the case but concluded the widows would have to litigate their case without access to these documents—documents the Court itself never saw.[11] Decades after the case was decided, the documents for which the executive branch had claimed privilege were made public. It turned out they contained no military or state secrets. Instead, they showed that government negligence had been to blame for the crash that gave rise to the widows' lawsuit.[12]

The *Reynolds* decision "gave a green light to the state secrets privilege, and it has been so used consistently by the Justice Department [since 1953]." Since *Reynolds*, "[i]n subsequent disputes over access to agency document, the government would regularly cite this decision as legal justification for withholding requested materials." This has been particularly true since the 9/11 attacks, "with the government now routinely citing 'state secrets' as the ground for denying private litigants access to agency information."[13]

Although application of the state secrets privilege in *Reynolds* itself did not result in dismissal of the case at bar, "[t]he possibility of dismissal after successful invocation of the state secrets privilege has always existed."[14] This makes the doctrine especially attractive to those interested in unrestrained presidential power. Successful use of the state secrets doctrine can make it possible to shield from scrutiny presidential decisions that overstep statutory or constitutional bounds. Since 9/11, both the Bush and the Obama administrations have used the state secrets privilege for this purpose.

The Bush administration relied on the state secrets privilege in seeking dismissal of civil cases involving the extraordinary rendition program and the warrantless surveillance program.[15] In *El-Masri v. United States*, the Bush administration argued that the state secrets privilege required dismissal of a lawsuit involving extraordinary rendition. Khaled El-Masri claimed that, in 2004, CIA agents had sent him to a secret prison in Afghanistan, where he was detained for five months without charges, beaten, and drugged. A European human rights organization had previously concluded that El-Masri's claims were "substantially accurate."[16] The Third Circuit, however, accepted the Bush administration's invocation of the state secrets privilege and dismissed the case without even reviewing *in camera* the documents claimed to contain privileged and secret information.[17]

In another extraordinary rendition case, Maher Arar claimed that U.S. authorities detained him at Kennedy Airport in New York City in 2002 and then sent him to Syria, where he was held for almost a year in a small, grave-like cell, tortured, and forced to sign a false confession.[18] A Canadian judicial report stated "categorically there is no evidence that Arar did anything wrong or was a security threat." The judicial report concluded that Canadian intelligence officials had "passed false warnings and bad information about Arar to the United States." Canada's prime minister wrote a letter of apology to Arar and his family and awarded him $9.75 million in compensation.[19] When Arar filed a lawsuit in a U.S. district court in 2004, the Bush administration asked the court to dismiss the case on the basis of the state secrets privilege. The district court and the Second Circuit on appeal both ruled for the government, finding it unnecessary to decide the state secrets question.[20]

In both *El-Masri* and *Arar* the Bush administration invoked the state secrets privilege in an effort to prevent judicial review of an extraordinary rendition program that brushed aside legal limits on presidential power. The federal anti-torture statute makes it a crime to conspire to commit torture outside the United States.[21] The United States is a party to the United Nations Convention against Torture and Other Cruel, Inhuman, or Degrading Treatment or Punishment (CAT), which "prohibits the transfer of persons to countries where there is a substantial likelihood that they will be tortured."[22] Both the federal anti-torture statute and the CAT, as implemented under U.S. law, could apply to U.S. officials involved in extraordinary rendition. In addition, the U.S. War Crimes Act could apply to U.S. officials involved in extraordinary rendition.

However, in a March 13, 2002, memo, the Office of Legal Counsel described presidential authority to "transfer . . . prisoners [captured during military engagements] to third parties" as "exclusive and virtually unfettered."[23] The OLC memo "conclude[d] that as Commander in Chief and Chief Executive, the President has the plenary constitutional power to detain and transfer [to other countries] prisoners captured in war." In the OLC's view, the president could "dispose of the liberty of captured enemy personnel as he sees fit."[24] The law, in the OLC's view, posed no obstacle to extraordinary rendition; legal limits could simply be brushed aside. Louis Fisher also observes that the extraordinary rendition program departed from the rule of law because, in the past, "presidents had no independent authority to transfer someone from the United States [or in U.S. custody] to a receiving country for trial. They depended on extradition procedures set forth in treaties and statutes."[25] According to the logic of the March 2002 OLC memo, the president's plenary power in this area would obviate the need for congressional authorization. The March 2002 OLC memo asserted extraordinary claims about presidential power. When it was made publicly available in 2009, Scott Horton remarked that "[i]f we had to boil the [OLC] memo down to one sentence it would be 'the executive is the law, and no other law matters.'"[26]

The Bush administration turned to the state secrets privilege to prevent the courts from reviewing its actions and testing the legitimacy of its claims of unfettered power, like those asserted in the 2002 OLC memo on extraordinary rendition.[27] The Bush administration made similar use of the state secrets privilege to block review of its warrantless surveillance program, though ultimately lawsuits against private companies under FISA were dismissed after Congress granted retroactive immunity to the telecommunications companies involved in the surveillance program.[28] For the Bush administration, the state secrets privilege served as a useful complement to its vision of unrestrained presidential power, giving it a tool to insulate controversial legal conclusions from judicial scrutiny. As we'll see in Section III, although President Obama promised to reject the Bush administration's approach to the state secrets privilege, the Obama administration has similarly used the privilege in an effort to shield expansive application of presidential power from judicial review.

# SECTION III

# THE BARACK OBAMA ADMINISTRATION
# AND NATIONAL SECURITY POWER

The George W. Bush administration left a troubling legacy with regard to presidential power: if the president believes unilateral action is necessary for national security, constitutional and statutory limits on presidential power can be set aside or navigated around. At times, the Bush administration expressly claimed the authority to set aside the rule of law and exercise plenary power with impunity. At other times, it used congressional acquiescence to add a thin legalistic veneer to what was actually the unrestrained exercise of power. In still other cases, it reduced clear statutory limitations on presidential power to faux law that, as applied by the administration, set no meaningful limits.

After Bush left office, it was important to make clear that his administration's approach to presidential power would not stand as precedent. As the Bush years came to a close, Harold Koh rightly predicted that "the next eight years will determine whether the pendulum of American policy will swing back from where it has been pushed, or whether it will stay stuck in the direction in which it has been pushed since September 11th."[1] The results, however, are not encouraging. In the area of war power, the Obama administration has not relied on plenary or inherent authority but instead has drained statutory and constitutional limits of substantive meaning, allowing it to use military force largely at its discretion. In its use of surveillance, the Obama administration continued the post-2007 Bush approach by stretching claimed statutory support to implausible lengths in an effort to provide justification for illegitimate unilateral executive action. The Obama administration has used faux law, the appearance of limits on power, to enable it to continue to hold prisoners at Guantanamo without trial or meaningful hearing, as the Bush administration did. In its use of the state secrets privilege, the Obama administration has claimed to change course but has essentially followed the Bush administration's approach. Congress has, in most cases, either remained passive or enabled extraconstitutional presidential action, as it did during the Bush years.

Some observers conclude that the Obama administration found ways to act compatibly with the rule of law, with its power limited by constitutional checks and balances.[2] Reality is more complicated. By embracing a vision of presidential power—the unitary executive theory—that expressly placed the president above the law, the Bush administration changed the parameters for evaluating presidential action. Arguments that claim to tie presidential power to what is actually illusory statutory authority look like a step forward, only because they seem restrained in contrast with the shocking excesses of the unitary executive theory. If executive branch lawyers are trying to find statutory support for presidential action, that seems like progress (as it also did when Yoo's successors at the OLC seemed to move away from the unitary executive approach). But, since 9/11, we have had only the illusion of constraint. Both the Bush and the Obama administrations have exercised unconstrained power in the area of national security, often, especially for Obama, by incorrectly claiming that their actions were justified by statutory grants of authority.

As a presidential candidate, Barack Obama employed rhetoric suggesting that, if elected, he would make a sharp break with the Bush administration with regard to the use of national security power.[3] After winning election and taking office, President Obama promised to "abid[e] by the rule of law" in defending the nation against terrorist threats.[4] Obama brought into the executive branch lawyers with a reputation for championing checks and balances and limits on presidential power.[5] Outside observers concluded that President Obama had rejected the idea of unchecked presidential power. In 2009, Glenn Greenwald declared that Obama's selection of David Barron and Martin Lederman as OLC lawyers had made clear that the Obama administration would respect "real limits [on presidential power] when [statutory] law or the Constitution dictates."[6] Also in 2009, Bruce Ackerman praised Harold Koh, another Obama administration lawyer, as "one of the few lawyers who [has] probed deeply into the constitutional implications of presidential unilateralism and how it might be controlled."[7] Jack Goldsmith writes that "Koh urged [Obama] to reject the Bush paradigm and 'unambiguously reassert [America's] historic commitments to human rights and the rule of law as a major source of our moral authority.'"[8]

Despite these hopeful initial signs, the Obama administration did not meaningfully move away from the Bush administration's approach to presidential power. On the surface, there has been change. The Obama administration does not speak the language of the unitary executive theory. Unlike Bush, Cheney, and John Yoo, Obama and his executive branch lawyers did not invoke "expansive rhetoric about the Commander in Chief's untouchable power."[9] But there was more rhetorical than substantive change here. Although Obama "broke from Bush in dropping 'war on terror' language [that embraced plenary power]," Obama ended up "adopting many of the Bush policies." Jack Goldsmith concludes that "[t]he [Obama] administration took the same basic position [regarding national security power] as its predecessor but placed it in prettier wrapping."[10]

That appears to be a useful observation, but I would modify the central part of Goldsmith's conclusion. He argues that Obama followed Bush—not the early unitary executive approach but an approach taken later in the Bush administration, after Congress, the courts, and other actors had attempted to rein in presidential power. As noted, in Goldsmith's view, the Obama administration continued many of the Bush administration's policies but toned down its chest-thumping rhetoric. Goldsmith concludes that this rhetorical shift "reflect[s] [the Obama administration's] genuine ideological and intellectual commitment to a more limited conception of executive power and a more regularized conception of the rule of law." Goldsmith also emphasizes that, although Obama adopted many of Bush's policies, the Obama administration adopted the late Bush approach, meaning a model of presidential power accountable to Congress, the courts, and other actors, rather than the unitary executive model of the early Bush years. Goldsmith concludes that, because Obama followed the approach developed later in the Bush administration, the lesson "is that the Commander in Chief is deeply constrained by law and politics, even in this endless war."[11]

The Obama administration at times did indeed use different arguments—ones that seem to recognize limits on presidential power—to reach the same conclusion as Bush: that the president has broad, unchecked authority to decide how best to defend the nation. This is not, however, evidence of a restrained presidency. The Obama administration has not proved that effective checks on presidential power have prevailed. At times, Obama has used subtler arguments than Bush to achieve the functional equivalent of plenary power—most notably, in the use of military force. At other times, Obama (like Bush) has relied on congressional acquiescence to produce the appearance of restraint, with the president acting pursuant to statutory authority. But this turns out to be an illusion. Congressional acquiescence does not provide reassurance that presidential power is limited.

Most centrally, the Obama administration has exercised unchecked power when it comes to using military force—for example, in the targeted killing of U.S. citizens who are suspected terrorists and in the authorization of military operations in Libya or against ISIS without congressional approval. When it comes to military detention and surveillance, the Obama administration can argue that it has not acted unilaterally in these areas. In fact, at first glance it looks as if Congress has effectively checked presidential power at Guantanamo, preventing the president from acting unilaterally to close the prison there. However, even at Guantanamo, there are areas of continuity between the Bush and the Obama administrations. Many of the prisoners at Guantanamo have been held for years, though they have never been charged with any offense and have been cleared for release because there is no evidence that they engaged in terrorism.[12] The fact that dozens of such prisoners continue to be indefinitely detained is evidence that the Obama administration has been unable to restore the rule of law at Guantanamo. The Obama administration claims that, for some prisoners at least, it planned to reject the Bush military tribunal model but was blocked by Congress. However, the administration always planned to use military trials for some prisoners, and even though the military tribunal system is now authorized by statute, it is still marked by significant flaws. As for surveillance, the Obama administration claims that the bulk metadata collection and Section 702 surveillance programs revealed by Edward Snowden operated subject to statutory constraints. But, as we'll see, the Obama administration's argument here depends on implausible methods of interpretation that render statutory limits meaningless.

Like the Bush administration, the Obama administration has advanced the state secrets privilege in court in an effort to block judicial review of presidential action. This is an important tool in keeping presidential power free of meaningful restraint. Although the Obama administration claimed to break with the Bush administration by limiting its use of the state secrets privilege, we will see that this claim does not stand up to scrutiny.

Even when it comes to torture, where the Obama administration did decisively reject the Bush administration's approach by explicitly requiring that prisoners in U.S. custody or control be subject only to interrogation methods authorized by the Army Field Manual,[13] there have been problems in terms of making it clear that the rule of law applies.

None of this is to say that the Bush and the Obama approaches to national security power are identical. The Obama administration has not followed the early Bush approach, which relied on the unitary executive theory to simply set aside laws that set limits on presidential power. But that does not mean the Obama administration has recognized meaningful limits on its power. Instead, it has in many cases found new ways to reach the same conclusion as the Bush administration: when the president wants to take action in the name of national security, statutory and constitutional limits will not stand in the way.

# 10

## THE OBAMA ADMINISTRATION

## AND THE USE OF MILITARY FORCE

As a candidate for the presidency in 2007, Barack Obama claimed to reject the Bush administration's embrace of the unitary executive theory. In an interview with then–*Boston Globe* reporter Charlie Savage, Obama promised to respect statutory and constitutional limits on presidential power. Obama seemed to make clear that he did not agree with the view endorsed by John Yoo's September 25, 2001, memo that decisions involving the use of military force are for the president alone to make. Candidate Obama correctly explained "[t]he President does not have power under the Constitution to unilaterally authorize a military attack in a situation that does not involve stopping an actual or imminent threat to the nation." Outside this limited self-defense scenario, congressional authorization would be necessary. In fact, Obama noted, "[h]istory has shown us time and again . . . that military action is most successful when it is authorized and supported by the Legislative branch. It is always preferable to have the informed consent of Congress prior to any military action."[1]

Obama's words in 2007 reflected an accurate understanding of the Constitution. Candidate Obama recognized that presidential power is limited by the Constitution and by statute and the president can unilaterally order the use of military force only in emergency circumstances involving self-defense when there is no time to check with Congress first. As president, however, Obama took a different view. When it came to the use of military force, the Obama administration found ways to justify unilateral presidential action outside the limited self-defense context. Unlike the Bush administration, the Obama administration did not rely on plenary or inherent power to reach these conclusions, but the result is the same: the Obama administration failed to recognize meaningful statutory or constitutional limits on presidential authority to order the use of military force.

In order to compare the Obama administration's approach to the use of military force with the Bush administration's, I will consider the Obama administration's actions with regard to Libya (2011), Syria (2013), and ISIS (2014), as well as the targeted killing program used to kill Anwar al-Aulaqi, a U.S. citizen.

## LIBYA

In March 2011, President Obama ordered military action against Libya, citing the need to protect civilians from the dictator Muammar Gaddafi.[2] Although Gaddafi was certainly a threat to Libyan civilians, there was no indication that the dictator posed any threat to the United States. On the basis of what he had said in 2007, it would have been reasonable to expect President Obama to seek congressional authorization before acting. Instead, he pointed to a United Nations Security Council resolution authorizing member states to use military force in Libya.[3] Of course, a UN resolution cannot substitute for constitutional processes.[4] However, Obama did not follow the constitutional framework he invoked in 2007—he did not seek congressional approval. Instead, he relied on an April 1, 2011, memo written by Caroline Krass of the Office of Legal Counsel.[5]

In order to consider whether the Obama administration's approach to the use of military force is different from the Bush administration's approach, it is useful to begin by comparing Krass's April 1, 2011, memo (Authority to Use Military Force in Libya) with John Yoo's September 25, 2001, memo (The President's Constitutional Authority to Conduct Military Operations against Terrorists and Nations Supporting Them). There are some obvious differences: Yoo's memo was not available to the public for more than two years,[6] while Krass's memo was immediately available to the public; Yoo's memo addressed the question of presidential authority to order the use of military force in general, while Krass's memo more narrowly focused on the specific question of presidential authority to order the use of military force in Libya in the spring of 2011. However, by considering the reasoning in each memo—how presidential power to order the use of military force is justified—it is possible to reach some initial conclusions.[7]

Yoo's September 2001 memo relied most centrally on claims of plenary or inherent power to support unilateral presidential authority to order the use of military force, even preemptively against nations or people who have not attacked the United States.[8] He invoked the unitary executive theory, claiming that the Framers of the Constitution intended to assign to the president "inherent executive powers that are unenumerated in the Constitution." He concluded that, because presidential power over the use of military force is inherent and plenary, it cannot be limited by Congress: the president can "take whatever actions he deems appropriate" when deciding how "to use military force to defend the Nation." Such "decisions, under our Constitution, are for the President alone to make[,]" and no statute "can place any limits on the President's determinations [regarding the use of military force]." Yoo also cited interbranch practice as a source of authority: in his view, past presidents who had ordered the use of military force without congressional authorization had created precedent for unilateral presidential authority in this area.[9]

In addition, Yoo's memo relied on the misconceived (and now discredited)[10] sole organ doctrine. As discussed in Section I, the idea that the president has "delicate, plenary and exclusive power . . . as sole organ of the federal government in the field of international relations—a power which does not require as a basis for its exercise an act of Congress[,]" flies in the face of the constitutional text.[11] Justice Sutherland's dicta in *Curtiss-Wright* took John Marshall's 1800 speech out of context and ignored the basic structure of the Constitution. Marshall was not describing any "plenary" presidential power over foreign affairs: he was merely observing that the president is the "sole organ" of the nation when carrying out treaties duly ratified by the Senate. Marshall understood that the Constitution clearly divides power over foreign affairs between the president and Congress, rejecting the then-prevailing British model that concentrated such power in the hands of the monarch.[12]

Yoo's memo also either misreads or misrepresents Alexander Hamilton's writings. While Yoo suggests Hamilton's writings support a vision of presidential control over the use of military force, Hamilton in fact acknowledged that the Constitution divides such power between the president and Congress. Yoo cites Hamilton in Federalist No. 23 to support claims about broad *presidential* power but fails to make clear that Federalist No. 23 described the powers of the federal government *as a whole*— that is, the joint powers of the president and Congress over the common defense of the nation—and Federalist No. 23 also acknowledged limits on such powers.[13] Yoo also enlists Federalist No. 70, seizing on what looks like helpful language about "energy in the executive." Yoo claims Federalist No. 70 supports the conclusion that "it is clear that the Constitution secures all federal executive power in the President to ensure a unity in purpose and energy in action."[14] It is true that Hamilton, in Federalist No. 70, emphasized the need for "unity" in the executive.[15] However, Hamilton was not arguing for, as Yoo suggested, "the centralization of authority in the President . . . in matters of national defense, war and foreign policy."[16] By "unity," Hamilton meant that there should be one national executive—instead of the plural executive that had been proposed by George Mason and others.[17]

To the extent that Federalist No. 70 left any doubt as to the question of "centraliz[ed] authority in the President alone," Federalist No. 69 (which Yoo did not take into account in any way) reveals Yoo's error in relying on Hamilton. In Federalist No. 69, Hamilton responded to critics of the proposed Constitution who worried the document would create an American monarch by specifically explaining why the American president would have less power than the British monarch, including in areas of national defense and foreign affairs.[18] Federalist No. 69 is a powerful refutation of Yoo's claim that the president has plenary power over foreign affairs and the use of military force. Rather than engaging with Federalist No. 69, Yoo simply ignored it, presenting instead a deceptive image of Hamilton as a supporter of plenary presidential power.[19]

At first glance, Krass's April 1, 2011, memo seems to take a very different approach from Yoo's memo. Where Yoo relied on plenary power, the sole organ doctrine, and the unitary executive theory to support his conclusion that decisions regarding the use of military force "are for the President alone to make,"[20] Krass appeared to take an approach that recognized limits on presidential power. On closer examination, some of this is not as it seems. Ultimately, Krass did recognize one important limit on presidential authority—the sixty-day War Powers Resolution deadline[21] (a limit that President Obama found a way to set aside). However, she also found room for very broad unilateral presidential power—as long as it was confined to the sixty-day WPR window.

One of the most striking differences between Yoo's memo and Krass's memo is the tone. Where Yoo speaks the language of the unitary executive— inherent presidential power to set aside statutory limits, congressional approval seen as "welcome [but] not constitutionally necessary"[22]—Krass's rhetoric avoids expressly making such broad endorsements of executive power. However, on closer examination, Krass endorses a view of presidential power that bears (to an extent) a resemblance to Yoo's description.

For example, while Krass did not directly embrace the sole organ doctrine, she concluded that "the historical gloss on the 'executive power' vested in Article II of the Constitution [shows] that the President bears the 'vast share of responsibility for the conduct of our foreign relations' . . . and accordingly holds *independent authority in the areas of foreign policy and national security.*"[23] Although Krass did not cite *Curtiss-Wright* and the sole organ doctrine, she came very close to Yoo's position here by suggesting (contrary to the text of the Constitution) that the President bears primary responsibility with regard to foreign affairs (and national security). That impression is reinforced by Krass's citation to Justice Jackson's concurring opinion in *Youngstown Sheet*, an opinion typically associated with limits on presidential power.[24] Krass did not focus on what Jackson had to say about restraint—instead, she cited that part of his opinion suggesting the president might possess power to act unilaterally when it comes to foreign affairs. In addition, although Krass, unlike Yoo, did not attempt to remake Hamilton into a champion of unrestrained presidential power, her memo does include indirect references to the mythic idea of an energetic executive who can act quickly to respond to emergencies where the slower-moving legislature cannot.[25]

These are areas where Krass's memo bears a resemblance to Yoo's, but it would be incorrect to say she followed his precise approach on these points. She did not endorse the unitary executive, and (unlike Yoo) nothing in her memo embraces the notion that the president can set aside statutory limits on power. However, on one important point, Krass's memo very closely tracks Yoo's: the importance of interbranch practice in shaping constitutional meaning—the idea that the scope of presidential power can be shaped simply by what presidents do and Congress allows.[26]

Since presidents beginning with Truman have relied on congressional acquiescence or passivity in unilaterally ordering the use of military force, relying on interbranch practice allowed Krass to downplay the role of the constitutional text in setting limits on presidential power. In doing so, she was following an approach relied on, in part, by Yoo in his September 25, 2001, memo. Yoo, like Krass ten years later, relied on "the normative role of historical practice in constitutional law."[27] Both Yoo and Krass argue that the historical record shapes constitutional meaning—in other words, because previous presidents had unilaterally ordered the use of military force even when the United States was not directly threatened, Bush or Obama could do the same.[28] Krass and Yoo cite many of the same specific examples as precedent—President Reagan's order to bomb Libya in 1986, President George H. W. Bush's intervention in Panama in 1989, President Clinton's military operations in Haiti, Bosnia, and Yugoslavia in the 1990s.[29] Krass's memo concluded that the president can unilaterally order the use of military force even if the United States is not acting in self-defense as long as two conditions are satisfied: (1) the president "reasonably [determines] that such use of force [is] in the national interest" and (2) the use of force does not rise to the level of a "war" under the Constitution.[30]

By relying on past practice to determine the scope of presidential authority, Krass was able to navigate around constitutional and statutory limits. Under her analysis, the president can authorize the offensive use of military force without Congress's approval if he or she independently determines that an important national interest is at stake.[31] What this means in practice is that, in Krass's view, during the sixty-day WPR window presidents may unilaterally order the use of military force even when neither the United States nor its armed forces have been attacked. The Constitution does not support Krass's conclusion. Congress, of course is assigned the power to declare war.[32] The evidence shows that the Framers of the Constitution meant to assign Congress all power "to take the country from a state of peace to a state of war."[33] Records from the Constitutional Convention indicate that the Framers intended an emergency exception to exist—in other words, that presidents (who, unlike members of Congress, would always be on duty) could take unilateral action "to repel sudden attacks."[34] However, as Nancy Kassop observes, "this sole exception makes the rule all the more plain: presidents can act on their own *only* in defensive circumstances. Any offensive military action, regardless of size, duration, or purpose, must be authorized by Congress. Offensive versus defensive was the crucial distinction for the framers."[35]

Unlike Yoo, who (rather implausibly) brushes aside the Declare War Clause as a mere formality not intended to "constrain the President's independent and plenary constitutional authority over the use of military force,"[36] Krass does not dismiss the Declare War Clause as irrelevant. Or, at least, she does not seem to do so. Her April 2011 memo "acknowledge[s] one possible constitutionally-based limit on . . . presidential authority to employ military force [offensively] in defense of important national interests—a planned military engagement that constitutes a 'war' within the meaning of the Declaration of War Clause may require prior congressional authorization." However, this apparent limitation may not be very meaningful in practice, given Krass's definition of "war" under the Constitution: "[t]his standard generally will be satisfied only by prolonged and substantial military engagements, typically involving exposure of U.S. military personnel to significant risk over a substantial period." When the president orders limited military operations that do not involve ground troops, Krass concluded, such action "[avoids] the difficulties of withdrawal and risks of escalation," factors that might otherwise indicate a constitutional need for congressional approval. The "airstrikes and associated support missions" Obama ordered in Libya simply did not rise to the level of war under the Constitution, as defined by Krass.[37] The problem, as Louis Fisher has observed, is that this is not a very meaningful limit on presidential power. If "war" depends in large part on the commitment of ground troops, then presidents would remain free to "pulverize another country" with air and missile strikes without seeking congressional authorization—especially if the operations were concluded quickly.[38]

Despite the fact that Krass does not expressly rely on inherent presidential power, the sole organ doctrine, or other arguments claiming presidential authority to set aside constitutional and statutory limits on power, it is difficult to significantly distinguish her conclusions about the scope of presidential war power from Yoo's—at least during the sixty-day WPR period. Yoo concluded that the president alone can decide how to use military force to respond to any terrorist threat—whether or not the perceived threat has actually materialized.[39] Krass concluded that, during the sixty-day WPR window, the president can order the use of military force whenever, in his or her view, such actions would serve "sufficiently important national interests," so long as military operations would not rise to the level of a "war" under the Constitution.[40] During the sixty-day WPR window, then, Yoo and Krass agreed that the president can order the offensive use of military force without congressional approval.[41] Krass concluded that such operations cannot rise to the level of a "war," whereas Yoo concluded that the president has complete authority as to the "method . . . and nature" of military operations, but, as noted, Krass's definition of war leaves presidents plenty of room for unilateral action.

There is one significant difference between Krass's and Yoo's approach, however. Krass did not dismiss the relevance of the WPR. She did find a way to work around language in the law that seems to restrict unilateral presidential action to the sudden-attack context, dismissing this language as a "policy statement."[42] But, unlike Yoo, Krass never suggested the president could simply ignore the WPR.[43] She acknowledged that the sixty-day WPR window eventually requires the termination of military operations unilaterally ordered by the president, unless Congress provides authorization once the clock expires.[44] Accordingly, Krass reportedly advised President Obama that he could not continue military operations in Libya after the sixty-day WPR deadline was reached without obtaining congressional authorization.[45]

If President Obama had accepted Krass's advice, it would be fair to conclude that the Obama administration recognized meaningful limits on presidential authority to use military force in a way the Bush administration did not. But President Obama decided not to follow OLC's advice. Instead, he relied on advice from State Department legal adviser Harold Koh and White House counsel Robert Bauer, who concluded that the WPR simply did not apply because military operations did not rise to the level of "hostilities."[46] The WPR describes presidential authority to "[introduce] United States Armed Forces into hostilities or into situation where imminent involvement in hostilities is clearly indicated by the circumstances."[47]

Like both Yoo and Krass, Koh turned to past practice to define the scope and limits of presidential power—here, in a statutory context. In testimony before the Senate Foreign Relations Committee, Koh argued that the meaning of the term "hostilities" under the WPR ought to be determined on the basis of "historical [interbranch] practice." Koh concluded that historical practice showed U.S. military operations in Libya did not rise to the level of hostilities under the WPR.[48] Following Koh's reasoning, the Obama administration submitted a June 15, 2011, report to the U.S. House of Representatives claiming that "U.S. military operations [in Libya] are distinct from the kind of 'hostilities' contemplated by the [WPR's] 60 day termination provision. U.S. forces are playing a constrained and supporting role in a multinational coalition. . . . U.S. operations do not involve sustained fighting or active exchanges of fire with hostile forces, nor do they involve the presence of U.S. ground troops, U.S. casualties, or a serious threat thereof, or any significant chance of escalation into a conflict characterized by these factors."[49]

This approach brings to mind Peter Shane's concept of "faux law." In Shane's terms, the Obama administration created "legitimating documents, formal pieces of paper that sanction the President's expansive assertions of unilateral power." The legal analysis contained in the report to Congress and in Koh's testimony provides the illusion that the Obama administration recognizes limits on executive power by "generat[ing] what looks like legal authority for even utterly unprecedented claims."[50] But the apparent limits on power are a mirage. As Louis Fisher recognized, according to the Obama administration's reasoning, "if the United States conducted military operations by bombing at 30,000 feet, launching Tomahawk missiles from ships in the Mediterranean and using armed drones, there would be no 'hostilities' in Libya under the terms of the War Powers Resolution, provided that U.S. casualties were minimal or non-existent. Under the administration's June 15 report [to Congress], a nation with superior military forces could pulverize another country (perhaps with nuclear weapons) and there would be neither hostilities nor war."[51] A "limitation" on presidential power to use military force that broadly permits the president to order the offensive use of force, for as long as he or she wants, including by ordering devastating bomb and missile attacks, cannot reasonably be called a meaningful limitation on power.

What does the Libya episode tell us about the Obama administration and presidential power? When it comes to the use of military force, the Obama administration reached conclusions that share important things in common with those reached by the Bush administration. There are differences—the Obama administration did not expressly rely on inherent power, the sole organ doctrine, or presidential authority to set aside statutory limitations—but the results were very similar. The Obama administration concluded that it could broadly authorize the use of military force without congressional authorization as long as military operations (1) served an important national interest and (2) did not rise to the level of hostilities.[52] In practice, however, these are not meaningful limits on presidential power. The "important national interest" test is subjective and, both Koh and Krass concluded, could include "preserving regional stability and supporting the credibility and effectiveness of the U.N. Security Council."[53] Caroline Krass's analysis offered at least one meaningful limit on presidential power: the sixty-day WPR window. However, Harold Koh's narrow definition of "hostilities" turned even this into an illusory limitation.

In the end, the Obama administration essentially concluded it could order the offensive use of military force without congressional authorization so long as military operations were "limited" in the sense that they did not involve ground troops or "full military engagement."[54] To be sure, that is not the same as Yoo's conclusion that the president has "independent and plenary constitutional authority over the use of military force."[55] But the Obama administration has created "disturbing precedent"[56] that could readily be cited with approval by some future John Yoo in the Office of Legal Counsel, who might reasonably read the Obama administration's actions as supporting the conclusion that presidents can order the offensive use of military force without congressional approval as long as they (1) can identify some important national interest to be served and (2) avoid using ground troops or planning a prolonged engagement (if the initial operations unexpectedly turn into a prolonged engagement, that might be all right, too).

Jack Goldsmith, who argues that both Bush and Obama have effectively been constrained by law, devotes just one sentence (and one short footnote) in *Power and Constraint* to President Obama's actions in Libya.[57] He suggests that President Obama's unilateral action in Libya was not something the framers of the Constitution would have found legitimate but seems to dismiss the possibility of meaningful limits in this area, claiming that "legal checks on unilateral uses of military force are weak at best, especially with regard to low-level uses of force that do not involve ground troops." Goldsmith correctly describes how presidential power has been used—as he observes, "[e]very modern president has claimed the power, under Article II of the Constitution, to use military force abroad without congressional authorization."[58] That is an accurate description of historical practice since the Korean War—as Yoo and Krass noted with approval when they relied on past practice as a source of constitutional meaning. But past practice that is itself unconstitutional cannot serve as legitimate precedent.[59] The key question, as Goldsmith acknowledges and as Justice Jackson predicted, is whether Congress will act as a check on presidential power.[60] In the 2013 Syria episode, Congress seemed to do so. But, on closer inspection that too turns out to be an illusion. With Syria, the Obama administration continued to champion unilateral presidential power to use military force, unrestrained by meaningful limits under the law.

## SYRIA

In August 2012, President Obama warned the Syrian dictator Bashar al-Assad that he would be crossing a "red line . . . [if] we start seeing a whole bunch of chemical weapons moving around or being utilized [in the civil war that had raged in Syria since the spring of 2011].[61] On August 25, 2013, an Obama administration official was quoted as saying "[t]here is very little doubt at this point that a chemical weapon was used by the Syrian regime against civilians."[62] The Obama administration was reportedly considering a "limited military strike" to punish Syria.[63] Administration officials believed that military action would serve "important national interests" by preventing regional instability and "enforcing [a] norm against using chemical weapons."[64] Given the Libya precedent, it seemed likely that the Obama administration had concluded it could act without congressional authorization—in fact, public debate over the legality of presidential action focused mainly on questions of international law, not the U.S. Constitution (unlike in Libya, the UN Security Council had not authorized member states to use force in Syria).[65]

This time, however, the script was different. More than 140 members of Congress (including 21 Democrats) signed a letter warning President Obama that "[e]ngaging our military in Syria when no direct threat to the United States exists and without prior congressional authorization would violate the separation of powers that is clearly delineated in the Constitution."[66] President Obama moved away from what had looked like inevitable unilateral military action against Syria, instead deciding to seek congressional authorization for any strike.[67]

This seems, at first glance, like an encouraging development for those interested in setting limits on presidential power under the law. However, even as the Obama administration seemed to recognize limits on its power by seeking congressional authorization, it also suggested it reserved the option to act without congressional approval. Charlie Savage of the *New York Times* reported that White House counsel Kathryn Ruemmler "said the president believed a strike [against Syria] would be lawful, both in international law and domestic law, even if neither the Security Council nor Congress approved it."[68] President Obama personally made clear that he believed "I always reserve the right and responsibility to act on behalf of America's national security." Obama made this statement during a press conference after he was "asked what he [would] do if Congress rejects his request to use military force as a way to respond to Assad's alleged use of chemical weapons. While the president did not say he would go ahead with his plan even without the ok of Congress, he did not rule that out."[69]

Secretary of State John Kerry similarly declared that "[c]onstitutionally, every president, Republican and Democrat alike, has always reserved to the presidency, to the commander-in-chief of the armed forces, the right to make a [unilateral] decision with respect to American security. . . . Bill Clinton went to Kosovo over the objections of many people and saved lives and managed to make peace because he did something that was critical at the time. Many presidents have done that. Reagan did it. Bush did it. A lot of presidents have made a decision that they have to protect the nation. . . . [P]resident [Obama] reserves the right in the presidency to respond as appropriate to protect the security of our nation." When Secretary Kerry was asked if President Obama would face a backlash if he ordered military action in the event that Congress rejected authorizing legislation, Kerry said that "I am not going to speculate about it because I hope Congress will exercise its best judgment [by supporting the president's] unbelievably limited and tailored [plan]."[70]

Ultimately, the potential constitutional crisis suggested by the possibility that President Obama might order military action even if Congress voted against legislation authorizing the use of military force never came to be. The Syrian crisis was resolved, at least for the time being, through diplomatic channels.[71] However, what this episode means for presidential power under the U.S. Constitution remains unclear. One view is that Obama's decision to propose authorizing legislation from Congress will set limits on future presidents. In this view, future presidents who seek to order the offensive use of military force without congressional approval will have "the [Syria] precedent cited against him or her."[72] But this is far from clear. President Obama has suggested that his decision to go to Congress was more a political than a legal one—meaning that he was not required to seek legislative approval; he merely believed it was prudent under the circumstances.[73]

President Obama's statement brings to mind similar assertions of power made by the Bush administration. For instance, after the Supreme Court's decision in *Hamdi v. Rumsfeld*,[74] in which eight justices rejected unrestrained presidential power, emphasizing checks and balances (as highlighted in Justice O'Connor's plurality opinion, which declared that "a state of war is not a blank check for the President when it comes to the rights of the Nation's citizens"), a Bush administration spokesperson insisted the decision was a victory for supporters of broad presidential power, declaring that "[t]he Justice Department is pleased that the U.S. Supreme Court . . . upheld the authority of the President as Commander in Chief of the armed forces to detain enemy combatants, including U.S. citizens. This power . . . is one of the most essential authorities the U.S. Constitution grants the President to defend America from our enemies."[75] True believers in unrestrained presidential power never accept limits on power—even when those limits seem to be imposed by Congress or the courts. For those committed to presidential power, there is always a way around the apparent check—whether through an assertion of reserved power that suggests any limits on power will be subject to the president's discretion or through a presidential signing statement that similarly renders statutory limits optional.

If presidents continue to stake out claims to largely unrestrained presidential power, as Presidents Bush and Obama have, then the key actor in determining whether meaningful limits can be enforced will be Congress. In this sense, the Syria episode can be seen as a hopeful one: Congress demonstrated it is capable of asserting itself when its members act together. But the test of this episode's enduring value as a limit on presidential power depends on what Congress does in the future. Judging from its response to military action against ISIS, the early indications are not hopeful.

## ISIS

The Islamic State of Iraq and Syria, or ISIS,[76] is a hideous group. Its actions are like something out of a nightmare. However, it is far from obvious what course of action should be taken against ISIS. The use of military force may well be part of the plan, but, as President Obama acknowledges, it is not the entire solution.[77] Moreover, despite ISIS's atrocities, the president does not have unilateral authority to order military action against the group (unless ISIS directly poses an imminent or actual threat to the United States). Nonetheless, the Obama administration has gone to war against ISIS, with a passive Congress failing to weigh in. The Obama administration's actions against ISIS suggest that the 2013 Syria episode may be an exception to the rule of unrestrained presidential authority to use military force.

The fact that ISIS might not exist but for the U.S. invasion of Iraq in 2003 should itself be a cautionary tale when one considers how to use military force. ISIS has its origins in the terrorist group al Qaeda in Iraq, which formed after the 2003 invasion.[78] By mid-2014, ISIS forces had occupied cities in Iraq and Syria. By the summer of 2014, ISIS was threatening the cities of Baghdad and Erbil, where American diplomats and military advisers were stationed. There were reports that ISIS had trapped forty thousand Yazidis, adherents to a minority religious faith, in northern Iraq and might be moving to massacre them.[79]

In August 2014, President Obama unilaterally ordered air strikes against ISIS in Iraq, arguing that this action was necessary to protect Americans as well as the trapped Yazidis.[80] In September 2014, President Obama expanded air strikes against ISIS forces in Syria.[81] Although Congress had not specifically authorized the use of military force against ISIS, Obama argued that he already "ha[d] the authority he need[ed] to take action."[82] President Obama suggested that existing congressional authorization—the 2001 and 2002 AUMFs—could authorize military action against ISIS.[83] But neither statute can reasonably be seen as applying to ISIS, which did not even exist when the 2001 and 2002 AUMFs were enacted.

The 2001 AUMF authorized the president "to use all necessary and appropriate force against those nations, organizations, or persons he determines planned, authorized, committed, or aided the terrorist attacks that occurred on September 11, 2001, or harbored such organizations or persons, in order to prevent any future acts of international terrorism against the United States by such nations, organizations or persons."[84] That certainly authorized the war in Afghanistan against al Qaeda and the Taliban, but it cannot apply to ISIS, a group that did not exist when the 9/11 attacks were carried out and is now a rival of al Qaeda.[85] The 2002 AUMF authorized the 2003 war against the Saddam Hussein regime in Iraq.[86] It is indeed "all-but-frivolous" to cite the 2002 AUMF as authority for the president to use military force now against ISIS.[87]

As it stands, the Obama administration lacks any plausible statutory authority to support its decision to go to war with ISIS. The administration has asked Congress for authorization that specifically relates to ISIS, but the administration has made clear it does not believe such authorization is necessary—on the basis of either its implausible reliance on the 2001 and 2002 AUMFs or a theory of unilateral authority to act.[88] However, since there is fortunately no currently known emergency threat to the United States demanding unilateral military action against ISIS, congressional authorization is necessary, though it may not come. In February 2015, the Obama administration asked Congress to pass an AUMF against ISIS. The draft legislation contained vague provisions, including a stipulation that "enduring offensive ground combat operations" are not authorized.[89] This suggests, of course, that some ground combat operations would be permissible, but it is difficult to know when they would reach the "enduring" threshold. In fact, Josh Earnest, the White House press secretary, said that language in the proposed ISIS AUMF was designed to be "intentionally" vague in order to ensure "that there aren't overly burdensome constraints that are placed on the commander in chief."[90] In any case, the possibility that President Obama or his successor might take advantage of ambiguous statutory language is likely moot. It appears unlikely that Congress will take any action on the draft legislation proposed by the administration.[91] If Congress takes no action, declining either to approve or to reject legislation, military action against ISIS will simply continue without congressional approval. The Obama administration's campaign against ISIS would mark the hopeful incipient precedent set by the 2013 Syrian episode as an exception to the rule that presidents since Truman claim broad unilateral authority to order the use of military force.

## TARGETED KILLING

On September 30, 2011, a U.S. drone missile strike in Yemen killed a number of reputed members of al Qaeda in the Arabian Peninsula (AQAP), including Anwar al-Aulaqi and Samir Khan.[92] Al-Aulaqi and Khan were U.S. citizens. The attack targeted al-Aulaqi, whom President Obama described as "the leader of external operations for [AQAP]." The U.S. government claimed that al-Aulaqi "inspired militants around the world and helped plan a number of terrorist plots, including the December 2009 attempt to blow up a jetliner bound for Detroit." Al-Aulaqi had been placed on a kill-or-capture list sometime around late 2009 after executive branch officials concluded he was a senior operational leader in AQAP "whose activities in Yemen pose[d] a 'continuing and imminent' threat of violence to United States persons and interests."[93] There are reports that al-Aulaqi had been linked to Nidal Hasan, who killed thirteen people at Fort Hood, Texas, in 2009, and to Umar Farouk Abdulmutallab, the attempted "underwear bomber" who tried to blow up a plane headed to Detroit on Christmas Day in 2009.[94] Anwar al-Aulaqi's father had filed a lawsuit in August 2010 claiming that the government could not place Anwar al-Aulaqi, as a U.S. citizen, on a kill-or-capture list after a "closed executive process" without trial or judicial review of any kind.[95] A federal district court dismissed the lawsuit in December 2010.[96] On October 14, 2011, a few weeks after a drone strike killed Anwar al-Aulaqi, another drone strike in Yemen killed his sixteen-year-old son, Abdulrahman al-Aulaqi.[97]

Critics have raised questions (both before and after the killings) about the legitimacy of the decision to target Anwar al-Aulaqi for killing and about the killings of Samir Khan and Abdulrahman al-Aulaqi (it is unclear whether Khan and the younger al-Aulaqi were targeted for killing; there is no indication that either was ever placed on the kill-or-capture list).[98] Some criticisms raised due process concerns. The lawsuit filed by Anwar al-Aulaqi's father in August 2010 focused on the executive branch's failure to provide any judicial process before authorizing the killing of a U.S. citizen. This lawsuit charged that "the United States . . . placed Anwar Al-Aulaqi on . . . 'kill lists' without 'charge, trial, or conviction' . . . after a 'closed executive process' in which defendants and other executive officials determine that 'secret criteria' have been satisfied."[99] Other critics argued that al-Aulaqi was not, in fact, a terrorist leader. Gregory Johnsen called Anwar al-Aulaqi "a midlevel religious functionary [for AQAP] who happens to have American citizenship and speak English. This makes him a propaganda threat, but not one whose elimination would do anything to limit the reach of the Qaeda branch." Johnsen said al-Aulaqi was "a minor figure in al Qaeda," not a "terrorist kingpin" or commander.[100]

These criticisms call into question the legitimacy of the Obama administration's decision to order the killing of Anwar al-Aulaqi. Since al-Aulaqi was killed without judicial hearing or trial, does that mean the executive branch denied him due process as required by the U.S. Constitution? If al-Aulaqi was not, in fact, a senior AQAP leader involved in planning attacks against the United States, was he a legitimate target under the laws of war and pursuant to the 2001 AUMF enacted by Congress?

For years, the Obama administration refused to publicly release a July 16, 2010, Office of Legal Counsel memo and other legal memos presenting the argument that the killing of Anwar al-Aulaqi was legally authorized and justified.[101] The July 2010 OLC memo was finally made available to the public in June 2014 when a federal court of appeals required disclosure of a redacted version of the memo (other memos remain secret for now).[102] It is important to emphasize that the 2010 memo is redacted, so not all of the OLC's reasoning is available, even for the memo that has been released. However, between the 2010 memo and other arguments presented by the administration (for example, in a 2012 speech Attorney General Eric Holder gave at Northwestern Law School),[103] it seems possible to construct the Obama administration's position and to consider whether the administration's approach is meaningfully different from the Bush administration's approach to the use of military force.

The July 2010 OLC memo was signed by David Barron, then acting head of OLC.[104] Like Caroline Krass in the Libya action discussed earlier,

Barron does not speak John Yoo's language of inherent or plenary power. But, again like Krass, Barron found ways to navigate around constitutional and statutory limits and to justify expansive presidential power without meaningful limits.

In considering whether the Obama administration has recognized meaningful limits with regard to the targeted killing program, there are two questions to take into account: (1) statutory limits and (2) constitutional limits (i.e., due process). On the surface, Barron acknowledges both—he does not rely on any notion of inherent presidential power to set aside statutory limits, and he concedes that due process must be provided before a U.S. citizen suspected of being a terrorist leader can be killed. However, closer examination shows that Barron's July 2010 memo concentrates power in the hands of the executive without meaningful limits set by the other branches of government.

Barron's memo considers possible statutory obstacles to the targeted killing of Anwar al-Aulaqi, specifically the War Crimes Act, as well as federal laws that prohibit U.S. nationals from killing other U.S. nationals outside the United States and prohibit conspiracy to murder, kidnap, or maim another person outside the United States.[105] Barron concluded that the decision to target al-Aulaqi for killing would not be unlawful under any of these statutory provisions because the killing would be legitimate under the "public authority" justification.[106] The common law based public authority justification permits public officials to take actions that would otherwise be criminal, including killing, as long as those actions are "done with proper public authority."[107] As applied to the al-Aulaqi case, Barron concluded that the public authority justification made it legitimate for the Department of Defense and the CIA to kill al-Aulaqi as part of the "lawful conduct of war."[108] In other words, since "high level [executive branch] officials ha[d] concluded . . . that al-Aulaqi [was] a leader of AQAP whose activities in Yemen pose[d] a 'continuing and imminent threat' of violence to United States persons and interests[,]" al-Aulaqi could be lawfully targeted as an enemy combatant.[109]

This sounds eminently reasonable—after all, "[t]here is precedent for the United States targeting attacks against particular commanders" in past wars, even when those commanders were not on the front lines and were targeted in a surprise attack, not at a moment when they were actively engaged in combat. For instance, during World War II, a daring and successful U.S. raid killed Admiral Isoroku Yamamoto, the mastermind of the attack on Pearl Harbor, when Admiral Yamamoto was behind enemy lines, in a plane on his way to carry out a review of Japanese troops.[110] Surely, Barron suggested, the Yamamoto precedent justified the Obama administration's decision to order the targeted killing of al-Aulaqi.[111] The problem, however, is that Barron's analysis depends on two assumptions: that (1) al-Aulaqi was, in fact, a "leader of AQAP forces [who were] part of al-Qaida forces" and, relatedly, that (2) Congress had authorized the president to make war against AQAP.[112]

Each assumption was flawed. It was not clear whether (1) al-Aulaqi was an AQAP commander involved in planning attacks against the United States and, if he was, (2) that Congress had authorized military action against AQAP. As noted, Gregory Johnsen argued that al-Aulaqi was a propagandist for AQAP, not a military leader.[113] The conclusion that al-Aulaqi was an AQAP military leader and, therefore, a legitimate target under the laws of war as an enemy combatant had been reached entirely within the executive branch, without any external review by the other branches of government. In fact, Barron himself did not have any independent way to test the sufficiency of the executive branch's conclusions: his memo notes that his analysis "rel[ied] on the sufficiency of the particular factual circumstances of the CIA [and DOD] operation *as they have been represented to us.*" In other words, Barron had no way to know whether it was accurate that al-Aulaqi was an AQAP leader involved in planning attacks against the United States. His analysis assumed that "[h]igh level government officials [had correctly] concluded" that this was the case.[114] The fact that the legitimacy of the al-Aulaqi killing depended on this unreviewable conclusion points to the failure to provide meaningful due process, a problem discussed in more detail below.

The Barron memo also concluded that the targeted killing had been carried out "pursuant to Executive war powers that Congress has expressly authorized."[115] But this conclusion, like the conclusion that al-Aulaqi was an AQAP leader, depended on a questionable assumption—this time, the assumption that Congress had authorized the use of military force against AQAP. The 2001 AUMF, which Barron relied on as express authority for the use of force against AQAP, does not actually expressly mention AQAP. It could not have done so, as the 2001 AUMF was enacted in September 2001 and AQAP did not come into existence until years later.[116] The 2001 AUMF provides "[t]hat the President is authorized to use all necessary and appropriate force against *those nations, organizations, or persons he determines planned, authorized, committed, or aided the terrorist attacks that occurred on September 11, 2001, or harbored such organizations or persons*, in order to prevent any future acts of international terrorism against the United States by such nations, organizations or persons."[117] The emphasized text clearly authorizes the president to use military force against al Qaeda and the Taliban, which harbored al Qaeda leaders, including Bin Laden, after

9/11.[118] It does not clearly apply to AQAP. One might argue that AQAP is covered by the AUMF as a co-belligerent of al Qaeda or an associated force. However, it is not possible to say, as Barron did, that Congress "expressly authorized" such action. At best, this is an implicit authorization to use force against a group like AQAP that is associated with al Qaeda, but even this is a reading contradicted by the 2001 AUMF's legislative history.[119] By exaggerating the authority granted by the 2001 AUMF, Barron turned an authorization with consciously defined limits (applying only to al Qaeda and the Taliban) into a more open-ended authorization with malleable limits to be defined by the president.

Barron's memo also effectively set aside constitutional limits on presidential power to order targeted killings of U.S. citizens. The section of Barron's memo that addresses due process considerations is heavily redacted. However, it seems possible to extract the central core of Barron's conclusion: due process was provided to al-Aulaqi because decision makers in the executive branch balanced his interest in not being wrongfully killed against the executive branch's interest in defending Americans from the "continued" and "imminent" threat al-Aulaqi posed.[120] In other words, as Attorney General Holder put it in his 2012 speech at Northwestern Law School, due process does not necessarily require judicial process.[121] Both Barron's and Holder's approach seem to recognize limits on presidential power: neither declared that the president can simply ignore the Due Process Clause. But this is deceptive. As Noah Feldman observed after the Barron memo was released: "This [notion that due process could be satisfied by a secret process within the executive branch] is not due process as it has existed since the Magna Carta in 1215. It is a travesty of due process. At a bare minimum, the accused must be able to defend himself and have his case decided by someone who isn't actively interested in the case as a party to it. Put another way, due process demands that no one may be a judge in his own case—which the president would be if adjudicating whether to kill an American abroad."[122]

Feldman's critique suggests why Barron's conception of due process does not place any meaningful limit on presidential power. Barron's memo cites the Supreme Court's 2004 *Hamdi* decision as precedent for the proposition that the process due to a U.S. citizen can be satisfied by a balancing of the private and public interests at stake.[123] But in *Hamdi*, eight justices made clear (in three separate opinions) that due process is (1) designed to check executive power and (2) must be provided by a court, not the executive branch itself.[124] Justice O'Connor's plurality opinion concluded "due process demands that a citizen held in the United States as an enemy combatant be given a meaningful opportunity to contest the factual basis for that detention before a neutral decisionmaker." Separation-of-powers principles require an "impartial adjudicator," not the executive branch alone, to provide due process. In fact, O'Connor reasoned, "the [Bush administration's] position that the courts must forgo any examination of the individual case and focus exclusively on the legality of the broader detention scheme cannot be mandated by any reasonable view of separation of powers, as this approach serves only to condense power into a single branch of government."[125]

Justice O'Connor further wrote that "it would turn our system of checks and balances on its head to suggest that a citizen could not make his way to court with a challenge to the factual basis for his detention by his Government, simply because the Executive opposes making available such a challenge." It was possible, O'Connor suggested, that due process could be provided "by an appropriately authorized and properly constituted military tribunal." But it was not possible for the executive branch to satisfy due process requirements itself, without judicial involvement. O'Connor suggested that entrusting due process to the executive branch alone would amount to "a blank check for the President when it comes to the rights of the Nation's citizens."[126]

Justice Scalia's dissenting opinion, joined by Justice Stevens, agreed with Justice O'Connor that due process is designed to set limits on executive power. Scalia defined the idea of limited executive power as a fundamental principle in a system concerned with individual liberty: "[t]he very core of liberty secured by our Anglo-Saxon system of separated powers has been freedom from indefinite imprisonment at the will of the Executive."[127] Due process under the Constitution is essential (along with the Suspension Clause) to preserving liberty and constraining the executive. The Due Process Clause and other constitutional limits make clear that the president does not possess unlimited power and reflect "the Founders' general mistrust of military power permanently at the Executive's disposal." Justice Scalia's dissent was limited to the specific facts of the Hamdi case, that is, a case involving a U.S. citizen accused of being an enemy combatant and imprisoned in the United States without trial.[128] However, the principle he emphasizes—that the Due Process Clause is designed to protect individual liberty by setting limits on executive power—is difficult to square with Barron's approach. If there is reason to be skeptical of unilateral presidential action when it comes to detaining a citizen who is a suspected enemy, surely there is even more reason to be skeptical when the president seeks to kill a citizen who is a suspected enemy leader.[129]

The central theme running through the three separate Hamdi opinions that rejected unilateral presidential action is the aversion to concentrated power in the hands of the executive. Justice Souter (in an opinion joined by Justice Ginsburg and echoing the views expressed by Justices O'Connor's and Scalia's opinions) observed that:

[i]n a government of separated powers, deciding finally on what is a reasonable degree of guaranteed liberty whether in peace or war (or some condition in between) is not well entrusted to the Executive Branch of Government, whose particular responsibility is to maintain security. For reasons of inescapable human nature, the branch of the Government asked to counter a serious threat is not the branch on which to rest the Nation's entire reliance in striking the balance between the will to win and the cost in liberty on the way to victory; the responsibility for security will naturally amplify the claim that security legitimately raises. A reasonable balance is more likely to be reached on the judgment of a different branch, just as Madison said in remarking that "the constant aim is to divide and arrange the several offices in such a manner as that each may be a check on the other—that the private interest of every individual may be a sentinel over the public rights."[130]

It is possible (though unlikely) that the redacted portions of Barron's memo consider what eight justices in *Hamdi* had to say about due process operating as a check on executive power, but it is not possible to see how Barron's and Holder's notion that due process can be satisfied by secret deliberations within the executive branch can be reconciled with *Hamdi*. Although Barron claims to follow *Hamdi*, his approach actually rejects the approach endorsed by eight justices in that case. Barron's memo concentrates power in the executive branch and renders due process meaningless in the context of targeted killing, leaving it entirely up to the executive branch to determine when it is necessary to kill a U.S. citizen who is suspected of being—but not proved to be—a dangerous terrorist leader. It is true that Barron does not go as far as John Yoo would—Yoo has written that it is unnecessary and dangerous to provide *any* process (even if solely within the executive branch) to U.S. citizens suspected of being terrorist leaders and targeted for killing.[131] On the surface, Barron seems to reject Yoo's approach because he accepts the need for due process. In the end, however, this is a distinction without a difference. Barron's approach found a way for the Obama administration's targeted killing program to operate without any meaningful statutory or constitutional limits, other than those voluntarily adopted by the president.

# The Obama Administration

# and Surveillance

In June 2013, Glenn Greenwald reported that the National Security Agency was "collecting the telephone records of millions of U.S. customers of Verizon" pursuant to a top-secret Foreign Intelligence Surveillance Court (FISC) order.[1] Edward Snowden, a former CIA cybersecurity expert and NSA contractor, had given Greenwald access to the secret FISC order.[2] It soon became clear that the Obama administration's bulk telephony[3] metadata collection program[4] "had been going on for years, and was directed at all major [U.S.] telecom carriers, not just Verizon."[5] In addition, Greenwald and Barton Gellman reported that the NSA was accessing online communications Americans engaged in while using popular Internet service providers such as Yahoo, Google, Microsoft, and Facebook.[6]

## Bulk Metadata Collection

Snowden's revelations showed that, pursuant to FISC orders, the Obama administration (specifically the NSA) was collecting and storing "nearly all call details generated by certain telephone companies in the United States." This information did not include the content of phone calls—it is "metadata" about the calls, meaning "[c]all detail records [that] typically include much of the information [appearing] on a customer's telephone bill: the date and time of a call, its duration, and the participating telephone numbers." Most of these records "are for purely domestic calls, meaning those calls in which both participants are located within the United States, including local calls."[7] Through the bulk metadata program, the NSA was collecting records for billions of telephone calls made each day by Americans and other people in the United States and storing that information in databases for five years.[8]

Before considering how the Obama administration claimed legal justification for this program and whether that justification is persuasive, it is essential to understand additional context—how bulk metadata collection began and how it works. Bulk collection began in late 2001, just after the September 11 attacks.[9] At first, "both content and Internet and telephony metadata were collected outside the ambit of FISA."[10] This surveillance and data collection was conducted pursuant to the President's Surveillance Program (PSP), without any FISC order or oversight. As discussed in Section II, John Ashcroft, James Comey, Jack Goldsmith, and other executive branch lawyers objected to the PSP, leading to a tense showdown with the White House in March 2004. When Ashcroft, Comey, and Goldsmith were prepared to resign, the Bush administration modified the PSP by seeking FISC approval for the first time in July 2004 for bulk collection of Internet metadata. However, "the remaining elements of the program, including collection of content and telephony metadata . . . continue[d] without [FISC] authorization." It was not until 2006 that the administration sought FISC approval for bulk telephony metadata collection.[11] This happened in the wake of reporting about the Terrorist Surveillance Program (the part of the PSP involving warrantless surveillance of the content of phone calls), when telephone companies "got nervous" and asked the NSA to seek a court order authorizing metadata collection.[12]

The stated goal of the bulk metadata program is "to enable the government to identify communications among known and unknown terrorism suspects, particularly those located inside the United States."[13] The NSA claimed authority to gather bulk telephony metadata pursuant to Section 215 of the Patriot Act, and the FISC endorsed the NSA's legal position.[14] Beginning in 2006, FISC orders required specific U.S. telephone companies to "provide the NSA with 'all call data records' generated by those companies."[15] Prior to December 2015, when the NSA received these records, it stored them in databases that permitted it to conduct searches or "queries." These queries are performed through "contact chaining"—"the process of identifying the connections among individuals through their calls with each other." The idea is that, once NSA identifies a suspected terrorist, it can then "identify unknown terrorist operatives [on the basis of] their contacts with known suspects, discover links between known suspects, and monitor the pattern of communication among suspects."[16]

From 2006 through January 2014, queries were conducted without FISC oversight; the FISA court's role was limited to issuing initial production orders to telephone companies, but it did not review specific searches of the records that were collected.[17] Once the NSA collected call records from those companies, it was up to the NSA to determine when it was appropriate to conduct searches or queries of those records.[18] Here's how that process worked: the NSA sought to identify "seed" terms—for example, one phone number that could then be used to search the database for other contacts. Before a seed term could be used as the basis for a search, a NSA official had to "[determine] that there is reasonable, articulable suspicion [RAS] that the selection term is associated with [international] terrorism . . . [and] a terrorist organization identified in the FISA court's orders."[19]

Once the NSA determined that the RAS test was met, it could then search its call record databases for all phone numbers found to be in contact with the seed for up to "three hops": the first hop is all phone numbers "directly in contact with the seed," the second hop is all numbers in contact with first hop numbers, and the third hop is all numbers in contact with second hop numbers.[20] As U.S. District Court Judge Richard J. Leon observed, in practice "it is possible to arrive at a query result in the millions within three hops while using even conservative numbers."[21] For instance, if the seed number has called or received calls from one hundred numbers (the first hop) and each of those one hundred numbers has also called or received calls from one hundred numbers (the second hop), with each of those second hop numbers also having called or received calls from one hundred numbers (the third hop), the NSA would search the metadata associated with one million phone records indirectly connected with a single seed number.[22] When the NSA "identifie[s] information [from its queries of the databases] believed to have potential counterterrorism value, it passes that information on to other federal agencies, including the FBI."[23]

A key question becomes whether the metadata program is legally justified.[24] The Obama administration claimed the authority to collect, store, and potentially search the metadata records associated with essentially all calls made in the United States. How did it justify this authority? It began with Section 215 of the Patriot Act, which amended FISA's "business records provision."[25] Under FISA's business records provision (originally enacted in 1998), the FBI[26] was permitted to seek an order from the FISC requiring a business "to release records in its possession for an investigation to gather foreign intelligence information or an investigation concerning international terrorism."[27] In making an application to the FISC, the FBI had to shows that there were "specific and articulable facts giving reason to believe that the person to whom the records pertain is a foreign power or an agent of a foreign power."[28] The FISC could issue production orders to four specific types of businesses only: "a common carrier, public accommodation facility, physical storage facility, or vehicle rental facility."[29]

The Patriot Act, initially enacted in 2001, "significantly extended the reach of FISA's business records provision."[30] Section 215 of the Patriot Act, as amended in 2006, permitted the FBI to "make an application for an order [from the FISC] requiring the production of any tangible things (including books, records, papers, documents, and other items) for an investigation to obtain foreign intelligence information not concerning a United States person or to protect against international terrorism or clandestine intelligence activities, provided that such investigation of a United States person is not conducted solely upon the basis of activities protected by the first amendment to the Constitution."[31] Under Section 215, "the FBI [was] no longer limited to seeking records from common carriers, public accommodations facilities, physical storage facilities, or vehicle rental facilities."[32] In order to support its application, the FBI needed to provide the FISC with "a statement of facts showing that there are reasonable grounds to believe that the tangible things sought are relevant to an authorized investigation (other than a threat assessment) . . . to obtain foreign intelligence information not concerning a United States person or to protect against international terrorism or clandestine intelligence activities."[33]

The Patriot Act significantly changed FISA's business records provision by (1) removing the limitation as to the types of businesses that could be subject to production orders and (2) removing the requirement that the FBI show "specific and articulable facts" to support its claim that the records pertained to "a foreign power or an agent of a foreign power."[34] Under the 2006 amended version of Section 215, the FBI needed only to show the FISC that there were reasonable grounds to believe the records it sought were "relevant to an authorized investigation . . . to obtain foreign intelligence information not concerning a United States person or to protect against international terrorism or clandestine intelligence activities."[35] In other words, "[t]his [now] meant that the [FBI], in order to obtain highly sensitive and invasive documents—such as medical histories, banking transactions, or phone records—needed to demonstrate only that those documents were 'relevant' to a pending investigation."[36]

In May 2006, when the Bush administration sought permission from the FISC to continue[37] carrying out the NSA's bulk telephony metadata program, it argued that the newly amended version of Section 215 provided the necessary legal authority. The executive branch argued that it should be given authority to collect *all* metadata records "because the NSA can effectively conduct metadata analysis only if it has the data in bulk." In other words, the executive branch argued "that essentially the entire nation's calling records are 'relevant' to every [international] counterterrorism investigation cited in the government's applications to the court."[38] The idea is that the government is looking for a "needle" of information in a "haystack" of records and that it can find these essential "needles" of information only by conducting comprehensive searches of massive amounts of data that will permit it to detect patterns underlying terrorists' communications.[39] The FISC accepted the executive branch's argument, agreed with its understanding and application of the term "relevant" under Section 215, and approved bulk telephony metadata collection.[40]

After President Obama took office, the metadata program continued as it had since 2006, pursuant to FISC orders: "[s]ince 2009 [until 2014], there [were] no major changes in the operation of the Section 215 program."[41] In justifying the continued use of the metadata program, the Obama administration relied on the same argument made by the Bush administration and accepted by the FISC since 2006: "[because] the government has reason to believe that conducting a search of a broad collection of telephony metadata records will produce counterterrorism information — and that it is necessary to collect a large volume of data in order to employ the analytic tools needed to identify that information — the standard of relevance under Section 215 is satisfied." In the Obama administration's view, "the entire repositor[y] of records" is relevant to ongoing investigations of international terrorism, even though "any particular record is unlikely to bear on the matter being investigated, because searching the entire repository is the only feasible means to locate the critical [information]."[42]

In other words, the Obama administration believed (and the FISC agreed) that *all* telephony metadata records sought from specified telephone companies ("potentially . . . the entire nation's calling records")[43] are relevant to ongoing investigations of international terrorism, even though the vast majority of these records admittedly have nothing to do with terrorism.[44] A publicly released 2013 FISC order endorsed the Obama administration's legal justification for the metadata program, just as the FISC had endorsed the same rationale put forth by the Bush administration beginning in 2006. The 2013 FISC order concluded that, "[b]ecause the subset of terrorist communications is ultimately contained within the whole of the metadata produced, but can only be found after the production is aggregated and then queried using identifiers determined to be associated with identified international terrorist organizations, the whole production is relevant to the ongoing investigation out of necessity."[45]

The Obama administration argued, as the Bush administration had argued beginning in 2006, "that essentially the entire nation's calling records are 'relevant' to every [international] counterterrorism investigation cited in the government's application to the [FISC]." As the Privacy and Civil

Liberties Oversight Board (PCLOB) tersely observed, "[t]his position is untenable."[46] In the PCLOB's words, the interpretation of Section 215 endorsed by the executive branch and the FISC "is circular and deprives the word 'relevant' of any interpretive value. [Under the administration's reasoning], [a]ll records become relevant to an investigation . . . because the government has developed an investigative tool that functions by collecting all records to enable later searching."[47] Although the Obama administration insists that the metadata program is limited to phone records and that "Section 215 [does not necessarily authorize] the collection and storage of *all* types of information in bulk,"[48] the PCLOB observed that the logic of the government's argument suggests otherwise: "[t]he implication of [the administration's and the FISC's] reasoning is that if the government develops an effective means of searching through *everything* in order to find *something*, then *everything* becomes relevant to its investigations. The word 'relevant' becomes limited only by the government's technological capacity to ingest information and sift through it efficiently."[49]

This inexorably elastic definition of the word "relevant" left Section 215 with no ability to set meaningful limits on executive authority to collect and search Americans' phone records. It is implausible to believe that Congress intended to give the executive branch this kind of authority. As Representative Jim Sensenbrenner (R-Wisconsin), an author of the Patriot Act, asked after the Snowden revelations revealed the scope of the metadata program: "[h]ow can every call that every American makes or receives be relevant to a specific investigation?" Sensenbrenner charged that "both the [Obama] administration and the FISA court are relying on an unbounded interpretation of [Section 215] that Congress never intended."[50] Sensenbrenner objected that "[t]he government must request specific records relevant to its investigation. . . . To argue otherwise renders [Section 215] meaningless. . . . It's like scooping up the entire ocean to guarantee you catch a fish."[51] Elizabeth Goitein of the Brennan Center for Justice agreed that such an "anemic definition of relevance [as that put forward by the administration][52] would render this limitation in [Section 215] meaningless . . . [and] would contradict a basic rule of statutory interpretation . . . [that] Congress meant its words to have effect."[53] Adina Schwartz points out that the administration's (and the FISC's) notion that "relevance [may be assessed] on a database-wide level," rather than by considering the relevance of individual records, "would seem to [logically suggest] that the government would not be barred from obtaining any information about anyone, so long as the information was included in a database and there was some reason to believe that some item or other about someone or other in the database might have some connection or other to an investigation of [international] terrorism or to obtaining foreign intelligence."[54]

The Obama administration and its defenders argue that Obama's approach to surveillance is different from Bush's because Obama, unlike Bush, obtained legal approval from the FISC. As Representative Steny Hoyer (D-Maryland) insists, "The difference between this program [under Obama] and the Bush program [is that] the Bush program was not sanctioned by law; this is pursuant to law. . . . I think that's a very important distinction that some people don't draw, but they ought to draw."[55] There are two central problems with this argument. First, the Bush administration also received FISC authorization for bulk telephony metadata collection beginning in 2006. It is true that from late 2001 to 2006 Bush authorized such collection unilaterally, without FISC approval, through the Presidential Surveillance Program.[56] That is an important point, as it means pre-2006 surveillance violated FISA. However, beginning in 2006, the Bush administration sought and gained approval from the FISC for the program, relying on the same rationale later advanced by the Obama administration. The metadata program, and the legal authority claimed for it, did not change until after the Snowden revelations in 2013.[57]

Second, the FISC order Representative Hoyer alludes to as providing legal sanction for the metadata program is simply another example of what Peter Shane describes as "faux law"—a "formal [document]" that "looks like legal authority for executive usurpation."[58] The fact that the FISC accepted the administration's argument that Section 215 provides authority for the metadata program does not prove that the argument is a good one or even a plausible one. In fact, the argument is utterly implausible, and the FISC harmed its own credibility by endorsing it.[59]

The Obama administration's definition of "relevant" under Section 215 is similar to its definition of "hostilities" under the War Powers Resolution (WPR). As discussed in chapter 10, Harold Koh defined "hostilities" so narrowly under the WPR that the term lost nearly all practical ability to limit unilateral presidential authority to order the offensive use of military force as long as the president did not deploy ground troops. Under Koh's definition, the WPR has little or no meaningful ability to set limits on presidential power. Similarly, the Obama administration's definition of "relevant" under Section 215 of the Patriot Act removes all meaningful statutory[60] limits on presidential power. In fact, "the operation of the [metadata] program bears almost no relationship to the text of the statute— which is designed to confer subpoena-like authority on the FBI, not to enable nationwide bulk data collection by the NSA." Accepting the Obama administration's statutory interpretation argument under Section 215 "requires an impermissible transformation of the statute. . . . Where [Section 215's] text uses limiting words (such as 'relevant'), those words must be redefined beyond their traditional meaning."[61]

The PCLOB concluded that "the government's interpretation of the word 'relevant' in Section 215 [is] unsupported by legal precedent and a subversion of the statute's manifest intent to place *some* restriction, albeit a flexible and generous one, on the scope of the items that can be acquired under its auspices."[62] This was the central problem with the Obama administration's approach: the point of the relevance standard under Section 215 is to set a limit on the government's ability to collect information, not to enable unlimited collection.[63] The NSA's goal is to collect everything—all telephony metadata records. Its logic is that unless it has all the records, it cannot conduct complete searches of the information, as complete searches depend on having access to "all calling records." But, as the PCLOB aptly observed, "[i]f Section 215's relevance requirement is to serve any meaningful function . . . relevance cannot be premised on the government's desire to use a tool whose very operation depends on collecting information without limit."[64]

It is true that the Obama administration has not embraced the inherent power/unitary executive rationale relied on by the Bush administration before 2006 to support metadata collection without FISC approval.[65] Therefore, Jack Goldsmith is correct when he argues that the Obama administration followed the late Bush administration approach—in this case, the approach the Bush administration began when it gained FISC approval for the metadata program in 2006. Goldsmith reassures us that "[t]here is no reason to think that Obama is circumventing surveillance laws the way the Bush administration did in its early years. But there is also no reason to think he has backed away from Bush's later surveillance practices."[66] That is correct: we now know, thanks to the Snowden revelations, that the Obama administration continued the Bush metadata program as it had existed since 2006 (i.e., pursuant to FISC approval).[67] But this cannot fairly be described as a constrained approach. The Obama administration (like the Bush administration beginning in 2006) simply found a new way to achieve the same result Bush had initially justified through the unitary executive theory. By claiming to respect statutory limitations, the Obama administration can argue that it recognized limits on presidential power. But, as in other areas, this is an illusion. The Obama administration relied on implausible statutory interpretation to render Section 215 meaningless as a limit on presidential power.

Ultimately, the Obama administration changed its approach to metadata collection only when it was forced to do so. In May 2015, the U.S.

Court of Appeals for the Second Circuit ruled that "the bulk telephone metadata program [was] not authorized by § 215 [of the Patriot Act]." The Second Circuit specifically rejected the Obama administration's argument that Section 215 authorized bulk metadata collection on the basis of a broad understanding of the term "relevance." The court concluded that the administration's definition of relevance under Section 215 was "unprecedented and unwarranted."[68] The court noted, however, that since it was deciding the case on statutory grounds, Congress could modify the statute to give the administration the authority it sought.[69]

Section 215 of the Patriot Act expired at midnight on May 31, 2015. On June 2, 2015, Congress enacted and President Obama signed into law the USA Freedom Act.[70] Under the new law, after a six-month transition period, private companies were to take over responsibility for storing metadata records and the government would have to seek FISC approval in order to search specific records (previously, after the NSA obtained a FISC order to collect records in bulk, it could then decide on its own how to conduct searches of the data).[71] This would change and limit the metadata collection program. However, the Obama administration asked the FISC to authorize continued bulk metadata collection during the six-month transition period, arguing that the Second Circuit's decision did not bind the FISC.[72] In other words, it argued that the old metadata collection program could continue during the transition period despite the Second Circuit's ruling and despite the fact that Section 215 had expired on May 31, 2015. The six-month transition period expired at the end of November 2015, and the government stopped storing metadata, which now remains with private companies. Under the USA Freedom Act, the government must now seek specific authorization from the FISC in order to search metadata stored by private companies.

Both Congress and the courts took steps to set limits on presidential power to engage in bulk metadata collection and surveillance. The Obama administration seems to have accepted these changes, though it remains to be seen whether this is an effective way of limiting presidential power in this area.

## THE SECTION 702 SURVEILLANCE PROGRAM

At first glance, the Obama administration's collection of intelligence pursuant to Section 702 of FISA looks more limited and more defensible than pre-2014 surveillance under the bulk metadata program. Section 702 permits the executive branch to put under surveillance only foreigners (non-U.S. persons in the language of the statute)[73] "who are reasonably believed to be located outside the United States" in order "to acquire foreign intelligence information."[74] Americans cannot be targeted for surveillance, and even non-Americans in the United States cannot be targeted.[75] Section 702 also prohibits "reverse targeting"—in other words, the government cannot "intentionally target a person reasonably believed to be located outside the United States if the purpose of such acquisition is to target a particular, known person reasonably believed to be in the United States."[76] The attorney general (AG) and the director of national intelligence (DNI) must certify to the FISC that surveillance will comply with Section 702, including by using minimization procedures designed to avoid unnecessarily gathering communications by or data related to Americans.[77] The FISC must review the certification and "issue a written opinion explaining the reasons why the court has held that the proposed targeting and minimization procedures do, or do not, comply with statutory and Fourth Amendment requirements."[78]

It would seem there are the makings of an argument that the Obama administration has been subject to meaningful limits when engaging in surveillance under Section 702. This surveillance program proceeds pursuant to a statute that permits the government to target for surveillance only foreigners (non-U.S. persons) reasonably believed to be outside the United States. Minimization procedures are used to ensure Americans' privacy is protected. The statute contains language designed to prevent the government from using foreign targets as a pretext for gaining access to communications by people in the United States (the so-called reverse targeting prohibition). The FISC exercises oversight of the program. This is not the Bush administration's Terrorist Surveillance Program, which secretly, in apparent violation of criminal law, authorized the NSA to intercept Americans' international communications without any FISC oversight, relying only on the president's reasonable belief that such communications were connected with al Qaeda or an affiliated organization. In fact, the Privacy and Civil Liberties Oversight Board concluded that the Section 702 program complies with both statutory law and the Constitution (unlike the bulk metadata program, which it concluded was unlawful, as discussed earlier in this section).[79]

On closer examination, however, the Section 702 program is not subject to meaningful statutory or constitutional constraints that effectively protect Americans' reasonable expectations of privacy. First, the statute itself allows the executive branch to gain access to Americans' communications without a warrant: "Americans cannot be 'targets' under [S]ection 702, but their communications with targets can be intercepted."[80] In 2013, the government directed Section 702 surveillance at more than eighty-nine thousand foreign targets; "[i]t is unknown how many U.S. citizens have been in contact with [these foreign] targets" and therefore themselves subject to surveillance.[81] This raises a constitutional problem, as discussed later.

Apart from the constitutional question, even assuming that statutory limits on surveillance would be meaningful if followed, "the government's implementation of the [program] exceeds statutory authority . . . [because] the government is claiming, and exercising, more authority than the statute actually provides."[82] As with the metadata program, the Obama administration has found ways to render statutory limitations under Section 702 ineffective. But, unlike the metadata program, Section 702 surveillance allows the government to collect and search the *contents* of Americans' communications.[83] Although Section 702 is designed to focus surveillance on non-Americans outside the United States, in practice the program allows for "large scale warrantless surveillance of Americans' international communications" and has even been used to "give the government broad authority to collect purely domestic communications as well." The program has operated without regard to constitutional or statutory limits.[84] The story of the Section 702 surveillance program under Obama ends up closely tracking the story of bulk metadata collection. The Obama administration has essentially followed the Bush administration's later (in this case, post-2007) approach, using FISC review of the program to provide a façade of legitimacy for a surveillance program that allows it to gather information about Americans in ways not permitted by either statutory law or the Constitution.

Section 702 of FISA[85] was enacted by the FISA Amendments Act of 2008 ("2008 FAA") and provides statutory authority for the attorney general and the director of national intelligence "to authorize jointly . . . [surveillance] targeting [non-U.S. persons] . . . reasonably believed to be located outside the United States to acquire foreign intelligence information."[86] The executive branch is not required to identify specific individuals targeted for surveillance: it is sufficient to attest that surveillance is "reasonably designed to" (1) "ensure that [it is] limited to *targeting* persons reasonably believed to be located outside the United States" and (2) "prevent the intentional acquisition of [purely domestic communication within the United States]."[87] Surveillance need not be solely aimed at gathering foreign intelligence: the AG and the DNI must attest in their certification to the FISC only that "a significant purpose of the acquisition is to obtain foreign intelligence information."[88] Section 702 surveillance is aimed at "electronic communications or electronically stored information."[89] Although "targeting" is not specifically defined by the statute, the PCLOB explains that "[t]he NSA targets non-U.S. persons by [using] 'selectors,' such as email addresses and telephone numbers." These "selectors" are provided to electronic communications service providers in order to acquire information.[90]

When the FISA court reviews certifications submitted by the AG and the DNI, its task is essentially to ensure that the certification complies with these targeting procedures, in other words, to determine whether the surveillance "is limited to targeting [non-U.S.] persons reasonably believed to be outside the United States" and contains "minimization procedures," meaning procedures that are "reasonably designed . . . to minimize the acquisition and retention, and prohibit the dissemination, of nonpublicly available information concerning unconsenting United States persons consistent with the need of the United States to obtain, produce, and disseminate foreign intelligence information."[91] This is a "narrowly circumscribed" role, as "[t]he FISC does not review or approve the government's targeting decisions. . . . The FISC reviews only the general procedures that the government proposes to use in carrying out its surveillance."[92] The FISC reviews "targeting procedures" but not "individual targeting determinations."[93] The executive branch is *not* required to submit an application to the FISA court that "articulate[s] any individualized suspicion regarding its targets [or Americans who communicate with them]," let alone satisfying Fourth Amendment requirements that a warrant be issued on the basis of probable cause and with specificity as to "the place to be searched."[94]

Once the FISC signs off on a certification prepared by the executive branch, "the government sends written directives to electronic communications service providers compelling their assistance in the acquisition of communications [by or about targeted persons]."[95] The PCLOB has explained how targeting works: "Section 702 targeting begins when an NSA analyst discovers . . . a foreign intelligence lead—specifically, information indicating that a particular person may possess or receive the types of foreign intelligence information described within one of the Section 702 certifications." The NSA analyst must assess whether the intended target is "a non-U.S. person reasonably believed to be located outside the United States based on the totality of the circumstances available."[96] The NSA analyst is also required to determine that using a particular selector (e.g., an e-mail address) to target a non-U.S. person "will be likely to acquire" foreign intelligence information described in an approved Section 702 certification. After these determinations are made, two senior NSA analysts must separately confirm that the request to use a particular selector "meets all of the requirements of the NSA targeting procedures." If each senior analyst approves the request, it is sent to an electronic communications service provider (or providers) "to initiate Section 702 acquisition."[97]

Snowden's revelations showed that the executive branch has received authority from the FISC to acquire information in two ways under Section 702: (1) PRISM collection and (2) upstream collection.[98] PRISM collection occurs when the FBI (on behalf of the NSA) asks an Internet service provider for communications sent to or from a "selector" associated with a specific person (e.g., an e-mail address). The provider "is compelled to give the communications sent to or from that selector to the government." The collection of communications through PRISM does not include phone calls.[99] As of 2011, more than 90 percent of NSA collection of Internet communications had come through PRISM.[100] Upstream collection "occurs with the compelled assistance . . . of the providers that control the telecommunications backbone over which [telephone and Internet] communications transit. . . . The collection therefore does not occur at the local telephone company or email provider with whom the targeted person interacts . . . but instead occurs 'upstream' in the flow of communications *between* communication service providers."[101] Unlike PRISM data collection, upstream collection does include phone calls. The upstream portion of Section 702 surveillance, though much smaller than the portion captured through PRISM, is still extensive: "[a]s of 2011, the NSA acquired approximately 26.5 million Internet transactions a year as a result of upstream collection." Upstream collection results in the acquisition of purely domestic communications. The FISC "estimated in 2011 that . . . Section 702 upstream collection could result in the government acquiring as many as tens of thousands of wholly domestic communications each year." Internet communications collected through PRISM are retained for five years, while data collected through upstream collection are retained for two years.[102]

Agencies (including the NSA)[103] with access to data collected through the Section 702 program are then able to run searches or queries "using terms intended to discover or retrieve communications content or metadata that meets the criteria specified in the query. These queries may include terms that identify specific U.S. persons and can be used to retrieve the already acquired communications of specific U.S. persons." Under minimization procedures used by executive branch agencies, "queries of Section 702-acquired intelligence [must] be designed so that they are 'reasonably likely to return foreign intelligence information.'" When communications by U.S. persons are collected by mistake, those communications are removed from agency databases.[104] However, Section 702 "allows the government to retain and disseminate communications—including those of U.S. persons—if the government concludes that the communications contain 'foreign intelligence information' . . . a phrase that is defined very broadly to encompass not just information relating to terrorism but information relating to 'the conduct of the foreign affairs of the United States.'"[105] There is no judicial oversight over the government's decision to "analyz[e], retai[n], or disseminat[e] U.S. communications." The ACLU's Jameel Jaffer concludes that "[Section 702] does not prohibit the government from acquiring Americans' communications en masse and mining them for foreign intelligence information . . . [in fact, the statute] is formulated to permit precisely this."[106]

Unlike under the original pre-2007 FISA warrant process, under the Section 702 program "the government never has to identify programmatic surveillance targets to the FISC; it is required only to provide the FISC with its targeting and minimization procedures. The government need not reveal the names of its targets, the basis for targeting them, their locations, or the facilities, phone lines, and e-mail addresses subject to interception."[107] Even if the executive branch conscientiously complies with the law by making sure it does not focus on U.S. persons or people inside the United States, it turns out that "the government [will] [sweep] up the communications of U.S. persons and individuals within the United States 'incidentally.'"[108] Indeed, Jaffer observes this is an intended goal of the program — to sweep up information about Americans.[109] Furthermore, "[b]ecause FISC proceedings are secret, the public has no way of knowing whether the FISC actually receives the information it would need to provide an independent assessment of the targeting procedures, and the very limited review that the FAA requires the FISC to conduct is insufficient to provide effective oversight."[110] In passing the 2008 FAA, Congress gave the executive branch broad surveillance powers subject to very limited judicial oversight, deciding to trust an executive that had very recently proven it is not to be trusted.

The Section 702 program changed the standards previously applicable under FISA. Before Section 702 of FISA was enacted, the executive branch typically needed to show probable cause that a target of surveillance was a foreign power or an agent of a foreign power in order to obtain a warrant from the FISC.[111] In other words, before Section 702 was enacted, "FISA generally foreclosed the government from engaging in [electronic surveillance] without first obtaining individualized and particularized orders from the FISC."[112] Under Section 702, as mentioned, no individualized showing of probable cause is required (in fact, the FISC does not make individualized determinations of any kind), and no determination must be made that targets are associated with a foreign power. The executive branch also does not "[specify] to the FISC the particular non-U.S. persons who will be targeted." Instead, the government "identif[ies] categories of foreign intelligence information regarding which the Attorney General and Director of National Intelligence [seek to] authorize acquisition through the targeting of non-U.S. persons reasonably believed to be located abroad."[113]

This new standard, if on the books in 2001, would have made it relatively simple for the Bush administration to gain FISC approval for the once-illegitimate Terrorist Surveillance Program (TSP) (or something very much like it) through which President Bush authorized the NSA to "[intercept] . . . the content of communications into and out of the United States where there was a reasonable basis to conclude that one party to the communication was a member of [al Qaeda] or related terrorist organizations."[114] At the time President Bush secretly created this program in 2001 (without providing notice to the FISC), it violated FISA, as a federal district court found in August 2006 when it enjoined the TSP.[115]

After the TSP was made public, the executive branch complained that it had to "[expend] 'considerable resources' to obtain [FISA] court orders based upon a probable cause showing" that targeted individuals were "agents of a foreign power (such as an international terrorist group) and that they used the specific communication facilities (such as email addresses) [for] which the government was seeking to conduct electronic surveillance."[116] In 2007, the Bush administration "pressed Congress for amendments [to FISA] that would permit large-scale warrantless surveillance of Americans' international communications."[117] Congress responded with passage of the temporary Protect America Act of 2007 (since replaced by the 2008 FAA), which "eliminated the requirement for the government to seek . . . individual [court] orders [from the FISC] in order to engage in surveillance of international communications that targets non-U.S. persons." The goal of Section 702 was to create "a separate procedure to facilitate the targeting of persons reasonably believed to be outside the United States in order to acquire foreign intelligence information."[118]

Although Section 702 seems to focus on surveillance targeting foreigners outside the United States, in practice the Section 702 program's "effect is to give the government broad authority to monitor *Americans'* international communications." The ACLU's Jaffer argues that "[t]his is by design."[119] Jaffer charges that, although "[t]he government has argued . . . surveillance of Americans' communications under [Section 702] is 'incidental' to surveillance of foreign targets . . . the surveillance of Americans' communications under [Section 702] is not 'incidental' in any ordinary sense of that word." Jaffer explains that "[i]ntelligence officials who advocated for passage of the [2008] FAA . . . indicated that their principal aim was to allow the government broader authority to monitor Americans' international communications. Indeed, when legislators proposed language that would have required the government to obtain probable-cause warrants before accessing Americans' international communications, the White House issued a veto threat."[120]

As mentioned, Section 702 prohibits so-called reverse targeting, in which the government intentionally selects a target outside the United States with the real goal of gaining access to communications made by "a particular, known person reasonably believed to be in the United States."[121] However, Jaffer notes, the "[reverse targeting] prohibition is narrow—it applies only if the purpose of the government's surveillance is to target a '*particular, known* person reasonably believed to be in the United States.'"[122] This statutory language leaves a wide loophole, as Jaffer observes. For instance, the government "can target *Al Jazeera* or the *Guardian* in order to monitor their communications with sources in the United States" as long as the government does not specifically know who those sources are in advance. Since Section 702 allows the executive branch to engage in programmatic "dragnet surveillance," as opposed to individualized surveillance, "surveillance under [Section 702] is likely to invade the privacy of thousands or even millions of people [inside the United States,]" even without taking into account the ways in which the administration oversteps statutory bounds, as discussed later.[123]

Section 702 has significant problems as enacted, and it is distinctly possible that the statute is unconstitutional because it violates the Fourth Amendment and/or the First Amendment.[124] The PCLOB claims it is uniquely difficult to "[e]valuat[e] the constitutionality of the Section 702 program . . . [because] [u]nlike [under] the typical Fourth Amendment inquiry, where the legitimacy of 'a particular search or seizure' is judged 'in light of the particular circumstances' of that case, evaluating . . . Section 702 [surveillance] requires assessing a complex surveillance *program* . . . that entails many separate decisions to monitor large numbers of individuals." This seems to miss the point. There is no obvious constitutional problem with PRISM or upstream collection of purely foreign communications— that is, communications outside the United States that don't involve U.S. persons.[125] But Section 702 collection—by design—leads to the acquisition of communications involving U.S. persons inside the United States—even purely domestic communications.[126]

This is where the constitutional problem arises. Current Section 702 surveillance allows the executive branch to search the content of Americans' communications without a warrant. The government may well have a good reason to conduct such searches in some circumstances. But, when it wants to do so, it should be required to "[seek] a warrant [from a court] based on probable cause." Under the existing program, "the government [is not prohibited] from acquiring Americans' communications en masse and mining them for foreign intelligence information." Because the FISC's role is limited essentially to reviewing targeting procedures, "there is no requirement that the government seek judicial approval before it analyzes, retains, or disseminates U.S. communications." Since "the statute does not call for individualized judicial authorization of specific surveillance targets" or individualized judicial authorization to search collected communications of nontargeted persons, "the government can conduct large-scale warrantless surveillance of *Americans'* international communications."[127] It is difficult to see how this is constitutionally permissible.[128]

However, even assuming that Section 702 is constitutional, the Obama administration has "exceed[ed] its statutory authority" in ways that render the limits contained in Section 702 illusory. First, by engaging in "about" surveillance, the administration has found a way to search "virtually every text-based communication entering or leaving the [United States]."[129] "About" surveillance occurs when the government "seeks to acquire communications about the target that are not to or from the target."[130] In other words, such surveillance would look for references to the target or the target's e-mail address in the body of a text-based communication that was neither sent to nor received from the target. "About" surveillance is part of upstream collection.[131] In order to conduct "about" surveillance, the Obama administration has reportedly been "systematically searching—without warrants—through the contents of Americans' [international] communications." This seems to involve "temporarily copying and then sifting through the contents of what is apparently most e-mails and other text-based communications that cross the border." According to computer scientists, this surveillance can be carried out systematically only if the government "gather[s] nearly all cross-border text-based data."[132] "About" collection can allow the government to acquire communications between two non-targets who are either "U.S. persons or persons located within the United States." Through the use of "about" collection, "there is a greater risk that the NSA will acquire *purely domestic* communications through upstream collection than through PRISM."[133]

If the reports are accurate,[134] "about" surveillance seems reminiscent of the bulk metadata program in its all- (or nearly all-) encompassing approach (though "about" surveillance includes content—unlike metadata collection). Although it is difficult to speak in certainties here as reporting about the program has not been confirmed by the government, it seems that "about" surveillance requires the government to sift through essentially all international communications engaged in by Americans. The government's apparent defense of "about" surveillance is also reminiscent of its defense of bulk metadata collection—that it needs access to *all* the international communications Americans make in order to determine which ones include references to targeted non-U.S. persons. The PCLOB, which concludes that Section 702 surveillance is lawful, also concludes that Section 702, "while silent on 'about' upstream collection, can permissibly be interpreted as allowing such collection as currently implemented."[135] This is an odd conclusion for the PCLOB to reach, given that it earlier concluded the bulk metadata collection program rendered statutory limits meaningless in that context. The overreach involved with "about" surveillance seems hard to distinguish from the metadata program.

Section 702 is clearly designed to limit the government's ability to acquire or search Americans' communications (although it also contemplates that some communications involving U.S. persons will be acquired).[136] The statute requires the government to target only non-U.S. persons reasonably believed to be outside the United States.[137] Minimization procedures required by the statute are designed to "minimize the acquisition, retention, and dissemination of U.S. person information consistent with the United States' foreign intelligence needs."[138] The point of the minimization procedures is to set limits on government surveillance in order to protect Americans' privacy. "About" surveillance turns the concept of minimization on its head, just as the government's sweeping definition of "relevance" removes any effective statutory limits under Section 215 of the Patriot Act. If, as suggested by reporting, the government is searching the contents of virtually all text-based communications entering or leaving the United States, then the government enjoys essentially unlimited access to search Americans' international communications.

As Jameel Jaffer observes, if "about" surveillance is compatible with Section 702, then "Congress [must have] understood itself to be authorizing the very thing FISA originally set out to prohibit—the indiscriminate searching of Americans' [international] communications for foreign intelligence information." In Section 702 of FISA, Congress authorized the executive branch to monitor the communications of foreign people or groups outside the United States who are "targeted," and to intercept communications "*to* or *from* a target." "About" surveillance allows searches of communications that were neither sent to nor received by a legitimate target under Section 702. As Jaffer observes, "the practice of 'about' surveillance is consistent neither with the statute's language nor with its legislative history."[139]

Section 702 surveillance also finds a way around statutory limits through the use of "backdoor" searches. As mentioned, Section 702 expressly prohibits "reverse targeting"—in other words, the government cannot "intentionally target a person reasonably believed to be located outside the

United States if the purpose of such acquisition is to target a particular, known person reasonably believed to be in the United States."[140] The statutory goal was "to limit the government's ability to use the surveillance of foreign targets as a pretext for the monitoring of Americans [whom the government knew or believed to be in contact with the foreign targets]." In 2011, however, changes to NSA minimization procedures approved by the FISC gave the agency a "backdoor" way "to circumvent the [statutory] prohibition against reverse targeting by searching communications already acquired under [Section 702] for information about 'particular, known' Americans."[141] In other words, these new procedures[142] allow the NSA to search its database using "U.S. person identifiers"—phone numbers or e-mail addresses belonging to Americans.[143] As the ACLU's Jaffer observes, backdoor searches "render the [statutory] prohibition against reverse targeting all but meaningless, because they allow the government to use the surveillance of communications to, from or 'about' foreign targets as means of facilitating the surveillance of particular, known Americans."[144]

The government certainly has a legitimate and important interest in conducting surveillance aimed at gathering information related to terrorism and possible terrorist attacks against Americans. The PCLOB has concluded that "[t]he Section 702 program makes a substantial contribution to the government's efforts to learn about the membership, goals, and activities of international terrorist organizations, and to prevent acts of terrorism from coming to fruition."[145] But the program as currently implemented fails to comply with statutory and constitutional limits. Instead, the executive branch has decided to engage in broad "dragnet" surveillance that allows "the indiscriminate searching of Americans' communications for foreign intelligence information."[146]

The government's position seems to be that Americans can trust it not to abuse its access to their communications. Rick Ledgett, who at the time headed the NSA's Media Leaks Task Force, said in 2014 that concerns about NSA surveillance were "almost delusional . . . I wish I could get to the high mountaintop to scream [to Americans] 'you're not a target!'"[147] But, given the reality that the Obama administration's intelligence-gathering efforts under Section 702 are not meaningfully constrained by the law, Ledgett's plea depends on Americans concluding that the executive branch can, in large part, be trusted to self-regulate. As with bulk metadata collection, when it comes to intelligence gathering under Section 702, the Obama administration has relied on "faux" law presenting the illusion of limits on its surveillance authority. Checks and balances can't work this way—they depend on adherence to the rule of law, not having one branch of the federal government operate with broad authority to make its own rules.[148]

# 12

# THE OBAMA ADMINISTRATION
# AND MILITARY DETENTION

When President Obama took office, one of his first acts was to issue an executive order stating that the infamous Guantanamo prison in Cuba would close within one year.[1] In a speech Obama gave a few months later, the broader message was that the Bush administration had abandoned the rule of law at Guantanamo and the Obama administration would set things right.[2] As we will see, though, it is difficult to conclude that the administration has fulfilled Obama's promise to bring the rule of law to prisoners held at Guantanamo. Although the Obama administration argues Congress has stood in the way, that argument is not fully persuasive. The Obama administration had always planned to continue some of the Bush administration's approach with regard to detention and trial, even before Congress acted to limit its options.

However, the Obama administration's actions with regard to prisoners at Guantanamo cannot be categorized as neatly as its actions with regard to the use of military force or surveillance. When it came to military force and surveillance, the Obama administration saw legal limits on power merely as obstacles in its path. The president took action free of statutory or constitutional restraints; when, for example, one executive branch lawyer advised him that there were limits on how he could use military force in Libya, he simply found the advice he wanted from a different lawyer. Guantanamo is different in several ways. It is clear that Obama recognized the detention and limited trial system established there by the Bush administration was deeply flawed. Judging from Obama's actions—he has not sent any new prisoners there, and he reduced the prison population from about 250 to 107 by the end of 2015—it seems unlikely that the system he inherited is one he would have created on his own. The Bush administration argued that Guantanamo was a place outside the U.S. court system and that prisoners there should have no access of any kind to federal courts.[3] By contrast, the Obama administration has endorsed the Supreme Court's 2008 decision in *Boumediene* that prisoners at Guantanamo have a constitutional right to habeas review.[4] In addition, the Obama administration has tried or sought to try some Guantanamo prisoners in federal civilian court, winning a conviction in the Ahmed Ghailani case for his involvement in the 1998 U.S. embassy bombings in Kenya and Tanzania.[5] Along with Ghailani, the Obama administration planned to bring other prisoners from Guantanamo—including, most notably, Khalid Sheikh Mohammed—to the United States for civilian trial. As discussed later in this chapter, it was unable to do so when Congress passed legislation effectively preventing the transfer of prisoners from Guantanamo to the United States for any purpose.

All this seems to suggest that the Obama administration had every intention of making a clean break with the Bush approach when it came to Guantanamo. But the story is more complicated. Although some of President Obama's rhetoric and actions, especially when he first took office, suggested a dramatic change, there were always areas of continuity with the Bush administration. For instance, the Obama administration wanted to bring some prisoners to the United States for trial but planned to try others before military tribunals (even before Congress intervened), and it planned to hold still others indefinitely without trial of any kind, albeit at a facility inside the United States.

While the story is more nuanced when it comes to Guantanamo, part of the pattern observed in the preceding discussion about the use of military force and surveillance continues here. Although the Obama administration relied on statutory authority rather than plenary power, it reached some of the same conclusions as the Bush administration: that at least some prisoners could be tried by military tribunals while others could simply be held without any trial. Moreover, in the case of the Bergdahl prisoner exchange, discussed later, the Obama administration relied on a signing statement to justify unilateral action not permitted by statute. This was a page taken directly from the Bush administration's playbook.

In making sense of the Obama administration's ambivalent approach to Guantanamo, it is useful to begin with a speech President Obama gave in May 2009. The speech seemed to set some of the right goals, suggesting the administration was committed to the rule of law. But it also made clear that the Obama administration, from the start, was not in fact committed to fully restoring the rule of law to a detention system initially created to operate outside the U.S. legal system.

In his May 2009 speech, President Obama declared that the detention system established by the Bush administration at Guantanamo was a failure. It had become clear to other observers that the system was designed more for indefinite detention[6] than for prosecution and that, without meaningful judicial process, "[prisoners] held at the naval base represented a mix of terrorist fighters and innocent people erroneously swept up."[7] Obama seemed to agree with these criticisms, noting that only three prisoners at Guantanamo had been convicted by military tribunals and charging that "[i]nstead of bringing terrorists to justice, efforts at prosecution met setback after setback, cases lingered on, and in 2006 the Supreme Court invalidated the entire system [in *Hamdan v. Rumsfeld*]."[8]

President Obama also observed that the prison at Guantanamo had "set back the moral authority that is America's strongest currency in the world." In creating the prison, Obama said, "our government was [required to defend] positions that undermined the rule of law." In fact, as Obama rightly noted, "part of the rationale for establishing [a prison at] Guantanamo in the first place was the misplaced notion that a prison there would be beyond the law—a proposition that the Supreme Court soundly rejected." Obama worried that "instead of serving as a tool to counter terrorism, Guantanamo became a symbol that helped al Qaeda recruit terrorists to its cause. Indeed, the existence of Guantanamo likely created more terrorists around the world than it ever detained." The solution, Obama concluded, was to close the prison. The president explained that he had already begun this process as one of his first acts in office by "order[ing] the closing of the prison camp at Guantanamo Bay [in a January 2009 executive order]."[9]

President Obama acknowledged that the prison would not close immediately and said that he had also ordered "a review of all pending cases at Guantanamo." This review would, he said, "[clean] up something that is, quite simply, a mess—a misguided experiment that has left in its wake a flood of legal challenges that my administration is forced to deal with on a constant, almost daily basis." The review would resolve the difficult question of "what to do with the Guantanamo [prisoners]." The president admitted that "[t]here are no neat or easy answers here" but insisted that "the wrong answer is to pretend like this problem will go away if we maintain an unsustainable status quo." Obama declared that "[a]s President, I refuse to allow this problem to fester. I refuse to pass it on to somebody else. It is my responsibility to solve the problem. Our security interests will not permit us to delay. Our courts won't allow it. And neither should our conscience."[10]

Obama described each prisoner's case as falling into one of five categories. First were those who would be prosecuted in federal civilian courts.

A second group would be tried before military tribunals or commissions—but "[i]nstead of using the flawed commissions of the last seven years, [his] administration [would bring] our commissions in line with the rule of law." For a third group, prisoners whose release had been ordered by U.S. courts, the administration was "bound by the law . . . and . . . must abide by these rulings." A fourth group of prisoners would be transferred to other countries.[11]

The fifth group included the hardest cases, requiring the administration to address "the question of [prisoners] at Guantanamo who cannot be prosecuted yet who pose a clear danger to the American people." President Obama explained that "there may be a number of people who cannot be prosecuted for past crimes, in some cases because evidence may be tainted, but who nonetheless pose a threat to the security of the United States. Examples of that threat include people who've received extensive explosives training at al Qaeda training camps, or commanded Taliban troops in battle, or expressed their allegiance to Osama bin Laden, or otherwise made it clear that they want to kill Americans. These are people who, in effect, remain at war with the United States." President Obama emphasized that dangerous prisoners could not be released but also said that "we must recognize that these detention policies cannot be unbounded. They can't be based simply on what I or the executive branch decide alone." He rejected the Bush administration's approach as failing to comply with the rule of law and promised a new approach based on "clear, defensible, and lawful standards for those who fall into this category." President Obama further indicated that "[w]e must have fair procedures so that we don't make mistakes. We must have a thorough process of periodic review, so that any prolonged detention is carefully evaluated and justified."[12]

Someone hearing the president's speech in May 2009 could have reasonably believed that Obama was making a decisive break with the Bush administration on the issue of detention of suspected terrorists. In November 2001, the Bush administration had concluded the president had "inherent authority as Commander in Chief" to set up a military tribunal system and to decide whether to detain suspected terrorists indefinitely without trial of any kind.[13] The Supreme Court had rejected that argument and insisted that President Bush was bound by statutory and constitutional limits. But the Court's decisions had not closed Guantanamo, and about 250 prisoners remained there when President Obama took office, in January 2009.[14] Now, it seemed, President Obama would translate the logic of the Court's decisions into meaningful action that would ensure that prisoners once held arbitrarily and without legal process would receive meaningful judicial review.

However, as of this writing, President Obama has not fulfilled his promise to close Guantanamo. Instead, the administration has preserved much of the system established by the Bush administration. Although there are important differences between the Obama and the Bush approaches, there are also significant areas of overlap. Louis Fisher notes that Obama's "executive order [seeking to close Guantanamo] was the type of unilateral action that backfired repeatedly on George W. Bush."[15] Natsu Saito similarly criticizes President Obama for "simply issuing new Executive Orders and/or rescinding previous ones, not limiting the scope of executive power in any systematic way."[16] As Nancy Kassop observes, "two of the more high-profile policies that were prime candidates for reversal [by Obama] (housing [prisoners] indefinitely at the military prison at Guantanamo Bay and the use of military commissions to prosecute terrorist suspects) have been the subject of withering political battles, only to end up exactly where they began, with very little changes from the policies of the preceding Bush administration."[17] Moreover, even if President Obama had fulfilled (or at some point does fulfill) his promise to close Guantanamo, there is no guarantee that the administration will provide legal process to all prisoners. Critics charge that Obama's plan to close Guantanamo depended on the creation of a "Gitmo North" facility in the United States that would continue to hold some prisoners indefinitely without trial.[18]

In President Obama's defense, he was not writing on a blank slate. As he noted in his May 2009 speech, the Bush administration had left him a messy, poorly constructed detention system originally justified by reference to inherent power. Four Supreme Court rulings had rejected the idea of plenary executive control over what happens to prisoners at Guantanamo, but the prison remained in place when Obama took office. It is impossible to know, of course, whether President Obama would have unilaterally created an indefinite-detention system like the one established at Guantanamo if he had been in office after the 9/11 attacks. But we do know that Obama rejected the indefinite-detention approach for new prisoners. Faisal Shahzad, Umar Farouk Abdulmutallab, Ahmed Abu Khattala, and other terrorists captured since Obama took office have been tried and convicted in federal courts.[19] The Obama administration has not sent new prisoners to Guantanamo for detention without trial.[20]

In his May 2009 speech, President Obama seemed to set the right goals with regard to Guantanamo—most centrally, that the rule of law would control and detention policies would no longer be set by the executive branch alone. In the place of plenary executive power and indefinite detention, President Obama promised fair procedures and limits. It was clear even in May 2009, however, that it would be difficult to achieve these goals under the approach Obama outlined. Even if Guantanamo did close, there were indications that some prisoners would simply be held indefinitely at another prison. For those prisoners, the question was: would meaningful legal process be provided? For other prisoners slated for trial by military tribunal, what was the rationale for not trying them in federal civilian courts?

As time passed, it became clear that President Obama's approach, while not identical to President Bush's approach, had produced many of the same results: some suspected terrorists can be held without trial or meaningful hearing, others can be unnecessarily tried in military tribunals, and at times the administration can use unilateral action in an effort to bypass statutory limits on presidential action. When President Bush created the military detention system at Guantanamo, he originally relied on inherent power. After the Supreme Court rejected this approach in *Hamdi* and *Hamdan*, the Bush administration did not retreat from its position. Instead, it found ways to make it seem that it recognized limits on presidential power while in fact it continued to operate a detention and limited trial system on its own terms. The Combatant Status Review Tribunals (CSRTs) established after *Hamdi* gave the appearance that prisoners would receive legal process and an opportunity to challenge their detention. But the CSRT process was a sham, as discussed in Section II and later in this chapter. In addition, the military tribunals conducted with congressional approval pursuant to the 2006 Military Commissions Act essentially allowed the Bush administration to carry out military trials by using the same rules the Supreme Court had rejected in *Hamdan*—rules that five justices had said or suggested violated the Geneva Conventions.[21]

Although Obama promised a break with the Bush approach, his administration has basically followed the post-2004 Bush approach, relying on the appearance of legal process to superficially sanitize a system that has continued to hold some prisoners for years without a meaningful hearing, even those long since cleared for release, while trying others before military tribunals that still lack legitimacy. The rest of this chapter explains how the Obama administration has handled the issues President Obama spoke about in May 2009 with regard to prosecution, transfer, and continued detention of prisoners and why the administration has failed to make a decisive break with the Bush administration's approach.

## The Obama Administration and Military Tribunals

The Bush administration concluded it had inherent authority to order military trials for Guantanamo prisoners at its discretion, according to its own rules, and without congressional authorization.[22] The Supreme Court rejected this approach, as President Obama noted in his May 2009 speech. However, military tribunals continued under both the Bush and the Obama administrations. As discussed later in this chapter, although the Obama administration has suggested Congress is to blame for the continued use of military tribunals, the reality is that the administration's own plan for trying some prisoners has always included military tribunals. The Obama administration has proceeded to use military tribunals for several prisoners despite significant legal flaws in the system authorized by the 2009 Military Commissions Act (MCA). Obama promised that any military trials would comply with the rule of law. This promise depends on the possibility that military tribunals can in fact operate pursuant to meaningful statutory and constitutional limits. Congress has authorized military tribunals, most recently through the 2009 MCA.[23] The problem, of course, is that even military tribunals proceeding with statutory authorization may not be constitutionally permissible and may violate international law.

An important initial question to ask is: why use military tribunals at all? If they are a creature of military necessity, as the Supreme Court suggested in *Hamdan*, why use them outside the limited circumstances when ordinary courts are not available or charges under the laws of war could not otherwise be brought in civilian courts? Those circumstances are not present for prisoners at Guantanamo. In fact, trying prisoners before military tribunals may be a dangerous legal proposition. Salim Hamdan, who had been Osama Bin Laden's driver, was ultimately tried by a military tribunal pursuant to statutory law enacted after the Supreme Court rejected his initial military trial under rules created by the Bush administration. He was convicted of material support for terrorism by the military tribunal, but the D.C. Circuit Court of Appeals threw out the conviction, even though Congress had defined material support for terrorism as a crime under the 2006 Military Commissions Act.[24] The D.C. Circuit ruled in 2012 that Hamdan's conviction could not stand because "the relevant statute at the time of Hamdan's conduct . . . did not proscribe material support for terrorism as a war crime."[25] The D.C. Circuit's 2012 ruling in *Hamdan II*[26] raised the prospect that other convictions gained in military tribunals could similarly be vacated on appeal.[27] In fact, the D.C. Circuit's subsequent ruling in the *al-Bahlul* case has "effectively invalidat[ed] [the] use [of a material support for terrorism charge] at Guantánamo."[28]

There are additional reasons why military tribunals may pose legal problems, even when authorized by Congress. David Glazier argues that after the 2009 MCA, "the Guantánamo tribunals still fall short of applicable legal standards with respect to both procedural and substantive law, and will predictably continue to fail federal judicial challenges." Even though trials "conducted under the current MCA represent a substantial improvement over the early Bush Administration trial rules . . . [t]hey remain flawed in terms of both their written rules and actual trial practice."[29] Glazier raises concerns that military trials under the 2009 MCA will fail to meet fair trial standards under Common Article 3 of the Geneva Conventions.[30] In Glazier's view, the tribunals' procedural[31] flaws include (1) denial of equal protection of the law because only foreign nationals may be tried by the tribunals, (2) provision of unequal access by defendants to witnesses and other evidence, (3) admissibility of evidence obtained through coercion,[32] and (4) overreliance on classified material not available to defendants.[33] Glazier concludes that "[t]he military commissions have been tried for a full decade under two different administrations and have consistently failed to clear any credible legal bar due to their shortcomings in both procedure and substantive law. Meanwhile, federal courts have returned scores of terrorist convictions without legitimate controversy, and with none of the commissions' jurisdictional flaws."[34]

Despite these significant problems, the Obama administration has, as Glazier discusses, continued to use military tribunals—most prominently (but not only) in the trial of Khalid Sheikh Mohammed (KSM) and four co-defendants. The charges in the KSM case include allegations that the defendants helped plan the 9/11 attacks (with KSM as the mastermind). Glazier describes these charges as "rest[ing] on the strongest legal grounds of any Guantánamo case to date," but he concludes that even this case "has real flaws."[35] Some of the charges—terrorism and conspiracy—might not be valid offenses under the law of war (though they could readily be advanced as charges in federal court).[36] For these reasons, in addition to the procedural problems under the 2009 MCA discussed earlier, Glazier observes that, "even where a law of war trial is legally permissible, practical considerations may still suggest that it is not wise to conduct one."[37]

Attorney General Eric Holder agrees that it would have been better to try KSM in federal civilian court, as the Obama administration had originally planned. In late 2013, after proceedings had begun against KSM before a military tribunal, Holder said, "I was right [to have planned a trial in civilian court]. . . . I think the decision that I [originally] announced [to proceed in civilian court] . . . was the right one. And I think that the facts and events that have occurred since then demonstrate that." Holder pointed out that "[i]f you look at the history of the Article III [federal court] prosecutions, you will see that they don't take nearly as long as those that occur in the military system. . . . We hold people accountable [in federal court]."[38] The military tribunal proceedings against KSM support Holder's conclusions. The military tribunal held initial hearings in May

2012, but as of February 2015, a defense attorney noted that "[n]ot only is there no end in sight to the military commission, there's no middle in sight."[39] Critics refer to the KSM military tribunal proceedings as "the forever trial."[40] Shayana Kadidal, an attorney at the Center for Constitutional Rights, remarked that "[i]f [KSM and four co-defendants] had been brought to the United States in 2009, those trials would be long over."[41]

Given all these problems, why weren't KSM and his co-defendants tried in civilian court?[42] As noted, that had been the Obama administration's initial plan. On November 13, 2009, "the administration announced its decision to try . . . [KSM] . . . the most senior al Qaeda detainee, in a federal courthouse in New York City." Elected officials, including New York City mayor Michael Bloomberg, raised objections to a Manhattan trial, citing security concerns and expenses.[43] While the administration "spent much of 2010 investigating alternative sites for trying [KSM] in federal court," Congress ultimately passed legislation prohibiting the use of funds to transfer prisoners (including KSM) from Guantanamo to the United States.[44] On April 4, 2011, Attorney General Holder announced that KSM and four co-defendants would be tried in a military tribunal. Holder blamed members of Congress for "interven[ing] and impos[ing] restrictions blocking the administration from bringing any Guantanamo detainees to trial in the United States."[45]

Holder's point, that Congress had impermissibly interfered with prosecutorial discretion, was not implausible,[46] but the administration cannot escape all responsibility for continuing to use military tribunals by passing the blame to Congress. Even if KSM and his four co-defendants had been tried in civilian court, that would not have meant the Obama administration rejected the military tribunal system. In his May 2009 speech, President Obama said he supported the use of military tribunals to try some prisoners, as long as reforms were made.[47] With Congress passing the 2009 Military Commissions Act, Attorney General Holder announced plans to try Omar Khadr, Abd al-Rahim al-Nashiri, and three others by military tribunal. Holder made this announcement on the same day he announced the administration's plans to try KSM in federal civilian court.[48] Moreover, Congress's decision to pass legislation blocking the transfer of prisoners to the United States for trial did not have to be the last word on the matter. President Obama could have, for instance, explored the possibility of holding a federal civilian trial at Guantanamo, perhaps with jurors participating through video conference.[49]

The other problem with the administration's plan for prosecutions (in whatever venue) is that it applied only to some prisoners. As discussed below, the Obama administration had always planned to hold others without trial of any kind. That approach is fundamentally similar to the Bush administration's decision to hold prisoners at Guantanamo indefinitely without trial, although the Obama administration has used different rhetoric to justify its decision.

## PRISONERS DETAINED AT GUANTANAMO
## BUT NOT PROSECUTED

The Bush administration argued that it had plenary power to make decisions about the detention of enemy combatants, including suspected terrorists.[50] While the Supreme Court did not endorse this position and emphasized in the 2004 *Hamdi* decision that the executive branch is subject to checks and balances and the rule of law, the Bush administration continued holding prisoners at Guantanamo without trial.[51] The Court's decision did not fundamentally change what was a system of indefinite detention, from which most prisoners would be released only at the executive branch's discretion.

Although President Obama said in his May 2009 speech that some prisoners at Guantanamo would continue to be held without trial, he seemed to reject the Bush administration's views about plenary or inherent executive power, declaring "we must recognize that these detention policies cannot be unbounded. They can't be based simply on what I or the executive branch decide alone . . . [w]e must have fair procedures so that we don't make mistakes. We must have a thorough process of periodic review, so that any prolonged detention is carefully evaluated and justified."[52]

Despite these statements, however, "[t]he Obama Administration has contributed to the legalization and legitimation of war on terrorism [indefinite] detention." The Obama administration has not embraced the rhetoric of the unitary executive theory. Its approach is "more nuanced [than Bush's] . . . [as Obama] ground[s] [detention] authority in the AUMF [or other legislation] rather than in Article II's Commander-in-Chief Clause."[53] But the result is substantively the same: the Obama administration has held prisoners at Guantanamo without trial and without the kind of meaningful hearing the Court called for in *Hamdi*.

As discussed in Section II, the Supreme Court's 2004 decision in *Hamdi* concluded "due process demands that a citizen held in the United States as an enemy combatant be given a meaningful opportunity to contest the factual basis for that detention before a neutral decisionmaker."[54] Logically, this requirement must also apply to noncitizens held at Guantanamo, since the Fifth Amendment's Due Process Clause applies to "persons" and the Court has separately held that the Constitution applies at Guantanamo.[55] As also discussed in Section II, the *Hamdi* decision failed to effectively restrain presidential power. The Bush administration responded to the decision by creating Combatant Status Review Tribunals (CSRTs) to provide prisoners held at Guantanamo a chance to challenge their designation as enemy combatants (a status the Court had held could justify law of war detention). But the CSRTs were a sham, serving mainly "to validate a predetermined result" and giving the executive branch largely unchecked authority over the indefinite detention system at Guantanamo.[56] Prisoners received limited hearings and were not provided legal counsel.[57] Classified evidence not shown to the prisoner was often used to establish enemy combatant status justifying indefinite detention. Prisoners were not able to confront witnesses or, often, to even see the evidence used against them. It was difficult for prisoners to present their own evidence or call witnesses on their behalf: "the only evidence that the [prisoners] were permitted to offer in the vast majority of [CSRT hearings] was their own testimony." The tribunals nearly always (at least 93 percent of the time) found prisoners to be enemy combatants.[58]

When President Obama promised, in May 2009, to "[clean] up . . . [the legal] mess" at Guantanamo and to address the problem of "legal limbo" for most prisoners, this logically suggested that his administration would finally provide all prisoners the kind of meaningful hearing alluded to in *Hamdi*.[59] However, most of the 107 prisoners remaining at Guantanamo as of January 2016 have received only an insufficient CSRT hearing. Fourteen have also received Periodic Review Board (PRB) hearings, which may offer some promise of meaningful review but are difficult to fully evaluate and have not been extended to all prisoners.[60] PRBs were described in a March 2011 executive order,[61] but no hearings were held until October 2013.[62] President Obama cited the 2001 AUMF, rather than inherent or plenary power, as providing authority for his order.[63] Pursuant to the order, each prisoner held at Guantanamo for "continued law of war detention" would receive an initial PRB review within one year and, after that, a full review and hearing each three years.[64] In July 2013, the Obama administration announced that seventy-one prisoners at Guantanamo would receive PRB review.[65]

Pursuant to the 2011 executive order, prisoner reviews would be conducted by a PRB consisting of six "senior officials" named by six executive branch agencies. As in the CSRT hearings, prisoners would be assigned a personal representative but not a lawyer—though prisoners could retain private counsel at their own expense. The PRB's task is to determine whether continued detention "is necessary to protect against a significant threat to the security of the United States." Prisoners can make a statement to the PRB, introduce relevant information, and call witnesses who are "reasonably available." The executive branch is required to provide evidence to the PRB, including information that could be helpful to the prisoner. However, the PRB can in some circumstances provide the prisoner a summary of or substitute for the information it received from the executive branch. The executive order did not rule out categories of evidence, such as hearsay evidence and evidence obtained through coercion or torture, as inadmissible but simply stated that the PRB "shall consider the reliability of any information provided to it in making its determination."[66]

PRBs have many of the same defects as CSRTs. It is not clear that prisoners can receive a meaningful hearing without legal counsel or the opportunity to see evidence used against them. A new problem is that, unlike CSRTs, PRBs seek to determine whether prisoners will be dangerous if released rather than whether there was any legitimate reason to hold prisoners in the first place. In practice, however, the most salient problem with the PRB process has been that it is slow. The administration did not meet its deadline of holding all initial reviews within one year of the release of Executive Order 13567. As of December 2015, hearings had been held for twenty-one prisoners, with eighteen prisoners receiving final determinations. PRBs have cleared fifteen of these prisoners for transfer from Guantanamo.[67] More than four years after the executive order regarding PRBs was issued, forty-six prisoners still at Guantanamo and eligible for PRB review have not yet received an initial hearing. At this rate, Human Rights First calculates that "initial PRB reviews will not be completed until 2020."[68]

Critics argue that even those prisoners who have received PRB hearings are not guaranteed a meaningful opportunity to dispute the legitimacy of their detention—or a meaningful opportunity to make the government justify their detention. The PRBs do not determine the legitimacy of the government's decision to detain prisoners in the first place. Instead, they determine whether prisoners would be dangerous if released. The PRB process can be described as supporting a system of preventive detention based on predictions about the possibility that prisoners who have never been charged with a specific offense will be dangerous in the future if released.[69] Zak Newman of the ACLU points out that the PRBs can make decisions based on secret evidence and that prisoners cleared for transfer are not actually guaranteed release.[70]

These are fair concerns to raise, but, if we are to judge from the limited PRB results so far, this process has provided meaningful review for at least some prisoners. Fifteen of the twenty-one who have received hearings have been cleared for transfer. The problems seem to be that (1) the PRB process has been much too slow, as most prisoners eligible for review have not yet received even an initial (let alone "periodic") review yet; (2) only some of the prisoners cleared for transfer by the PRB because they were determined not to pose a danger to the United States have actually been released;[71] and (3) the PRB process lacks transparency, so it is difficult to know whether those prisoners who have received hearings and not been cleared for transfer received a meaningful hearing.[72] It is reasonable to conclude that PRBs, if used for all eligible prisoners, could be a useful piece of broader system of review, though they are not sufficient by themselves.

The Obama administration might respond to criticisms of the PRB system by pointing out it is not in fact the only process available to prisoners and that it can be seen as part of a larger system of review. Prisoners at Guantanamo have the constitutional right to file a petition for habeas corpus review in federal court, and many have done so.[73] But scholars have questioned the substance of these habeas reviews. The Supreme Court's 2008 ruling in *Boumediene* did not provide much guidance to the D.C. district court that would hold habeas reviews for Guantanamo prisoners.[74] Formulating rules to apply in these reviews has been left to the district court and the D.C. Circuit Court of Appeals, which have created "a detention standard . . . accept[ing] that terrorism suspects may be confined militarily without trial if the government demonstrates, by a preponderance of the evidence, that they were 'part of' or 'purposefully and materially support[ed]' al Qaeda, the Taliban, or associated forces."[75] The D.C. Circuit has based this standard of review on statutory language. However, this standard can lead to strange results. For example, Ghaled Nassar Al-Bihani worked as a cook for a paramilitary outfit allied with the Taliban in Afghanistan after 9/11 and, though he carried a weapon, did not use it in combat. He was captured by the Northern Alliance in late 2001, handed over to the United States, and sent to Guantanamo.[76] When his habeas case reached the D.C. Circuit, a three-judge panel concluded he could be lawfully held as someone who was "part of" and "purposefully and materially supported" al Qaeda and the Taliban.[77] In May 2014, a PRB cleared him for release.[78] However, he has not yet been released and has now been held for more than thirteen years on the basis of his service as a cook for a military unit allied with the Taliban.

Critics argue that the habeas review provided in the D.C. Circuit is simply not meaningful. Jonathan Hafetz argues that "[t]he D.C. Circuit . . . has construed the government's evidentiary burden as a limited one, freely admitted hearsay, limited detainees' ability to rebut the government's allegations, and warned district courts not to scrutinize the government's evidence too closely, citing the danger of interfering with the executive during wartime." Hafetz notes that "[o]ne D.C. Circuit panel, moreover, went so far as to rule that district judges must presume the accuracy of government intelligence reports unless rebutted by the petitioner, prompting the dissenting judge to note that the ruling 'comes perilously close to suggesting that whatever the government says must be treated as true.' With such a ruling, the dissent explained, 'it is hard to see what is left of the Supreme Court's command in *Boumediene* that *habeas* review be 'meaningful.'"[79] Hafetz published a study with other Seton Hall Law School researchers in which the authors claimed "[i]t is an open secret that *Boumediene v. Bush*'s promise of robust review of the legality of the Guantanamo detainees' detention has been effectively negated by [D.C. Circuit] decisions . . . beginning with *Al-Adahi v. Obama* [in 2010]."[80]

Of course, it is not President Obama's fault that courts are not providing meaningful habeas review. However, it does make it essential for the administration to provide some other process, perhaps through PRB hearings. Otherwise, prisoners at Guantanamo will continue to be held indefinitely without meaningful judicial review of the legitimacy of their detention. As Clive Stafford Smith puts it: "[i]f the courts refuse to do their job [of applying meaningful habeas review], and if President Obama reneges on his 2009 promise [to close Guantanamo], what hope does an innocent detainee have?"[81] One might respond that Congress could act. That is certainly true in theory, but has not happened in practice. Congress has failed to set limits on executive discretion at Guantanamo.

Under these circumstances, the Obama administration's record regarding the detention system at Guantanamo appears difficult to distinguish substantively from Bush's approach. The Obama administration has not relied on plenary power to justify indefinite detention, but Congress[82] has enabled such detention and the courts have failed to make habeas review meaningful. The result is that the Obama administration, like the Bush administration, has indefinitely detained prisoners without charge, trial, or even meaningful hearing.

### PRISONER TRANSFER AND RELEASE

As discussed earlier, the Obama administration has argued that Congress effectively forced it to convene military tribunals, although the reality is that the Obama administration always planned to hold military tribunals for some prisoners. Similarly, the Obama administration has blamed Congress for passing legislation that makes it more difficult to transfer or release prisoners from Guantanamo to other countries than it was in the past. As with military tribunals, however, the slow pace of transfer for prisoners already cleared for release cannot be blamed entirely on Congress. Although Congress has set limits on prisoner transfers since 2011, it has also provided waiver authority allowing the executive branch to transfer prisoners if certain conditions are met. However, from 2011 to 2013, only four transfers took place, although more than eighty prisoners held during that time period had been cleared for transfer.[83] From July 2013 through January 2015, thirty-nine more prisoners were transferred to other countries, but as of September 2015, more than fifty prisoners cleared for release still remained at Guantanamo.[84] While the Obama administration has been slow to use statutory authority that could allow the transfer of prisoners cleared for release, it has, in other circumstances, acted unilaterally to release prisoners without complying with statutory requirements, as discussed later in this chapter with regard to the Bowe Bergdahl prisoner exchange.

In January 2010, the Guantanamo Review Task Force created by President Obama issued a report noting that it had approved 126 prisoners for transfer (44 of whom had already been released by January 2010).[85] In the words of the State Department envoy designated in 2013 to facilitate transfers from Guantanamo, the Task Force's decision represented the unanimous conclusion of six executive branch departments and agencies that "th[ese] [prisoners] should be transferred because [they] present such a low threat, a low risk, and it's in the national interest to transfer th[ese] prisoners from Guantanamo."[86] The Task Force also designated an additional thirty prisoners from Yemen for "conditional detention," indicating that these prisoners might be transferred to Yemen in the future "if the current moratorium on transfers to Yemen is lifted and other security conditions are met."[87]

In December 2010, Congress passed legislation (as part of the 2011 National Defense Authorization Act) prohibiting the use of funds to transfer or release Guantanamo prisoners to other countries. However, the bill authorized the secretary of defense to transfer prisoners after providing "written certification, with the concurrence of the secretary of state, that the government or foreign country [where the prisoners would be transferred] is not a designated state sponsor of terrorism or a designated foreign terrorist organization [and] maintains effective control over each detention facility in which an individual is to be detained [when relevant]."[88]

President Obama did not veto this legislation, but when he signed the 2011 NDAA into law he included a signing statement. In his signing statement, Obama objected that "[w]ith respect to section 1033, the restrictions on the transfer of detainees to the custody or effective control of foreign countries interfere with the authority of the executive branch to make important and consequential foreign policy and national security determinations regarding whether and under what circumstances such transfers should occur in the context of an ongoing armed conflict. We must have the ability to act swiftly and to have broad flexibility in conducting our negotiations with foreign countries. . . . Despite my strong objection to these provisions, which my Administration has consistently opposed, I have signed this Act because of the importance of authorizing appropriations for, among other things, our military activities in 2011. Nevertheless, my Administration will work with the Congress to seek repeal of these restrictions, will seek to mitigate their effects, and will oppose any attempt to extend or expand them in the future."[89]

In National Defense Authorization bills passed since December 2010, Congress continued to include the prohibition on using funds to transfer or release prisoners from Guantanamo to other countries and also included a provision allowing the executive branch to bypass the prohibition if it provides the kind of written certification described by the law.[90] The 2014 NDAA streamlined the certification process by permitting transfer to other countries when the secretary of defense determined that a prisoner was no longer a threat to U.S. national security, actions were taken to "substantially mitigate" the risk that the prisoner would engage in activity threatening the United States or Americans, and transfer was in the national interest.[91] The statute also required the secretary of defense to provide detailed notification to Congress at least thirty days before transferring or releasing a prisoner.[92] The 2015 NDAA contained the same "relaxed" transfer provisions.[93] In a signing statement for the 2014 NDAA, President Obama called these changes "a positive step" but also argued that the changes did not "eliminate all of the unwarranted limitations on foreign transfers and, in certain circumstances, would violate constitutional separation of powers principles." Obama stated that "[i]n the event that the restrictions on the transfer of Guantanamo detainees in sections 1034 and 1035 operate in a manner that violates constitutional separation of powers principles, my Administration will implement them in a manner that avoids the constitutional conflict."[94]

Despite the administration's complaints that Congress had placed onerous restrictions in the way of releasing prisoners from Guantanamo after 2010, the administration had actually been able to take actions to increase the number of prisoners released months before Congress eased the statutory certification process. In April 2013, prisoners at Guantanamo had begun a hunger strike to protest their ongoing detention as eighty-six prisoners cleared for release years earlier were still being held.[95] In May 2013, President Obama announced he was lifting a moratorium on prisoner transfers to Yemen and was appointing a new State Department envoy to facilitate transfers.[96]

Following Cliff Sloan's appointment in July 2013 as the new State Department envoy (as well as that of Sloan's counterpart at the Department of Defense assigned to work on prisoner transfers), the administration dramatically changed its approach. After transferring just four prisoners from Guantanamo from 2011 through mid-2013, the administration transferred nine prisoners in the month of December 2013 alone—again, before new legislation easing the statutory certification process required for prisoner transfer went into effect.[97]

In all, thirty-nine prisoners were transferred from Guantanamo between July 2013 and early January 2015.[98] This was a positive development, as the prisoners released had been cleared for transfer since January 2010. The question, though, is: why did it take so long to transfer these prisoners? The Obama administration's defense—that Congress stood in the way for years—is not fully convincing. Even during the period from 2011 to 2014 when the strictest certification requirements were in place, it was possible to transfer prisoners. The Obama administration demonstrated this could be done after July 2013. Placing the blame on Congress does not fully explain the results: the pace of release has been largely under the administration's control.[99] In fact, when Sloan, the State Department envoy, resigned from his position in December 2014, news reports cited a government official who "said that Mr. Sloan was unhappy that a number of prisoners who had been cleared for release by the president's national security team had been held up by [Secretary of Defense] Hagel."[100] Although Sloan denied reports that he left because he was frustrated by executive branch delay, the numbers speak for themselves. As of January 2016, forty-eight prisoners cleared for release in January 2010 still remained at Guantanamo.[101] Their release to other countries has never been blocked by Congress.

Even as the Obama administration has been slow to make use of existing statutory procedures for prisoners cleared for transfer, it has demonstrated its willingness to set aside statutory requirements when it decides it is necessary to unilaterally release prisoners not cleared for transfer. On May 31, 2014, President Obama announced that Sergeant Bowe Bergdahl, who had been held by the Taliban for more than five years, would be returning to the United States in exchange for the release of five Taliban prisoners held at Guantanamo.[102] The Taliban prisoners had not been cleared for transfer, and the administration did not comply with statutory certification procedures before releasing them to Qatar, where they would be subject to a one-year travel ban.[103] President Obama explained that he had acted without notifying Congress because "[w]e were concerned about Sergeant

Bergdahl's health."[104] Other administration officials "stressed that once negotiations began they had to move quickly, for fear that a lag or a leak about the arrangements could put Bergdahl's life in jeopardy."[105]

President Obama remarked that "[t]he United States has always had a pretty sacred rule, and that is: we don't leave our men or women in uniform behind."[106] That is indeed an essential promise to keep. However, the administration did not comply with statutory law in achieving Bergdahl's release and has failed to take the necessary actions to legitimize its actions. A National Security Council press release issued on June 3, 2014, claimed the requirement that the executive branch provide written notice to Congress at least thirty days before transferring prisoners from Guantanamo "should be construed not to apply to this unique set of circumstances, in which the transfer would secure the release of a captive U.S. soldier and the Secretary of Defense, acting on behalf of the President, has determined that providing notice as specified in the statute could endanger the soldier's life."[107] In other words, the Obama administration was claiming this was an emergency action and there was no time to consult Congress. That is not an implausible position (depending on the facts). The problem is that the administration did not seek retroactive approval from Congress to legitimize its emergency action. Such approval is necessary to legalize unilateral presidential action that would otherwise not be permissible.[108]

By seeking retroactive approval for emergency action, a president acknowledges the rule of law and limits on presidential power. In contrast, by acting unilaterally and not seeking congressional approval after the fact, the Obama administration operated as if it had inherent authority to order the transfer. In fact, the June 3 NSC press release suggested President Obama was relying on a signing statement, noting that "[t]he President also has repeatedly expressed concerns regarding th[e] statutory notice requirement. For example, the President's FY 2014 NDAA signing statement indicated that 'Section 1035 does not . . . eliminate all of the unwarranted limitations on foreign transfers and, in certain circumstances, would violate constitutional separation of powers principles. The executive branch must have the flexibility . . . to act swiftly in conducting negotiations with foreign countries regarding the circumstances of detainee transfers.'"[109]

It is not clear precisely what this means. If the administration meant only that Congress cannot prevent the president from acting unilaterally in an emergency when there is no time to comply with statutory requirements, that is plainly correct—as long as the president later obtains retroactive approval for the emergency action. But if the NSC press release meant that the president has authority to simply ignore statutory provisions that, in the president's view, interfere with necessary prisoner transfers, that is a position difficult to distinguish from the Bush administration's approach. Christopher S. Kelley has explained that the Bush administration used signing statements as part of a strategy to advance its conception of the unitary executive and expansive, unchecked presidential power.[110] As a presidential candidate in 2007, Barack Obama promised that "I will not use signing statements to nullify or undermine congressional instructions as enacted into law." Then-candidate Obama observed that "[t]he problem with th[e] [George W. Bush] administration is that it has attached signing statements to legislation in an effort to change the meaning of the legislation, to avoid enforcing certain provisions of the legislation that the President does not like, and to raise implausible or dubious constitutional objections to the legislation." Candidate Obama declared that "it is a clear abuse of power to use [signing] statements as a license to evade laws that the president does not like or as an end-run around provisions designed to foster accountability."[111] With the Bergdahl prisoner exchange however, President Obama "seems to have done precisely what he promised not to do as a candidate . . . stak[ing] out a position that is very hard to distinguish from the Bush administration's inherent power approach."[112]

## OBAMA'S GUANTANAMO LEGACY

President Obama has promised not to pass along the problems of Guantanamo to his successor. It remains to be seen whether he can achieve this goal before his presidency ends. To date, however, Obama's promise to restore the rule of law with regard to prisoners at Guantanamo has not been kept. Even if Guantanamo is ultimately closed before he leaves office, with all prisoners either released or provided with the meaningful legal process necessary to justify their conviction or continued detention, the legacy will be troubling. For years, the Obama administration continued to run a detention system that had many of the same problems President Obama had rightly criticized during the Bush years. Under Obama, Guantanamo has been a place where hardened terrorists coexist with prisoners unconnected with al Qaeda or the Taliban, the latter never charged with any offense and long since cleared for release.

When the Bush administration opened Guantanamo, it believed it was creating "the legal equivalent of outer space"—a place where the rule of law would not apply.[113] Although the Obama administration never took precisely that approach and in fact has managed to release or successfully prosecute in federal court more than a hundred prisoners, for the prisoners who remain the similarities are striking. They have been held in a system that gives most of them no meaningful opportunity to challenge the basis for their detention, while others are needlessly tried in a military tribunal system that still remains unable to provide fair procedural standards and may be incapable of trying defendants for the putative war crimes they are charged with. The result is a system that fails to bring dangerous terrorists to justice even as it continues to hold others who should never have been detained in the first place. These are the same central flaws endemic to the system the Bush administration first created at Guantanamo.

The Obama administration's actions at Guantanamo cannot be reduced to a pithy summary explaining that the Bush administration's approach has simply been extended under cover of rhetorically milder justifications. The situation is much too complicated for that. But it is also important to note the areas of continuity between the Bush and the Obama administrations when it comes to Guantanamo. For prisoners there who have been cleared for release but are still held, the fact that indefinite detention is now supported by statutory authority does not make a difference. President Obama inherited a knotty problem, one that has undoubtedly been complicated by restrictions Congress set with regard to transfer of prisoners to the United States for purpose of trial. Obama set the right goal: to bring the rule of law to Guantanamo. But his administration has not achieved that goal, and Congress is not the only reason why.

# THE OBAMA ADMINISTRATION

# AND TORTURE

On the question of torture, the Obama administration has its strongest case for arguing that it has made a decisive break with the Bush administration's approach. As discussed in chapter 7, the Bush administration authorized torture of prisoners, including by waterboarding and sleep deprivation. In the 2002 Yoo-Bybee memo, the Bush administration initially relied in part on the unitary executive theory as justification for its argument that the president had the power to simply set aside criminal laws prohibiting torture. When it moved away from the unitary executive approach, the Bush administration continued to find ways to justify torture by relying on OLC interpretations and applications of the U.S. anti-torture law that rendered statutory limits on presidential power meaningless.[1]

As a candidate for the presidency, Obama spoke out against torture, and as president he took steps to prevent its use as soon as he took office.[2] In a January 22, 2009, executive order, President Obama prohibited interrogators from "rely[ing] upon any interpretation of the law governing interrogation—including interpretations of Federal criminal laws, the Convention Against Torture, Common Article 3, Army Field Manual 2–22.3, and its predecessor document, Army Field Manual 34–52—issued by the Department of Justice between September 11, 2001, and January 20, 2009."[3] Rejecting the Bush-era OLC memos on torture was certainly a good start.[4]

Obama's executive order further prohibited the use of any interrogation method not authorized by the Army Field Manual.[5] The Army Field Manual specifically prohibits waterboarding.[6] Matthew Alexander, a former military interrogator who has been critical of torture, concluded that "[t]he adoption . . . of the Army Field Manual as the standard for interrogations across the government, including the C.I.A., was a considerable improvement." However, Alexander noted that the Army Field Manual, which does not expressly prohibit sleep deprivation, left room for what he described as "abuse" of prisoners, including by "limiting [prisoners] to just four hours of sleep in 24 hours."[7] In addition, Alexander said that "some interrogators feel the manual's language contains a loophole that allows them to give a detainee four hours of sleep and then conduct a 20-hour interrogation, after which they can "reset" the clock and begin another 20-hour interrogation followed by four hours of sleep."[8]

A 2013 report concluded that the Army Field Manual "permits methods of interrogation that are recognized under international law as forms of torture or cruel, inhuman, or degrading treatment . . . includ[ing] sleep deprivation."[9] As Alexander notes, the Obama administration could claim credit for changes that made interrogation practices "better than before," but the bar set by the Bush administration was a low one. Alexander recommended that the Army Field Manual be revised to expressly prohibit sleep deprivation, solitary confinement for more than two weeks, all stress positions, and imprisonment in confined spaces.[10]

Obama's January 2009 executive order took some significant positive steps, including rejecting the Bush-era OLC memos on torture. There is not enough information available to determine whether the Obama administration has exploited the loopholes Alexander identified in the Army Field Manual or, if some form of sleep deprivation or other dubious interrogation methods are in fact being used, how the Obama administration believes this can be legally justified. There is no reason to assume, without evidence, that the Obama administration is doing any of these things. But, as Alexander observes, given the post-9/11 record, it is essential to be as clear as possible that abuse is not authorized and not permitted. Moreover, since President Obama's actions came through executive order, "these limitations [e.g., that interrogators must comply with the Army Field Manual] are not part of U.S. [statutory] law and could be overturned by a future president with the stroke of a pen."[11]

This relates to a larger concern some observers have identified. Although the Obama administration took important action to reject torture and the justifications the Bush administration relied on, "it is unclear whether it has taken sufficient steps to prevent a future administration from resorting to torture or cruel treatment, particularly if terrorists succeed again in conducting horrific crimes against Americans as they did on September 11."[12] The Obama administration decided not to prosecute anyone for authorizing or carrying out torture during the Bush years. Even before he took office, Obama suggested he was reluctant to punish those involved, explaining he had "a belief that we need to look forward as opposed to looking backwards."[13] In August 2009, Attorney General Holder began a formal investigation of CIA interrogations after 9/11.[14] Holder's review of more than one hundred cases resulted in a decision to open criminal investigations in two cases where prisoners had been killed during interrogation. Ultimately, however, no charges were brought in those two cases or in any cases involving torture.[15] The decision not to bring charges may itself be a violation of U.S. treaty obligations.[16] Not only did the Obama administration decide not to prosecute anyone for acts of torture authorized and committed during the Bush years; it also declined to organize a fact-finding investigation that could have focused public attention on torture and pressured Bush administration officials to take responsibility for their acts.[17]

Christopher Pyle is sharply critical of these decisions, noting that they may have been motivated by political calculations: "[p]rosecuting President Bush and his aides would only inflame Republicans, [Obama] reasoned, leading them to accuse Democrats of being 'soft on terrorists' and undermining the fight against al Qaeda." Pyle observed that it is dissonant for "President Obama [to] . . . denounce torture . . . [while refusing to] characterize those who did it as criminals."[18] Moreover, although Obama's executive order on torture prohibited interrogators from relying on Bush-era OLC memos, President Obama also "assured" CIA interrogators who had "[relied] in good faith upon the [OLC] legal advice that they [would] not be subject to prosecution."[19] In Pyle's view, because of these decisions to not hold anyone accountable for torture, "[u]nder Obama, as under Bush, ours is no longer a government under law. It is a government of options—options to torture, assassinate, or even wage war at the president's direction."[20]

In other words, future administrations may conclude that the law does not limit their discretion regarding interrogation methods, even methods that amount to torture. The Constitution Project's Task Force on Detainee Treatment wondered, "[c]an [torture] [h]appen [a]gain?"[21] Charlie Savage reported in September 2012 that "the future of American government practices when interrogating high-level terrorism suspects appears likely to turn on the outcome of the [2012 presidential] election." Savage explained that "[Republican presidential candidate Mitt] Romney's advisers have privately urged him to 'rescind and replace President Obama's executive order' and permit secret 'enhanced interrogation techniques against high-value detainees that are safe, legal and effective in generating intelligence to save American lives,' according to an internal Romney campaign memorandum." The campaign document was prepared by Romney's national security law subcommittee, which included Steven Bradbury. Bradbury is the author of Bush-era OLC memos (discussed in Section II) that found ways to navigate around statutory limits on torture. Romney himself said that he did not believe waterboarding was torture.[22] Of course, President Obama could not have prevented his rival from reauthorizing waterboarding if Romney had won the 2012 election. But Obama's failure to hold torturers accountable may embolden future presidents who believe waterboarding and other forms of torture are a good idea.

Critics also argue that, although the Obama administration took steps to reject torture as a part of interrogation, it did not actually end torture. They point to the forced feeding of prisoners during hunger strikes at Guantanamo.[23] A United Nations spokesperson suggested the force-feeding could, depending on the circumstances, be "prohibited by international law."[24] Human Rights Watch claimed that "the procedures [used at Guantanamo] raise serious concerns that U.S. forced feedings are violating medical ethics, medical care standards and human rights obligations."[25] As Julian Ku points out, however, "not all forced feeding is illegal[,]" and it is difficult to determine conclusively whether the Obama administration's methods rise to the level of torture or other illegal conduct.[26]

Unlike in the other areas discussed—the use of military force, surveillance, and detention—there is a clear break between the Bush and the Obama administrations when it comes to torture. The Obama administration did not find new ways to justify waterboarding,[27] sleep deprivation, or other forms of torture the Bush administration authorized for the interrogation of prisoners. Despite its refusal to continue to authorize these methods, the Obama administration in this area is not unblemished. Critics point out that the administration's decision not to hold anyone accountable for torture carried out during the Bush years is itself a failure to impose limits on presidential power. Former U.S. senator Mark Udall charged that that "[s]ome of these people [who engaged in torture during the Bush years] are still employed by the CIA [under Obama]."[28]

Even if the Obama administration itself does not torture or abuse prisoners, future presidents and executive branch officials may believe that, if they choose, they can safely set aside laws prohibiting torture. In fact, as noted, there is evidence that Obama's opponent in 2012, Mitt Romney, was considering reinstating waterboarding or other forms of torture if he won the election, and some candidates for the presidency in 2016 have suggested a similar approach. Of course, President Obama has no way to guarantee that his successors will recognize legal limits on their authority when it comes to torture and abuse of prisoners. But it is reasonable to conclude that "if torturers are not punished, then torture could happen again."[29] Like the military detention and (limited) trial system created at Guantanamo, torture occurring during the Bush administration was a problem not of Obama's creation. But, also as with Guantanamo, the

Obama administration's failure to apply the rule of law to set limits on actions taken by a previous administration has troubling implications. The Bush administration's theory was that it could authorize and carry out torture with impunity. The Obama administration's actions have effectively vindicated that theory.

# 14

# THE OBAMA ADMINISTRATION

# AND SECRECY

Barack Obama's presidential campaign criticized the Bush administration for having "invoked a legal tool known as the 'state secrets' privilege more than any other previous administration to get cases thrown out of civil court."[1] After the election, however, "the Obama administration disappointed critics of the state secrets privilege by defending or extending the Bush administration's assertions of the privilege."[2] As in other areas, at first glance the Obama administration seemed to have made a break with the Bush administration's approach. Upon closer examination, however, it becomes clear that the Obama administration has "echoed the state secrets argument made by [the Bush administration]."[3]

In early 2009, the Obama administration surprised many observers by continuing to assert the state secrets privilege in court cases involving extraordinary rendition and warrantless surveillance. In *Mohamed v. Jeppesen*, an extraordinary rendition case filed during the Bush years, the Obama administration caught a federal judge off guard by continuing to "[press] ahead with an argument for preserving state secrets originally developed by the Bush administration."[4] In *Jewel v. NSA*, a lawsuit filed in the fall of 2008 to challenge the Bush administration's warrantless surveillance program, the Obama administration had an opportunity to provide a legal response that would describe its position regarding state secrets. The Obama administration responded to the lawsuit in *Jewel* by filing a motion to dismiss on the basis of the state secrets privilege.[5] Glenn Greenwald remarked that the *Jewel* filing showed that "the Obama DOJ now is [identical] to the Bush DOJ when it comes to its claims of executive secrecy." Greenwald concluded that "[w]hat's being asserted here by the Obama DOJ is the virtually absolute power of presidential secrecy, the right to break the law with no consequences, and immunity from surveillance lawsuits so sweeping that one can hardly believe that it's being claimed with a straight face."[6]

In response to these criticisms, the Obama administration announced in a September 2009 Department of Justice memo what it described as "new . . . policies and . . . procedures" that would apply to its use of the state secrets privilege in court. Attorney General Holder's September 2009 memo promised to "narrowly [tailor]" the department's use of the state secrets privilege, invoking it "only to the extent necessary to protect against the risk of significant harm to national security." Holder further indicated that, even when the privilege was used, the administration would not always seek dismissal of the underlying litigation. Holder stated that the Department of Justice would "not defend an invocation of the privilege" to "conceal violations of the law" or to "prevent embarrassment" to the government or a government official.[7]

The September 2009 DOJ memo established a procedure aimed at limiting use of the privilege to circumstances where release of information in the context of litigation would reasonably be expected to significantly harm national security or U.S. foreign relations. When a government department or agency believed it was necessary to invoke the state secrets privilege, it would submit information to the DOJ based on officials' personal knowledge showing why the information in question needed to be protected from disclosure. An assistant attorney general would review the agency submission to determine "whether or not the Department should defend the assertion of the privilege in litigation." A committee of senior DOJ officials would then determine whether the assistant attorney general's recommendation was justified. Finally, the deputy attorney general and the attorney general would review the committee's recommendation.[8]

Attorney General Holder's memo insisted that the administration would invoke the state secrets privilege only "when genuine and significant harm to national defense or foreign relations is at stake" and, even then, "only to the extent necessary to safeguard those interests."[9] This suggested a meaningful break with the Bush administration, which had used the state secrets privilege to insulate claims of unrestrained presidential power from judicial review. It was certainly a rhetorical shift, as Holder's memo in no way suggested that the Obama administration would use the state secrets privilege to protect executive branch decisions justified by reference to plenary or inherent power. However, even after the Holder memo was released, "in practice the Obama administration's approach continued to be difficult to distinguish from . . . [that of] the Bush administration."[10]

In 2010, Christina Wells noted one problem with the Holder memo: even assuming it provided some accountability within the Obama administration itself, "[n]othing in the policy . . . require[d] that executive officials provide to *courts* any of the justifications or evidence ostensibly required during administrative review." As Wells observed, the state secrets privilege is asserted in the courts; if invoked successfully, it prevents any judicial review of documents for which the privilege is claimed. Since the Holder policy applied only to internal executive branch review, it "allows government officials [after the internal review process is completed] to broadly assert the privilege [in court] based on little or no evidentiary support." Wells, writing in 2010, worried that the Holder policy might become "little more than a symbolic gesture."[11]

In fact, this is precisely what happened. The Holder memo did not stop the Obama administration from continuing the Bush administration's approach of using the state secrets privilege to seek dismissal of lawsuits challenging extraordinary rendition and warrantless surveillance. As discussed, each of these programs had been implemented by the Bush administration. The Obama administration's continued use of the state secrets privilege was acting to insulate the Bush administration's application of and justification for unrestrained presidential power. This may seem odd: why protect actions taken by a previous administration—especially an administration of a different political party? By continuing the Bush administration's approach to the state secrets privilege, however, the Obama administration was protecting the principle of unrestrained presidential power as a general proposition. As discussed throughout Section III, the Obama administration has its own interest in this principle.

The Obama administration has used the state secrets privilege to block judicial scrutiny of the extraordinary rendition program, most centrally in *Mohamed v. Jeppesen Dataplan, Inc.*, a lawsuit initiated during the Bush years that raised some bloodcurdling allegations. One plaintiff alleged that American officials had transported him to Egypt, where he was "subjected to electric shock through electrodes attached to his ear lobes, nipples, and genitals." Another plaintiff claimed he had been transferred to Morocco, where "Moroccan security agents . . . cut him with a scalpel all over his body, including on his penis, and poured 'hot stinging liquid' into the open wounds." A third plaintiff claimed he had been "deprived of sleep and threatened with sexual torture, including sodomy with a bottle and castration."[12] Plaintiffs filed suit against Jeppesen, a private company they said had helped U.S. officials transport them to countries outside the United States where they were tortured. The Bush administration had intervened in the case and invoked the state secrets privilege to win dismissal of the litigation by a federal district court.[13] By the time the Obama administration became involved, the case was on appeal to the Ninth Circuit.

Although there was "voluminous publicly available evidence supporting [plaintiffs'] allegations, including that Jeppesen knew what was going on when it arranged flights described by one of its own officials as 'torture flights,'"[14] the Obama administration followed the same approach as the Bush administration, continuing to argue that the state secrets privilege required dismissal. This position was hard to reconcile with the Holder memo. If information about plaintiffs' allegations and the extraordinary rendition program as a whole was publicly available, how could disclosure of information relevant to their claims significantly harm national security or U.S. foreign relations? If some unreleased information did raise these concerns, why couldn't the lawsuit proceed while the government sought to prevent disclosure of this specific information?

The Obama administration ultimately convinced the Ninth Circuit *en banc* to affirm the district court's decision and dismiss plaintiffs' claims pursuant to the state secrets privilege.[15] In a 6-5 decision, the Ninth Circuit concluded that the case should be dismissed under *Reynolds* because "there is no feasible way to litigate Jeppesen's alleged liability without creating an unjustifiable risk of divulging state secrets."[16] Like the Supreme Court in *Reynolds*, the Ninth Circuit did not review the disputed documents *in camera*. It relied only on declarations and certifications the government submitted to support its state secrets claim.[17] Judge Hawkins, writing for the five dissenters, criticized the majority for agreeing to accept the government's claim at face value and pointed out that in *Reynolds* itself "avoidance of embarrassment—not preservation of state secrets—appears to have motivated the Executive's invocation of the privilege."[18] Without seeing the documents at issue in *Jeppesen*, the Ninth Circuit had no way to determine whether the government had a similar motivation here—other than the court's belief in the sufficiency of the Obama administration's internal review process.

The Obama administration successfully used the state secrets privilege to shield the Bush administration's extraordinary rendition program from judicial scrutiny. The Obama administration has also invoked the state secrets privilege to block litigation involving surveillance conducted by both the Bush and the Obama administrations. The *Jewel v. NSA* lawsuit was filed in September 2008 and challenged both the Terrorist Surveillance Program conducted by the Bush administration and the Section 702 surveillance program described in chapter 11. The Obama administration responded to the complaint by filing a motion asking the federal district court to dismiss the claims on the basis of the state secrets privilege.[19] The district court ruled that some evidence should be excluded from the litigation because it involved state secrets but denied the administration's request to dismiss the entire case.[20] However, the Obama administration continued to press the state secrets argument and in February 2015 the district court agreed that allowing the litigation to continue would "[risk] exceptionally grave damage to national security."[21]

The district court's February 2015 ruling in *Jewel* was based on a classified brief submitted by the government, so it is not possible to know what specific arguments the government made. However, the district court made clear that it was ruling on the basis of the state secrets privilege, citing the Ninth Circuit's *Jeppesen* decision to bolster its conclusions.[22] By invoking the state secrets privilege, the Obama administration was able to shield from scrutiny its upstream data collection program under FISA Section 702, pending possible appeal.

Although the Holder memo indicated that the state secrets privilege would be used sparingly and only when necessary to protect sensitive information, the Obama administration has in fact applied it overbroadly to defend expansive claims of presidential power. The Obama administration has also used the state secrets privilege in an effort to block litigation by people placed on a government no-fly list compiled by the FBI. In January 2006, Rahinah Ibrahim filed a lawsuit in federal court alleging she had been illegally detained at a San Francisco airport after being improperly placed on the no-fly list and that she had later been prevented from reentering the United States. Ibrahim is a Malaysian woman who, at the time, was studying at Stanford University. Although the government admitted it had no evidence that Ibrahim was linked to terrorist activity or had a criminal record of any sort, it argued that the state secrets privilege compelled dismissal of the case.[23] The district court judge, however, allowed the case to continue. After Ibrahim's attorneys took the depositions of several witnesses, including an FBI agent who conceded he had made a mistake in placing Ibrahim on the no-fly list, the judge ordered the government to remove her from the no-fly list.[24]

In another no-fly list case, *Mohamed v. Holder*, the Obama administration again sought to use the state secrets privilege to win dismissal of case. Gulet Mohamed, a U.S. citizen, claimed the government had improperly placed him on the no-fly list, preventing him from returning to the United States from a trip abroad. When Mohamed attempted to renew his student visa at an airport in Kuwait, he was detained by two men who handcuffed him and transported him to an undisclosed location, where he was tortured. He was later brought to a deportation facility, but Kuwaiti officials told Mohamed they could not deport him because the U.S. government had placed him on the no-fly list. After he was released, Mohamed bought a plane ticket to the United States but was not allowed to board his flight.[25]

Mohamed filed a lawsuit claiming that being placed on the no-fly list violated his constitutional rights.[26] The government moved to dismiss his claims on grounds not involving the state secrets privilege. The federal district court denied the motion in part, allowing the litigation to continue. At this point, the government invoked the state secrets privilege in an effort to win dismissal of the case (the government's motion is still pending in court).[27]

The Obama administration has also defended secrecy in other ways, including by "stepp[ing] up the prosecution of government whistleblowers who uncovered illegal actions [and] using the 1917 Espionage Act eight times during [Obama's] first administration to prosecute leakers (it had been so used only three times in the previous ninety-two years)."[28] In fact, "[t]he Obama Administration has undertaken more leak prosecutions than all prior Administrations combined."[29] Edward Snowden is the most well known person to have made information public during the Obama years (as discussed earlier in chapter 11). He has not been prosecuted as he remains outside U.S. jurisdiction, but the administration has charged him with violation of the Espionage Act.[30] Snowden's revelations exposed presidential overreach in the area of bulk metadata collection and Section 702 surveillance that had begun under President Bush but continued under President Obama.[31] Glenn Greenwald notes that the charges are ironic in light of Obama's "repeated pledges of unprecedented transparency and specific vows to protect 'noble' and 'patriotic' whistleblowers."[32] In 2008, the Obama campaign had declared it would "[p]rotect [w]histleblowers[,]" who are "[o]ften the best source of information about waste, fraud, and abuse in government." The Obama campaign argued that "[s]uch acts of courage and patriotism [carried out by whistleblowers], which can sometimes save lives and often save taxpayer dollars, should be encouraged rather than stifled as they have been during the Bush administration. We need to empower federal employees as watchdogs of wrongdoing and partners in performance."[33]

Greenwald argued that Snowden's revelations could not have helped terrorists, who "already knew, and have long known, that the U.S. government is doing everything possible to surveil their telephonic and internet communications." The beneficiaries of Snowden's revelations, Greenwald argued, were the American public, which learned about surveillance carried out by the executive branch that was not subject to meaningful legal restraint and was directed at Americans' communications.[34] Daniel Ellsberg, who had made the Pentagon Papers public in 1971, agreed that "Snowden was the one person in the . . . NSA who did what he absolutely should have done. . . . We all [i.e., government officials] took the same oath to protect and defend the Constitution. There are people who violate it all the time." Ellsberg argued that Snowden had acted to expose wrongdoing and government overreach.[35]

Although Snowden is the most well known person to expose government secrets during the Obama administration, he is not alone. Others who have done the same have been prosecuted by the Obama administration and imprisoned. After reports that the CIA had destroyed videotapes of Abu Zubaydah's interrogation, former CIA operative John Kiriakou confirmed to the media that the CIA had waterboarded Zubaydah. Although Kiriakou argued that waterboarding had helped save American lives, his former colleagues at the CIA were furious and "thought [Kiriakou] was a traitor."[36] Kiriakou spoke with reporters about other aspects of the CIA's interrogation program, and in January 2012 the Obama administration charged him with illegally providing classified information to journalists. Kiriakou was convicted and sentenced to thirty months in prison. Ironically, no one who authorized or carried out waterboarding has been prosecuted. Kiriakou concedes that "I've made mistakes and I've said too much. It's something that I have to constantly remind myself of—that saying less is better than saying more. I often fail at that." But Kiriakou's defenders argue that his prosecution "seems disproportionate and more like persecution. There appears to be a vindictiveness about this."[37]

Thomas Drake, an NSA official, was prosecuted by the Obama administration for speaking to a reporter about concerns Drake had that an NSA surveillance program "turned into a boondoggle that cost more than a billion dollars and violated U.S. citizens' privacy rights." Drake tried to raise his concerns with his supervisor, in testimony before Congress, and with the Defense Department's inspector general, but he believed that his reports were being ignored. Drake subsequently spoke with a *Baltimore Sun* reporter. After the reporter published articles about the NSA program, Drake was charged with violating the Espionage Act. Drake insisted he had provided only unclassified information to the reporter.[38] Drake ultimately entered into a plea bargain, agreeing to plead guilty to a misdemeanor.[39] Drake was sentenced to a year's probation and community service. The federal judge presiding over the case sharply criticized the government for putting Drake through "four years of hell[,]" only to drop significant charges against him as a trial date approached. The judge said that the prosecution's actions "[didn't] pass the smell test."[40] Law professor Mary-Rose Papandrea calls the decision to prosecute Drake "questionable at best" and evidence of "a disturbing level of prosecutorial overzealousness."[41] Drake explained his actions by saying that "I did not take an oath to support and defend government illegalities, violations of the Constitution or turn a blind eye to massive fraud, waste and abuse."[42]

Lucy A. Dalglish, executive director of the Reporters Committee for Freedom of the Press, worries that the Obama administration's actions will "have a chilling effect [on potential whistleblowers]—sources will be less likely to turn information over to reporters. . . . As a result citizens will have less of the information they need about what is going on in our country and who they should vote for." Dalglish concluded that the Obama administration "is clearly making a point of going after people who have access to sensitive and classified information. They are aggressively pursuing government employees who have access to that information and release it to journalists [even if the purpose of the disclosure is to call attention to government overreach]."[43] The Obama administration has also directly pressured journalists, including by threatening to prosecute those who publish information received from whistleblowers. The Obama administration investigated reporter James Rosen for pursuing information from a State Department employee regarding U.S. intelligence about North Korea. Steven Aftergood pointed out that "[a]sking for information has never been deemed a crime."[44] Glenn Greenwald argued that the Rosen investigation showed that the Obama administration was seeking "to criminalize the acts of journalists who report on what the U.S. government does in secret, even though there is no law that makes such reporting illegal and the First Amendment protects such conduct." Greenwald argued that the Obama administration's actions against Rosen and other journalists went beyond the kind of threats the Bush administration had made against the press, as "the Bush DOJ [unlike the Obama DOJ] never went so far as to formally accuse journalists in court filings of committing crimes for reporting on classified information."[45]

The Obama administration's record on prosecuting those who publicly expose information[46] about government wrongdoing or overreach and pressuring reporters who publish information gained from whistleblowers or leakers complements its use of the state secrets privilege as a device to insulate executive action from judicial review. Christina Wells's prediction that the Holder policy might become "little more than a symbolic gesture" has been proved correct.[47] The September 2009 Holder memo suggested that the Obama administration's use of the state secrets privilege would be subject to limits and would not be used to shield expansive assertions of presidential power from judicial scrutiny. But the limits described in the Holder memo have proven to be illusory, and the Obama administration has invoked the privilege in much the same way the Bush administration did, in efforts to block litigation aimed at uncovering the abuse of presidential power. As discussed, this has been part of a broader approach aimed at protecting government secrets in order to defend broad presidential power—an approach that also relied on criminal prosecution of those who seek to publicly disclose evidence of presidential overreach. When the administration has invoked the state secrets privilege in court, it has not always succeeded. In some cases, federal courts have rejected the administration's attempt to shield its actions from scrutiny. But that, of course, is insufficient to demonstrate the Obama administration's own ability to recognize restraints on presidential power where the Bush administration did not.

# CONCLUSION

As a presidential candidate, Barack Obama correctly observed that the Bush administration had dangerously refused to recognize meaningful limits on presidential power, including through its use of the unitary executive theory but also by relying on implausible methods of statutory interpretation. As president, however, Obama missed the opportunity to make a decisive break with the Bush approach. Although Obama has not relied on the unitary executive theory and his administration has used softer rhetoric that purports to accept some limits on power, he and his administration have often reached the same conclusion as the Bush administration: that the president can make decisions about national security free from meaningful constraints. There are significant areas of continuity between the Bush and the Obama administrations, including their conclusions about the scope of the president's authority to (1) use military force, (2) order surveillance, and (3) rely on the state secrets privilege. Even in areas where the Obama administration has deviated in some respects from the Bush administration—on military detention and trial at Guantanamo and on torture—there are areas of overlap, in part because the Obama administration has failed to hold Bush administration officials accountable for violations of the law.

It is worth considering why this happened. There are various theories. Jack Goldsmith suggests that Obama's views changed once he got access to classified information that convinced him he needed the kind of power the Bush administration had claimed.[1] Nancy Kassop points to a struggle between political and legal officials in the Obama administration, with the political group getting its way on many issues, including whether to bring prosecutions for torture and whether to try Guantanamo prisoners in federal court.[2] Michael Glennon argues that Obama, like other presidents (as well as members of Congress and federal judges), simply does not make most national security decisions.[3] Glennon's thesis—that unelected, high-level national security bureaucrats are largely responsible for policymaking in this area—is provocative and compelling. There are open questions to resolve, however. It would be useful, if it is possible, to identify these bureaucrats with far more specificity (though Glennon does identify some) in order to test the thesis more fully. It would be useful to speak with former executive branch officials and members of Congress about Glennon's thesis, assuming they would speak openly and forthrightly. It is also important to note that, as Glennon concedes, at least *some* decisions are made by the president. We can see evidence of that in the Obama administration. President Obama did not continue every Bush administration policy, and Obama's decision to reject torture, in particular, presumably was not supported by the national security bureaucrats Glennon describes.

Moreover, even if Glennon is correct that high-level bureaucrats make most national security decisions, with the president simply signing off passively, those decisions still must be justified. The public justification for national security decisions comes from the president, Congress, and the courts. If it is essential to subordinate presidential national security power to the rule of law, then it is important to ensure that presidents are actually subject to meaningful legal constraints.

Although the Obama administration's record may disillusion those who believe it is essential to set meaningful limits on presidential power, there are reasons for hope. The Obama administration was sometimes constrained—most notably when members of Congress insisted that the president needed statutory authorization before ordering military action against the Assad regime in Syria in 2013 but also in other areas, including torture and, to some extent, the detention system at Guantanamo.

This suggests a possible way forward. The lesson of the Obama presidency may simply be a reminder that the Framers of the Constitution were right to conclude that no one can be trusted with unconstrained power—people are not angels.[4] As Christopher Pyle observes, "[f]ew presidents willingly give up power or seek to leave their office 'weaker' than they found it. Few now have what it takes to stand up to the national security state or to those in Congress and the corporations that profit from it."[5] In the Madisonian framework, the natural response would be to suggest that Congress, the courts, and the people must set limits on presidential power.[6] However, as Pyle and Glennon observe and as a review of the post-9/11 record shows, members of Congress are often passive and deferential in this area. Glennon argues that judges, too, are unable to set limits on national security power,[7] and discussion of the FISA court in Section III supports Glennon's conclusions. But the fact that Congress and the courts have usually failed to effectively limit presidential national security power since 9/11 does not mean that they are incapable of doing so. Change, of course, will be far from easy. First, members of Congress must be convinced that they have a central role to play in defining constitutional power, including presidential power.[8] Second, as Glennon points out, "an informed, engaged electorate" is indispensable. Glennon rightly describes this as a difficult goal to achieve—not because Americans are ignorant but because there are powerful forces working against their interest in "becom[ing] more informed."[9] Americans would undoubtedly benefit from a press and an education system that did a better of job of contributing to "public understanding of the constitutional allocation of powers."[10]

Executive branch lawyers have also shown the potential for setting limits on presidential national security power. Peter Shane is right that executive branch lawyers "must understand their unique roles as both advisers and advocates . . . in their advisory function, government lawyers must play a more objective, even quasi-adjudicative, role. They must give the law their most conscientious interpretation." Many of the executive branch lawyers discussed in Sections II and III—John Yoo, David Addington, Jay Bybee, Steven Bradbury, Harold Koh, David Barron—failed to do this. Even those who sometimes acted conscientiously, like Jack Goldsmith and Caroline Krass, did not always succeed in setting meaningful limits on presidential power. It is essential that the OLC have "some measure of independence to it" and that lawyers in this office and throughout the executive branch do not experience "political and professional pressure" that prevents them from giving objective opinions about the scope and limits of presidential power.[11]

There are no easy answers here, only the beginnings of ways to respond to the problem of unchecked presidential power that has been especially pronounced in the years since 9/11. Harold Koh was right to predict in 2008 that the next eight years would be crucial when it came to the scope of presidential power, but not in the way that he meant. Koh believed that an Obama presidency would put things back on the right track by restoring the rule of law and discrediting extravagant claims of presidential power. Unfortunately, the Obama presidency has fundamentally continued the Bush approach and has failed to recognize limits on presidential power. If those limits are to be restored, it will be up to Obama's successors and, perhaps more important, to future members of Congress, judges, executive branch lawyers, the press, and the public at large to set things right.

# NOTES

## Introduction

1.  Harold Koh, "Repairing Our Human Rights Reputation," *Western New England Law Review* 31 (2009): 17.

2.  Harold Koh, "Setting the World Right," *Yale Law Journal* 115 (2006): 2374.

3.  Ibid., 2355.

4.  Barack Obama, Executive Order 13491, "Ensuring Lawful Interrogations," January 22, 2009; see also Asa Hutchinson, James R. Jones, Talbot "Sandy" D'Alemberte, Richard A. Epstein, David P. Gushee, Azizah Y. al-Hibri, David R. Irvine, Claudia Kennedy, Thomas R. Pickering, William S. Sessions, and Gerald E. Thomson, "The Report of the Constitution Project's Task Force on Detainee Treatment" (Washington, D.C.: The Constitution Project, 2013), 312, 320. The Constitution Project's report suggests, however, that we cannot know with certainty that extraordinary rendition has ended since "the [Obama] administration asserts it retains the right to render detainees to foreign custody in reliance on 'diplomatic assurances' that they will not be tortured, with some increased safeguards to ensure detainees' humane treatment, but it is not clear if any renditions have occurred [during the Obama administration]." Ibid., 312.

5.  Human Rights Watch, "Getting Away with Torture: The Bush Administration and Mistreatment of Detainees" (New York: Human Rights Watch, 2011); Eric Posner, "Why Obama Won't Prosecute Torturers," Slate.com, December 9, 2014. President Bush, Vice President Dick Cheney, and other administration officials have been convicted in absentia of war crimes by other countries. Yvonne Ridley, "Bush Convicted of War Crimes in Absentia," Foreign Policy Journal, May 12, 2012; Sophia Pearson, Christie Smythe, and Joel Rosenblatt, "CIA Officials Linked to Torture Face Future Stuck on U.S. Soil," Bloomberg, December 10, 2014.

6.  Elizabeth Holtzman with Cynthia L. Cooper, *Cheating Justice: How Bush and Cheney Attacked the Rule of Law and Plotted to Avoid Prosecution—and What We Can Do about It* (Boston: Beacon Press, 2013); John W. Dean, "Barack Obama and the Foreign Intelligence Surveillance Act Amendments: In Pledging to Work to Remove Retroactive Immunity for FISA Violations, What Kind of Action Is Obama Contemplating?," *FindLaw*, July 2, 2008.

7. Jack Goldsmith, *Power and Constraint: The Accountable Presidency after 9/11* (New York: W. W. Norton, 2012).

8. Eric A. Posner and Adrian Vermeule, *The Executive Unbound: After the Madisonian Republic* (New York: Oxford University Press, 2011).

9. Louis Fisher, "Military Operations in Libya: No War? No Hostilities?," *Presidential Studies Quarterly* 42, no. 1 (March 2012): 176.

10. Robert J. Spitzer, "Comparing the Constitutional Presidencies of George W. Bush and Barack Obama: War Powers, Signing Statements, Vetoes," *White House Studies* 12, no. 2 (October 2013): 125–146.

11. Richard M. Pious, "Prerogative Power in the Obama Administration," *Presidential Studies Quarterly* 41, no. 2 ( June 2011): 263–290.

12. Ibid., 265.

13. Michael J. Glennon, *National Security and Double Government* (New York: Oxford University Press, 2015), 113.

14. Ibid., 29–72.

15. Ibid., 13.

16. Ibid., 16–28.

17. Ibid., 33.

18. Ibid., 59.

19. Ibid., 60.

20. Ibid., 99.

21. Ibid., 65.

22. As discussed in Section I, the Bush administration's theory of presidential power did have historical antecedents, but its application of the unitary executive theory, as discussed in Section II, was something new and led to unprecedented presidential decisions to set aside all statutory and constitutional limits on presidential power, even when that meant setting aside criminal law. At least, these decisions are unprecedented in the sense that the Bush administration was able to carry out these decisions with impunity—with assistance from the Obama administration, as discussed in Section III.

23. Ibid., 99–108.

24. Ibid., 118.

25. The Obama administration has not expressly repudiated the sole organ doctrine and relied on it in a brief submitted to the Supreme Court in *Zivotofsky v. Kerry*. Brief for Respondent John Kerry, Secretary of State, *Zivotofsky v. Kerry*, U.S. Supreme Court, docket no. 13–628 (2014).

26. Executive branch lawyers in the Bush administration never expressly repudiated the unitary executive theory but, beginning in 2004, did not always rely on it to justify national security decisions, as discussed in Section II.

27. As discussed in Section I, I borrow the term "faux law" from Peter Shane. Peter M. Shane, *Madison's Nightmare: How Executive Power Threatens American Democracy* (Chicago: University of Chicago Press, 2009), 141.

28. James Madison, Federalist No. 51, in Alexander Hamilton, John Jay, and James Madison, *The Federalist Papers*, ed. Michael A. Genovese (New York: Palgrave Macmillan, 2009), 119–122.

# Chapter 1.
## The Constitution and Presidential National Security Power

1. Peter M. Shane, *Madison's Nightmare: How Executive Power Threatens American Democracy* (Chicago: University of Chicago Press, 2009), 20.

2. Ibid., 20–21.

3. Ibid., 25.

4. Michael J. Glennon, *National Security and Double Government* (New York: Oxford University Press, 2015).

5. There are, of course, other sorts of presidential power—for instance, the power to pardon, appointment power, the power to oversee administrative agencies, the power to respond to natural disasters. See e.g. Jeffrey Crouch, *The Presidential Pardon Power* (Lawrence: University Press of Kansas, 2009); Shane, *Madison's Nightmare*, 143–174. This book focuses on presidential power in the context of national security.

6. See Louis Fisher, "Teaching the Presidency: Idealizing a Constitutional Office," *PS: Political Science and Politics* 45, no. 1 (January 2012): 17: "Following the terrorist attacks of September 11, studies on the presidency have been divided between those who urge the concentration of power in the president in times of emergency, and those who insist that the executive branch lacks both the competence and the authority to exercise power unchecked by Congress, the courts, and the general public."

7. See e.g. John Yoo, *Crisis and Command: The History of Executive Power from George Washington to George W. Bush* (New York: Kaplan, 2009); Eric A. Posner and Adrian Vermeule, *The Executive Unbound: After the Madisonian Republic* (New York: Oxford University Press, 2011) (Posner and Vermeule argue that there are *political* checks on presidential power but generally reject the viability of legal checks under the Constitution).

8. See e.g. Louis Fisher, *Defending Congress and the Constitution* (Lawrence: University Press of Kansas, 2011); James P. Pfiffner, *Power Play: The Bush Presidency and the Constitution* (Washington, D.C.: Brookings Institution Press, 2008); Shane, *Madison's Nightmare*; Christopher H. Pyle and Richard M. Pious, *The Constitution under Siege: Presidential Power versus the Rule of Law* (Durham, NC: Carolina Academic Press, 2010). These scholars have made the case against unchecked presidential power in other works as well—the books and articles cited here are not an exhaustive list of their work.

9. *Youngstown Sheet & Tube Co. v. Sawyer*, 343 U.S. 579, 641–642 (1952) (Jackson, J., concurring). Justice Jackson did not endorse this interpretation of the Commander in Chief Clause; he was describing how others defined its meaning. Jackson concluded that the commander in chief power was much more limited and the Framers of the Constitution had not intended to give the president a "monopoly of 'war powers.'" Ibid., at 644.

10. See e.g. Memorandum opinion from John C. Yoo, Deputy Assistant Attorney General, for Timothy Flanigan, Deputy Counsel to the President, *The President's Constitutional Authority to Conduct Military Operations against Terrorists and Nations Supporting Them* (September 25, 2001) (hereinafter September 25, 2001, Yoo memo); Memorandum opinion for Alberto Gonzales, Counsel to the President, *Standards of Conduct for Interrogation under 18 U.S.C. §§ 2340–2340A* (August 1, 2002). David Barron and Martin Lederman conclude that neither the text of the Constitution nor the historical record support the

conclusion that the Commander in Chief Clause gives the president authority to make any decision related to the conduct of a military campaign. David J. Barron and Martin S. Lederman, "The Commander in Chief at the Lowest Ebb—Framing the Problem, Doctrine and Original Understanding," *Harvard Law Review* 121, no. 3 (2008): 689; Barron and Lederman, "The Commander in Chief at the Lowest Ebb—A Constitutional History," *Harvard Law Review* 121, no. 4 (2008): 941.

11. Alexander Hamilton, Federalist No. 69, in Alexander Hamilton, John Jay, and James Madison, *The Federalist Papers*, ed. Michael A. Genovese (New York: Palgrave Macmillan, 2009) (hereinafter *The Federalist Papers*), 193–197.

12. Max Farrand, ed., *The Records of the Federal Convention of 1787* (New Haven: Yale University Press, 1937), 2:318–319; see also Louis Fisher, *Presidential War Power*, 3rd ed. (Lawrence: University Press of Kansas, 2013), 8–19.

13. Even then, however, the rule of law would require the president to acknowledge having taken extraconstitutional action and to seek retroactive approval from Congress legitimating his action—as President Lincoln did after taking unilateral action at the beginning of the Civil War.

14. September 25, 2001, Yoo memo.

15. Louis Fisher, "John Yoo and the Republic," *Presidential Studies Quarterly* 41, no. 1 (March 2011): 177.

16. Fisher, *Presidential War Power*, 1–16.

17. Ryan J. Barilleaux and Christopher S. Kelley, eds., *The Unitary Executive and the Modern Presidency* (College Station: Texas A&M University Press, 2010), 3. Advocates of the unitary executive theory also cite Article II's Oath and Take Care Clauses to support their assertion that the president can independently determine the scope of his power under the Constitution. Ibid. They may appear to recognize some limits—for instance, John Yoo conceded that the Constitution assigns some powers over foreign affairs and warmaking to Congress. September 25, 2001, Yoo memo. On closer examination, however, the concession is illusory. Yoo argued in the same memo that the president had plenary control over foreign affairs and the use of military force, rendering meaningless his concession that some of these "executive" powers were assigned to Congress by the Constitution. Ibid.

18. Alexander Hamilton, *Pacificus No. 1*, June 29, 1793, *The Papers of Alexander Hamilton*, Digital Edition, ed. Harold C. Syrett (Charlottesville: University of Virginia Press, Rotunda, 2011), vol. 15 (emphasis in original).

19. Ibid.

20. September 25, 2001, Yoo memo, 24.

21. *The Federalist Papers*, Federalist No. 69, 193–197.

22. Some scholars take a narrower view of the unitary executive theory, arguing that it stands for the idea that the president has plenary control over executive branch officials and administrative agencies. Steven G. Calabresi and Christopher S. Yoo, *The Unitary Executive: Presidential Power from Washington to Bush* (New Haven: Yale University Press, 2008). This narrower view is itself controversial because it is at odds with the principle that statutory law can limit executive power.

23. Mark Tushnet, "A Political Perspective on the Theory of the Unitary Executive," *University of Pennsylvania Journal of Constitutional Law* 12 (2010): 313, 315, 323–324.

24. Barilleaux and Kelley, *The Unitary Executive and the Modern Presidency*, 4. There are also antecedents in earlier presidencies—for example, the Truman administration's argument to a U.S. district court in the *Steel Seizure Case*.

25. See Section II.

26. John C. Yoo, "War and the Constitutional Text," *University of Chicago Law Review* 69 (Fall 2002): 1676: "in matters of national defense, war, and foreign policy . . . a unitary executive can evaluate threats, consider policy choices, and mobilize national resources with a speed and energy that is far superior to any other branch." See also William G. Howell with David Milton Brent, *Thinking about the Presidency: The Primacy of Power* (Princeton: Princeton University Press, 2013), 7: "The president's actions . . . must be decisive and, whenever possible, swift."

27. Posner and Vermeule, *The Executive Unbound*, 176–210.

28. William G. Howell and Jon C. Pevehouse, *While Dangers Gather: Congressional Checks on Presidential War Powers* (Princeton: Princeton University Press, 2007), 8.

29. Ibid.

30. Chris Edelson and Donna G. Starr-Deelen, "Libya, Syria, ISIS, and the Case against the Energetic Executive," *Presidential Studies Quarterly* 45, no. 3 (September 2015): 581–601.

31. Ibid.

32. Authorization for Use of Military Force, September 18, 2001, Public Law No. 107–40, 115 Stat. 224.

33. Edelson and Starr-Deelen, "Libya, Syria, ISIS, and the Case against the Energetic Executive."

34. Although Congress and the Supreme Court later ratified Roosevelt's action, the president initially acted unilaterally and did not believe action or authorization by the other branches was necessary to support his executive order, as discussed later in this section.

35. See Shane, *Madison's Nightmare*, 54: "the . . . case for a near-monarchical President in foreign and military affairs fails. It is . . . [not] based on a sound reading of constitutional text or history. The [Constitution] does not compel us to have an imperial presidency . . . [instead, it] provides profound roles for both Congress and the judiciary in setting the appropriate bounds of executive power."

36. Posner and Vermeule, *The Executive Unbound*.

37. Clinton L. Rossiter, *Constitutional Dictatorship: Crisis Government in the Modern Democracies* (Princeton: Princeton University Press, 1948).

38. *The Federalist Papers*, Federalist No. 47, 101.

39. Shane, *Madison's Nightmare*, 44. Posner and Vermeule argue that what the Framers intended is no longer relevant in a twenty-first-century world that requires strong executives to act quickly in order to meet new dangers. *The Executive Unbound*, 9, 18, 43–52, 60–61. However, Posner and Vermeule do not identify specific examples to support their claim that the nation cannot survive without allowing the executive to operate outside the rule of law, and they discount the danger of such extraordinary power, dismissing critics of their approach as "tyrannophobes." Ibid., 176–205. Posner and Vermeule are correct that, fortunately, the United States has never had a Hitler or a Stalin, but unchecked presidential power can be very dangerous even if it does not produce a dictator. Indeed, as Shane observes,

history "provides a compelling negative answer to the question whether presidential uni-lateralism generally serves the public interest." Shane, *Madison's Nightmare*, 55.

40. Chris Edelson, *Emergency Presidential Power: From the Drafting of the Constitution to the War on Terror* (Madison: University of Wisconsin Press, 2013), 18.

41. Annals of Congress, 6th Cong., 613 (1800), (Washington, D.C.: Gales & Seaton, 1834–56).

42. Ibid.

43. Ibid.

44. Louis Fisher, "Presidential Inherent Power: The 'Sole Organ' Doctrine," *Presidential Studies Quarterly* 37, no. 1 (March 2007): 140 (emphasis in original).

45. *U.S. v. Curtiss-Wright*, 299 U.S. 304, 320 (1936).

46. Fisher, "Presidential Inherent Power," 142.

47. *Curtiss-Wright*, 299 U.S. at 320.

48. U.S. Constitution, art. II, § 2; art. I, § 8.

49. Fisher, "Presidential Inherent Power," 140. In fact, even under the British model that the Framers rejected as giving too much power to the executive, the late eighteenth-century monarch no longer exercised absolute power over foreign affairs. Ibid.

50. September 25, 2001, Yoo memo. In a 2009 book, Yoo also favorably cited Sutherland's misinterpretation of Marshall's sole organ remark. Yoo, *Crisis and Command*, 290–292.

51. September 25, 2001, Yoo memo.

52. It is incorrect as a matter of historical record because many presidents have sought congressional authorization when conducting foreign affairs. For instance, presidents sought declarations of war in each world war and obtained congressional authorization for many other military actions, including during Vietnam, the first Gulf War, and even the 2003 invasion of Iraq. On other occasions, most notably during the Korean War, presidents acted unilaterally, without seeking congressional approval. However, such actions do not prove Yoo's point. They simply show that presidents sometimes exceed their constitutional authority. Extraconstitutional action does not create precedent for future action.

53. *Zivotofsky v. Kerry*, 576 U.S. ___ (2015).

54. Shane, *Madison's Nightmare*, 103.

55. Posner and Vermeule, *The Executive Unbound*, 3–5, 12–17, 60–61.

56. Shane, *Madison's Nightmare*, 112–142.

57. Ibid., 132.

58. Ibid. (emphasis added).

59. Ibid., 141. In the quoted excerpt, Shane is discussing presidential signing statements, but his analysis applies more broadly to legal opinions generated in the executive branch to justify plenary presidential power.

60. Louis Fisher, "Abraham Lincoln: Preserving the Union and the Constitution," *Albany Government Law Review* 3 (2010): 503.

61. Ibid., 524.

62. David Gray Adler, "The Framers and Executive Prerogative: A Constitutional and Historical Rebuke," *Presidential Studies Quarterly* 42, no. 2 (June 2012): 378, 379.

63. Pfiffner, *Power Play*, 28, 69–75; Fisher, *Defending Congress and the Constitution*, 235 ("the framers broke free of political systems [like the British] that centered war-making and foreign policy in the Executive").

64. Pfiffner, *Power Play*, 57.

65. Ibid.

66. Ibid., 58–61.

67. Ibid., 62.

68. Ibid., 229.

69. Ibid.

70. Shane, *Madison's Nightmare*, 5.

71. Ibid., 4.

72. Ibid., 27.

73. Ibid., 83.

74. Ibid., 103.

75. Pfiffner, *Power Play*, 229.

76. *Youngstown Sheet and Tube*, 343 U.S. 579, 650 ( Jackson, J., concurring).

77. U.S. Constitution, preamble.

78. See Shane, *Madison's Nightmare*, 55 (observing that advocates for unchecked presidential power may simply be arguing that their "vision of [unchecked] executive power is good for the United States, regardless of what the . . . drafters [of the Constitution] had in mind").

## Chapter 2.
## Presidential National Security Power before September 11, 2001

1. Although Roosevelt's actions in this regard were approved by Congress and the courts, he initially acted unilaterally in issuing the executive order that authorized the military to round up and intern Japanese Americans on the West Coast, and the executive order he issued suggested that Roosevelt believed he had plenary power to act, as discussed in this chapter.

2. Louis Fisher, "Teaching the Presidency: Idealizing a Constitutional Office," *PS: Political Science and Politics* 45, no. 1 ( January 2012).

3. James Madison, Federalist No. 51, in Alexander Hamilton, John Jay, and James Madison, *The Federalist Papers*, ed. Michael A. Genovese (New York: Palgrave Macmillan, 2009) (hereinafter *The Federalist Papers*), 120: "If men were angels, no government would be necessary. If angels were to govern men, neither external nor internal controls on government would be necessary. In framing a government which is to be administered by men over men, the great difficulty lies in this: you must first enable the government to control the governed; and in the next place oblige it to control itself. A dependence on the people is, no doubt, the primary control on the government; but experience has taught mankind the necessity of auxiliary precautions."

4. See Louis Fisher, "Abraham Lincoln: Preserving the Union and the Constitution," *Albany Government Law Review* 3 (2010): 503.

5. I divide discussion along these lines because advocates of plenary presidential power often argue that the September 11 attacks "changed everything," demanding a concentration of power in the hands of the executive in order to meet the terrorist threat. See e.g. *Meet the Press* Transcript for September 14, 2003, http://www.msnbc.msn.com/id/3080244 (Vice President Cheney declaring during interview with Tim Russert that "9/11 changed

everything"). Although I think this claim is unjustified, it is useful to divide discussion in this way in order to focus on the way in which arguments for plenary presidential power have been made since 9/11 and especially to focus on the similarities between Bush's and Obama's use of national security power.

6. There are also pre–World War II examples of presidents who either acted unilaterally or used congressional acquiescence to exercise broad power—for instance, John Adams and the Alien and Sedition Acts, Polk's use of deception to gain a congressional declaration of war against Mexico, McKinley's obtaining a declaration of war against Spain on the basis of "misleading and false statements," the Wilson administration's use of the 1917–18 Espionage and Sedition Acts to crack down on dissent during World War I. See Fisher, "Teaching the Presidency," 20–21.

7. The assertion of broad presidential power since World War II has been helped along by presidential scholars who have "trumpet[ed] the need for bold and unchecked presidential leadership." Ibid., 20–22.

8. Louis Fisher, *Nazi Saboteurs on Trial: A Military Tribunal and American Law* (Lawrence: University of Kansas Press, 2003), 25–29, 35–38.

9. Ibid., 1.

10. Ibid., 26–31, 35–38.

11. Ibid., 32–34, 40–42.

12. Ibid., 49, 51–52.

13. Ibid., 50, 52.; see also 7 Fed. Reg. 5101 (1942) (proclamation) and 7 Fed. Reg. 5103 (1942) (military order).

14. Fisher, *Nazi Saboteurs on Trial*, 51.

15. 7 Fed. Reg. 5101 (1942).

16. Fisher, *Nazi Saboteurs on Trial*, 172, 89–90.

17. 7 Fed. Reg. 5101 (1942); see also Fisher, *Nazi Saboteurs on Trial*, 51.

18. Fisher, *Nazi Saboteurs on Trial*, 52, 173.

19. Ibid., 101.

20. Ibid., 101. As Fisher notes, "[f]or the most part . . . the [tribunal] made up the rules as the trial went along." Ibid., 102.

21. Ibid., 53. Although the Articles of War gave the president authority to create, through regulation, procedures for military tribunals, Congress had provided that "nothing contrary to or inconvenient with [the] Articles [of War] shall be so prescribed." Article 38 of the Articles of War in effect in 1942, quoted in ibid., 101.

22. Ibid., 90.

23. Ibid.

24. Ibid., 172.

25. *Ex parte Quirin*, 317 U.S. 1 (1942).

26. Fisher, *Nazi Saboteurs on Trial*, 94.

27. By the time the Court issued its final written opinion in the case, six of the eight saboteurs had already been executed. Ibid., 109.

28. *Quirin*, 317 U.S. at 29, 47–48.

29. Fisher, *Nazi Saboteurs on Trial*, 134.

30. *Hamdi v. Rumsfeld*, 542 U.S. 507, 569 (2004) (Scalia, J., dissenting).

31. As Louis Fisher explains, "[t]he purpose of trying the eight Germans in secret was not to protect military secrets or safeguard national security. The need for secrecy was driven by two reasons: to conceal the fact that [one saboteur] had turned himself (and the others) in, and to mete out the death penalty." Fisher, *Nazi Saboteurs on Trial*, 172.

32. Ibid., 28, 35–38, 85.

33. Louis Fisher, *Military Tribunals and Presidential Power: American Revolution to the War on Terrorism* (Lawrence: University Press of Kansas, 2005), 114.

34. 7 Fed. Reg. 1407 (February 19, 1942).

35. The executive order does make reference to statutes relating to national defense, but none of these statutes so much as suggest that the president has authority to remove U.S. citizens and legal residents from their homes and place them in internment camps.

36. 7 Fed. Reg. 1407.

37. Peter Irons, *Justice at War: The Story of the Japanese Internment Cases* (New York: Oxford University Press, 1983), 64.

38. Ibid., quoting Memorandum of Biddle to Roosevelt, February 20, 1942, Official File 4805, Franklin D. Roosevelt Library, Hyde Park, New York.

39. Ibid., 64–65.

40. Jacobus tenBroek, Edward N. Barnhart, and Floyd W. Matson, *Prejudice, War and the Constitution* (Berkeley: University of California Press, 1968), 113; Irons, *Justice at War*, 65.

41. Irons, *Justice at War*, 65.

42. In a cover letter sent to Congress, Secretary Stimson explained that "[t]he purpose of the proposed legislation is to provide for enforcement in the Federal criminal courts of orders issued under the authority of Executive order of the President No, 9066, dated February 19, 1942." U.S. Army, Western Defense Command and Fourth Army, *Final Report: Japanese Evacuation from the West Coast, 1942* (Washington, D.C.: Government Printing Office, 1943), 30. Secretary Stimson's letter to Congress added that "The Bureau of the Budget has advised that there is no objection to the submission of this proposed legislation for the consideration of the Congress, as *the enactment thereof would not be in conflict with the program of the President.*" Ibid., emphasis added. Secretary Stimson's language gives no indication that the president or the executive branch believed Roosevelt needed Congress's authorization in order to issue the executive order: Congress's role was seen as simply providing for enforcement of the executive order. The italicized language suggests that Stimson believed Congress did not have the authority to contradict or interfere with the executive order issued by the president.

43. TenBroek, Barnhart, and Matson, *Prejudice, War and the Constitution*, 114; Irons, *Justice at War*, 66–67.

44. TenBroek, Barnhart, and Matson, *Prejudice, War and the Constitution*, 114.

45. Ibid.

46. Irons, *Justice at War*, 66–67.

47. Ibid., 66.

48. TenBroek, Barnhart, and Matson, *Prejudice, War and the Constitution*, 115. Senator Robert R. Reynolds (D-NC), who was the chair of the Military Affairs Committee, told those senators who were present for the vote that Japanese Americans represented a dangerous

"fifth column" on the West Coast, ready to aid the enemy in the event of invasion. Senator Reynolds repeated false charges that Japanese Americans had helped carry out the attack against Pearl Harbor. Senator Robert Taft (R-OH) raised the only objection to the legislation, arguing that the bill was the "sloppiest criminal law" he had seen and suggesting it was unconstitutional because of its vagueness. However, Senator Taft resigned himself to its passage during wartime, and Senator Reynolds "did not bother to answer [Senator Taft's] objections . . . [before] the bill passed by voice vote with no recorded dissent." Irons, *Justice at War*, 67–68.

49. Pub. L. No. 77–503, 56 Stat. 173 (March 21, 1942).

50. See *Hirabayashi v. United States*, 320 U.S. 81, 92 (1943); *Korematsu v. United States*, 323 U.S. 214, 217–218 (1944).

51. Louis Fisher, *Defending Congress and the Constitution* (Lawrence: University Press of Kansas, 2011), 264.

52. Ibid.

53. U.S. Constitution, art. I, § 8.

54. Louis Fisher, *Presidential War Power*, 3rd ed. (Lawrence: University Press of Kansas, 2013), 8. Under the War Powers Resolution, passed by Congress in 1973, the president might claim (thanks to sloppy draftsmanship) the authority "to use military force for any reason, anywhere in the world, for up to 90 days, without advance congressional approval." Fisher, *Defending Congress and the Constitution*, 271. However, this claimed statutory authorization for the president to use force is unavailing as it would violate the Constitution. Ibid. In any event, the War Powers Resolution was not available to Truman in 1950.

55. Fisher, *Defending Congress and the Constitution*, 265, quoting 91 Cong. Rec. 8185 (1945).

56. Ibid., 265, quoting 59 Stat. 621, § 6 (1945). In 1949, § 6 of the UN Participation Act was amended to permit the president limited authority "to provide military forces to the U.N." Ibid., 265. But even the 1949 amendments provided that "presidential discretion to deploy [military] forces was subject to stringent conditions: they can serve only as observers and guards, can perform only in a noncombatant capacity, and cannot exceed 1,000 in number." Ibid., citing 63 Stat. 735–36, § 5 (1949).

57. Although a UN resolution would have been constitutionally insufficient even if passed, in fact "Truman committed U.S. forces *before* the [Security] Council called for military action." Fisher, *Presidential War Power*, 98–99.

58. Arthur M. Schlesinger Jr., *The Imperial Presidency* (Boston: Houghton Mifflin, 1973), 133, quoting Department of State Bulletin, July 3, 1950. Secretary of State Acheson's memoirs explain why the president did not seek congressional sanction for sending troops to Korea and confirm that this was Truman's view: "There has never, I believe, been any serious doubt—in the sense of non-politically inspired doubt—of the President's constitutional authority to do what he did. The basis for this conclusion in legal theory and historical precedent was fully set out in the State Department's memorandum of July 3, 1950, extensively published. But the wisdom of the decision not to ask for congressional approval has been doubted. . . . The President agreed, moved also, I think, by another passionately held conviction. His great office was to him a sacred and temporary trust, which he was determined to pass on unimpaired by the slightest loss of power or prestige. This attitude would

incline him strongly against any attempt to divert criticism from himself by action that might establish a precedent in derogation of presidential power to send our forces into battle. The memorandum that we prepared listed eighty-seven instances in the past century in which his predecessors had done this. And thus yet another decision was made." Dean Acheson, *Present at the Creation* (New York: W.W. Norton, 1969), 414–415.

59. Fisher, *Defending Congress and the Constitution*, 266.

60. Fisher, *Presidential War Power*, 104.

61. Louis Fisher, "Unchecked Presidential Wars," *University of Pennsylvania Law Review* 148 (May 2000): 1637.

62. Fisher, *Presidential War Power*, 80; see also Memorandum opinion from John C. Yoo, Deputy Assistant Attorney General, for Timothy Flanigan, Deputy Counsel to the President, *The President's Constitutional Authority to Conduct Military Operations against Terrorists and Nations Supporting Them* (September 25, 2001): "Perhaps the most significant deployment without specific statutory authorization took place at the time of the Korean War, when President Truman, without prior authorization from Congress, deployed United States troops in a war that lasted for over three years and caused over 142,000 American casualties."

63. Maeva Marcus, *Truman and the Steel Seizure Case: The Limits of Presidential Power* (New York: Columbia University Press, 1977), 58–80.

64. Executive Order 10340, Directing the Secretary of Commerce to Take Possession of and Operate the Plants and Facilities of Certain Steel Companies, April 8, 1952.

65. Marcus, *Truman and the Steel Seizure Case*, 168.

66. Ibid., 94.

67. Ibid., 94–95, quoting President Truman's Special Message to Congress, April 9, 1952.

68. Ibid., 95.

69. Ibid., 95–99.

70. Ibid., 100, quoting remarks from the president's press conference of April 17, 1952.

71. Ibid., 95, quoting the president's press conference of April 24, 1952.

72. John Locke described this executive prerogative as "[t]h[e] power to act according to discretion, for the publick good, without the prescription of the Law, and sometimes against it." John Locke, *Two Treatises of Government*, ed. Peter Laslett (Cambridge: Cambridge University Press, 1988), 2nd Treatise, section 160. In other words, this is a form of emergency power that allows the executive to act against the law in the name of necessity.

73. Marcus, *Truman and the Steel Seizure Case*, 102–177.

74. Ibid., 106.

75. Ibid.

76. Judge Pine was presented with motions for a preliminary injunction that sought temporary relief, but he soon made clear that he was interested in resolving the larger issue of whether the president had "the constitutional power to seize the [steel] mills." Ibid., 108–118.

77. Ibid., 117.

78. Ibid., 119.

79. Ibid., 121.

80. Ibid., 125. Baldridge later claimed that he had been misunderstood and that the press made his position seem more extreme than it was, but Baldridge's argument before Judge Pine seem very clear. Ibid., 310, n. 107.

81. Ibid., 125.

82. Ibid.

83. April 27, 1952, letter from President Truman to C. S. Jones, reprinted in *Public Papers of Presidents of the United States, Harry S. Truman, 1945–1953* (Washington, D.C.: Government Printing Office, 1966), 301. The Department of Justice also moved away from its claim that the courts had no role to play in reviewing the president's actions. Patricia L. Bellia, "Story of the *Steel Seizure* Case," in *Presidential Power Stories*, ed. Christopher H. Schroeder and Curtis A. Bradley (New York: Foundation Press, 2009), 234–235, 266.

84. *Public Papers of Presidents of the United States, Harry S. Truman, 1945–1953*, 301.

85. Ibid.

86. Truman's letter stated that "[t]he powers of the President are derived from the Constitution, and they are limited, of course, by the provisions of the Constitution, particularly those that protect the rights of individuals." Ibid. However, Truman's claim to emergency presidential power seems to be an extraconstitutional one as the Constitution itself does not refer to such power. It is not clear whether Truman believed that constitutional provisions other than protections in the Bill of Rights could limit presidential power in this area.

87. Marcus, *Truman and the Steel Seizure Case*, 126–129.

88. *Youngstown Sheet & Tube Co. v. Sawyer*, 103 F.Supp. 569, 575–576 (D.D.C. 1952).

89. Ibid., at 573.

90. Ibid., at 573–574.

91. Ibid., at 574.

92. Ibid., at 575.

93. Ibid., at 577.

94. Ibid.

95. Marcus, *Truman and the Steel Seizure Case*, 130–135.

96. Ibid., 142–143. With Democrats having held the White House for the previous two decades, the Supreme Court in 1952 was composed entirely of justices nominated by Democratic presidents—five by Roosevelt and four by Truman. Ibid., 178, 182–191. In addition, the Court had deferred to presidential action taken in the name of national security in the *Quirin, Hirabayashi*, and *Korematsu* cases. Many, including Truman himself, expected the Court to reverse Judge Pine's decision. Ibid., 178–179.

97. Ibid., 154–163, 170–173.

98. Ibid., 154–157.

99. Ibid., 169.

100. Ibid., 150, 161.

101. Ibid., 170.

102. Ibid., 171.

103. Ibid.

104. Ibid., 176, emphasis in original.

105. Ibid., 177.

106. The decisions in *Quirin*, *Hirabayashi*, and *Korematsu* did not explicitly recognize such power but, as discussed in this chapter, it can be argued that those decisions had this effect, given the reality that the president had exercised unilateral power in each case (whether or not the Court acknowledged as much).

107. *Youngstown Sheet*, 343 U.S. 579 (1952).

108. Marcus, *Truman and the Steel Seizure Case*, 248.

109. *Youngstown Sheet*, 343 U.S. at 585.

110. Ibid., at 586.

111. Ibid., at 587.

112. By "formalistic" I mean an approach that seeks to clearly delineate between the powers of the different branches of government by describing certain powers as exclusively executive, others as exclusively legislative or judicial. Critics of formalism would likely point to Federalist No. 47, in which James Madison argued that the Constitution was not intended to make the different branches of the federal government "separate and distinct." *The Federalist Papers*, Federalist No. 47, 101–105. Instead, Madison argued, the separation of powers doctrine was intended to avoid "[t]he accumulation of all powers, legislative, executive, and judiciary, in the same hands." Ibid. This was accomplished by checks and balances, a system of overlapping powers rather than hermetically sealed branches of government, each operating independently and in isolation. Ibid.; see also Federalist Nos. 48 and 51, 107–110, 119–122. In Black's defense, he could respond that his approach was also aimed at vindicating Madison's principle by setting limits on presidential power.

113. *Youngstown Sheet*, 343 U.S. at 587–588.

114. Ibid., at 588.

115. Bellia, "Story of the *Steel Seizure* Case," 271. However, critics point to ambiguities and gaps in the tripartite test. See e.g. Patricia L. Bellia, "Executive Power in *Youngstown*'s Shadows," *Constitutional Commentary* 19 (2002): 87, 91: "Justice Jackson's tripartite framework for evaluating executive action is not a framework at all, nor did he necessarily intend it to be."

116. *Youngstown Sheet*, 343 U.S. at 635–636 (Jackson, J., concurring).

117. Ibid., at 637–638. The tripartite test also describes a third category of presidential action, when the president "acts in absence of either a congressional grant or denial of authority . . . rely[ing] upon his own independent powers, but there is a zone of twilight in which he and Congress may have concurrent authority, or in which its distribution is uncertain." Ibid., at 637. The problems of assessing the constitutionality of presidential action that falls into this category are addressed later in this chapter.

118. Ibid., at 639.

119. Ibid., at 640.

120. Ibid. The administration's argument here, supported by reference to the Commander in Chief and Take Care Clauses, anticipated the unitary executive theory, discussed in chapter 1. Jackson's opinion found no constitutional basis for such an argument. Ibid., at 640–646.

121. Ibid., at 640–641. For instance, Article II specifically grants the president power to grant pardons, make treaties (with the advice and consent of the Senate), appoint

ambassadors and judges, and "require the opinion, in writing, of the principal officer in each of the executive departments, upon any subject relating to the duties of their respective offices." U.S. Constitution, art. II, § 2.

122. *Youngstown Sheet*, 343 U.S. at 641 (Jackson, J., concurring).

123. Alexander Hamilton, *Pacificus No. 1*, June 29, 1793, *The Papers of Alexander Hamilton*, Digital Edition, ed. Harold C. Syrett (Charlottesville: University of Virginia Press, Rotunda, 2011), vol. 15. Hamilton argued that "the *executive power* of the nation is vested in the President; subject only to the *exceptions* and *qualifications* which are expressed in the [Constitution]." Hamilton acknowledged that, in some cases, there is a "division of the Executive Power [between the president and Congress]" and the two branches share a "concurrent authority." Ibid.

124. *Youngstown Sheet*, 343 U.S. at 579, 644 (Jackson, J., concurring).

125. U.S. Constitution, art. I, § 8, Amend. III.

126. *Youngstown Sheet*, 343 U.S. at 641 (Jackson, J., concurring).

127. Ibid., at 644.

128. Ibid., at 646.

129. Ibid., at 647.

130. Ibid., at 650, citing U.S. Constitution, art. I, § 9.

131. *Youngstown Sheet*, 343 U.S. at 650 (Jackson, J., concurring).

132. Ibid., at 651.

133. Ibid., at 652–653.

134. Ibid., at 637–638.

135. Marcus, *Truman and the Steel Seizure Case*, 171. In fact, decades later, in the 1981 *Dames & Moore* case, the Supreme Court accepted "a nearly identical" claim by the Carter administration that Congress had implicitly approved of unilateral presidential action based on Congress's "silence in the face of the Carter initiative." Neal Devins and Louis Fisher, "The Steel Seizure Case: One of a Kind?," *Constitutional Commentary* 19, no. 1 (Spring 2002): 83, citing *Dames & Moore v. Regan*, 453 U.S. 654 (1981).

136. *Youngstown Sheet*, 343 U.S. at 637 (Jackson, J., concurring).

137. Ibid.

138. Recall Hamilton's reference to concurrent power in *Pacificus*. Alexander Hamilton, *Pacificus No. 1*, June 29, 1793.

139. *Youngstown Sheet*, 343 U.S. at 637 (Jackson, J., concurring).

140. Ibid.

141. Iwan Morgan, *Nixon* (New York: Oxford University Press, 2002), 159–160, 175.

142. Ibid., 158.

143. After Nixon White House aide Tom Charles Huston.

144. Keith W. Olson, *Watergate: The Presidential Scandal That Shook America* (Lawrence: University of Kansas Press, 2003), 16–17; Morgan, *Nixon*, 175.

145. Olson, *Watergate*, 17–20; Morgan, *Nixon*, 175.

146. Olson, *Watergate*, 19–20. In 1971, Ellsberg made public the Pentagon Papers, a secret history of U.S. involvement in Vietnam, to the *New York Times* and *Washington Post*. Even though the Pentagon Papers mainly revealed information that cast previous administrations in a bad light, Nixon saw Ellsberg as dangerous because he had breached the wall of secrecy that Nixon saw as essential.

147. The Watergate burglary was "part of a larger strategy to effectively rig the 1972 presidential election." Chris Edelson, *Emergency Presidential Power: From the Drafting of the Constitution to the War on Terror* (Madison: University of Wisconsin Press, 2013), 119. The Nixon administration "used campaign contributions to fund political spying and sabotage, including hiring agents to infiltrate [possible Democratic opponent Senator Edmund] Muskie's campaign, spreading false stories about Muskie, stealing stationery from campaign offices in order to send fraudulent letters and press releases intended to discredit Muskie, disrupting campaign events, and tapping Muskie's and other Democratic candidates' phones." Ibid.

148. One special prosecutor, Archibald Cox, was fired in the infamous Saturday Night Massacre of October 20, 1973, when Nixon ordered the Justice Department to close the special prosecutor's office. To their credit, the top two Justice Department officials, Elliot Richardson and William Ruckelshaus, refused to fire Cox. Solicitor General Robert Bork ultimately carried out the task. However, a new special prosecutor, Leon Jaworski, was named on October 31, 1973, and he continued to seek production of the tapes.

149. *United States v. Nixon*, 418 U.S. 683, 703 (1974).

150. Justice Rehnquist recused himself from the case because he had served as a lawyer in the Office of Legal Counsel under Nixon.

151. Edelson, *Emergency Presidential Power*, 124, citing *United States v. Nixon*, 418 U.S. 683 (1974).

152. *United States v. Nixon*, 418 U.S. at 704.

153. Ibid., at 706.

154. 345 U.S. 1.

155. Barton Gellman, *Angler: The Cheney Vice Presidency* (New York: Penguin Press, 2008), 100.

156. Lee H. Hamilton, Chairman, U.S. House of Representatives Select Committee to Investigate Covert Arms Transactions with Iran, and Daniel K. Inouye, Chairman, U.S. Senate Select Committee on Secret Military Assistance to Iran and the Nicaraguan Opposition, *Report of the Congressional Committees Investigating the Iran-Contra Affair* (Washington, D.C.: Government Printing Office, 1987), 3–22.

157. Ibid., 18–19.

158. Ibid., 19.

159. Ibid., 457 (minority report) (emphasis added).

160. Ibid., 469 (minority report).

161. Ibid., 459.

162. Richard W. Stevenson, "Cheney Says 9/11 Changed the Rules," *New York Times*, December 21, 2005.

## Chapter 3.
## The George W. Bush Administration and National Security Power

1. Donna G. Starr-Deelen, *Presidential Policies on Terrorism: From Ronald Reagan to Barack Obama* (New York: Palgrave Macmillan), 1.

2. James P. Pfiffner, *Power Play: The Bush Presidency and the Constitution* (Washington, D.C.: Brookings Institution Press, 2008), 2.

3. Jack Goldsmith, *The Terror Presidency: Law and Judgment inside the Bush Administration* (New York: W. W. Norton, 2007), 205–206.

4. Ibid., 82–90, 97–98, 126.

5. Ibid., 148–149 (describing John Yoo's argument that the president, as commander in chief, could set aside any statute limiting his authority to interrogate prisoners as an "extreme conclusion [with] no foundation in prior OLC opinions, or in judicial decisions, or in any other source of law)"; see also Unclassified Report on the President's Surveillance Program, prepared by Inspectors General for Department of Defense, Department of Justice, Central Intelligence Agency, National Security Agency, and Office of the Director of National Intelligence, July 10, 2009, 21 (after learning of secret warrantless surveillance program known as President's Surveillance Program, it was "of particular concern to [Comey] and Goldsmith . . . that Yoo's legal analysis [justifying the program] entailed ignoring an act of Congress, and doing so without full congressional notification").

6. See Goldsmith, *The Terror Presidency*, 182.

7. Jack Goldsmith, *Power and Constraint: The Accountable Presidency after 9/11* (New York: W. W. Norton, 2012).

8. When Jack Goldsmith suggested that the administration could seek congressional approval for the military detention system set up after 9/11 before the Supreme Court weighed in, David Addington explained the administration's reasons for avoiding congressional approval unless absolutely necessary. Addington demanded of Goldsmith: "Why are you trying to give away the President's power?" Goldsmith, *The Terror Presidency*, 124. Goldsmith explains that "[Addington] believed that the very act of asking for Congress's help would imply, contrary to the White House line, that the President needed legislative approval and could not act on his own." Ibid.

9. See *Hamdan v. Rumsfeld*, 548 U.S. 557 (2006); Military Commissions Act of 2006, Pub. L. No. 109-366, 120 Stat. 2601 (2006).

10. Pfiffner, *Power Play*, 12.

11. Ibid., 12.

12. See Goldsmith, *The Terror Presidency*, 210 (describing the Bush administration's "open chest-thumping about the importance of maintaining and expanding executive power"). Vice President Cheney was a central player, if not the central player, in consistently advancing the argument for unilateral presidential power. He believed that the presidency had been dangerously weakened after Nixon's resignation from office, and Cheney, as vice president, was committed to rebuilding plenary presidential power in order to "restore it so that [Bush and Cheney] could 'hand off a much more powerful presidency' to their successors." Ibid., 86, 88–89, quoting interview with Vice President Cheney, *This Week*, ABC television broadcast, January 27, 2002. Goldsmith writes that Cheney and Addington's "unusual conception of presidential prerogative [i.e., a conception of plenary power] influenced everything they did to meet the post 9/11 threat." *The Terror Presidency*, 89–90. Yoo left the OLC in 2003 to return to academia but has continued to defend the idea of plenary presidential power.

13. Pfiffner, *Power Play*, 12.

14. Peter M. Shane, *Madison's Nightmare: How Executive Power Threatens American Democracy* (Chicago: University of Chicago Press, 2009), 132.

15. Military Commissions Act of 2006, Pub. L. No. 109-366, 120 Stat. 2601 (2006); FISA Amendments Act of 2008, Pub. L. No. 110-261, 122 Stat. 2436. The 2008 FAA took the place of the temporary Protect America Act, which expired in February 2008. Pub. L. No. 110-55, 121 Stat. 552; "What Happens If the Protect America Act Expires?," National Public Radio, February 14, 2008.

16. See e.g. Memorandum opinion from John C. Yoo, Deputy Assistant Attorney General, for Timothy Flanigan, Deputy Counsel to the President, *The President's Constitutional Authority to Conduct Military Operations against Terrorists and Nations Supporting Them* (September 25, 2001).

17. *Youngstown Sheet & Tube Co. v. Sawyer*, 343 U.S. at 635-636 (1952) (Jackson, J., concurring).

18. Ibid., at 636.

19. Goldsmith, *The Terror Presidency*, 140. Goldsmith suggests that the Bush administration acted unilaterally because it "was afraid of tying the President's hands in ways that would prevent him from doing what was necessary to protect the American people," not because there was no time to consult Congress.

20. Goldsmith describes this as a point of view based on the Bush administration's "unquestioned commitment to a peculiar conception of executive power." Ibid.

21. See Harold Hongju Koh, *The National Security Constitution: Sharing Power after the Iran-Contra Affair* (New Haven: Yale University Press, 1990), 157. Koh described congressional acquiescence as a problem when the president takes unilateral action by exploiting "statutory lacunae and pockets of unregulated activity." Ibid., 158. In such cases, the president counts on the likelihood of congressional inaction and does not seek statutory approval. Ibid., 117-118. However, deferential congressional endorsement of presidential action is another example of the same problem: acquiescence need not be silent.

## Chapter 4.
### The Bush Administration and the Use of Military Force

1. Jack Goldsmith, *The Terror Presidency: Law and Judgment inside the Bush Administration* (New York: W. W. Norton, 2007), 97, citing Memorandum opinion from John C. Yoo, Deputy Assistant Attorney General, for Timothy Flanigan, Deputy Counsel to the President, *The President's Constitutional Authority to Conduct Military Operations against Terrorists and Nations Supporting Them* (September 25, 2001) (hereinafter September 25, 2001, Yoo memo).

2. September 25, 2001, Yoo memo, 23-24: "In light of the text, plan, and history of the Constitution, its interpretation by both past Administrations and the courts, the long-standing practice of the executive branch, and the express affirmation of the President's constitutional authorities by Congress, we think it beyond question that the President has the plenary constitutional power to take such military actions as he deems necessary and appropriate to respond to the terrorist attacks upon the United States on September 11, 2001. Force can be used both to retaliate for those attacks, and to prevent and deter future assaults on the Nation. Military actions need not be limited to those individuals, groups, or states that participated in the attacks on the World Trade Center and the Pentagon: the

Constitution vests the President with the power to strike terrorist groups or organizations that cannot be demonstrably linked to the September 11 incidents, but that, nonetheless, pose a similar threat to the security of the United States and the lives of its people, whether at home or overseas."

3. Pub. L. No. 107–40, 115 Stat. 224 (2001).

4. September 25, 2001, Yoo memo, 23–24. In passing the AUMF, Congress did not give the Bush administration all the power it sought. After 9/11, "the Bush administration . . . had sought an even broader and more open-ended grant of authority [than Congress provided in the AUMF]." Jennifer Daskal and Stephen I. Vladeck, "After the AUMF," *Harvard National Security Journal* 5 (2014): 115. Yoo's memo concluded, however, that President Bush was not bound by the statutory limits Congress set.

5. September 25, 2001, Yoo memo, 24.

6. Ibid., 8: "Conducting military hostilities is a central tool for the exercise of the President's plenary control over the conduct of foreign policy." See also James P. Pfiffner, *Power Play: The Bush Presidency and the Constitution* (Washington, D.C.: Brookings Institution Press, 2008), 2, arguing that "President Bush . . . claimed powers once asserted by kings."

7. September 25, 2001, Yoo memo, 6.

8. Louis Fisher, *Defending Congress and the Constitution* (Lawrence: University Press of Kansas, 2011), 14–15. See also David Gray Adler, "The Framers and Executive Prerogative: A Constitutional and Historical Rebuke," *Presidential Studies Quarterly* 42, no. 2 (June 2012): 376, 378 (arguing that even if inherent power might be derived from Article II, it remains "specious").

9. Pfiffner, *Power Play*, 70–71; see also Fisher, *Defending Congress and the Constitution*, 235–241.

10. Federalist Nos. 47, 48, 51 in Alexander Hamilton, John Jay, and James Madison, *The Federalist Papers*, ed. Michael A. Genovese (New York: Palgrave Macmillan, 2009), 101–110, 119–122.

11. Adler, "The Framers and Executive Prerogative," 379–381.

12. U.S. Constitution, art. I, § 8. Congress is also assigned other war powers under Article I, section 8, including the power to "grant letters of marque and reprisal," to "make rules concerning captures on land and water," "to provide for calling forth the militia to execute the laws of the union, suppress insurrections and repel invasions," "to make rules for the government regulation of the land and naval forces," and "to raise and support armies . . . [and] to provide and maintain a navy." Ibid.

13. September 25, 2001, Yoo memo, 4.

14. Ibid., 4–5.

15. Max Farrand, ed., *The Records of the Federal Convention of 1787* (New Haven: Yale University Press, 1937), 2:318–319; see also Pfiffner, *Power Play*, 77.

16. Fisher, *Defending Congress and the Constitution*, 241.

17. Ibid.

18. M. Andrew Campanelli, Kai Draper, and Jack Stucker, "The Original Understanding of the Declare War Clause," *Journal of Law and Politics* 24 (Winter 2008): 49.

19. Pfiffner, *Power Play*, 75.

20. Jack Rakove, *Original Meanings: Politics and Ideas in the Making of the Constitution* (New York: Vintage Books, 1997), 263.

21. Louis Fisher, "Teaching the Presidency: Idealizing a Constitutional Office," *PS: Political Science and Politics* 45, no. 1 (January 2012): 18–19; Pfiffner, *Power Play,* 74.

22. Pfiffner, *Power Play,* 74, quoting John Jay, *The Federalist Papers,* Federalist No. 4. Fisher makes the same point, quoting Federalist No. 4 and concluding that "[t]he framers placed in Congress the authority to initiate war because they believed that executives, in their search for fame and personal glory, had a natural appetite for war and military initiatives, all of which inflicted heavy costs on the interests and liberties of their people." Fisher, "Teaching the Presidency," 18–19.

23. Pfiffner, *Power Play,* 74, quoting *Helvidius* in Gaillard Hunt, ed., *The Writings of James Madison* (New York: G. P. Putnam's Sons, 1900–10), 6:146 (emphasis in original).

24. Pfiffner, *Power Play,* 70–71; Fisher, *Defending Congress and the Constitution,* 235–241.

25. Fisher, "John Yoo and the Republic," *Presidential Studies Quarterly* 41, no. 1 (March 2011): 179.

26. Ibid., quoting Wilson.

27. David Grey Adler, "Presidential Power and Foreign Affairs in the Bush Administration: The Use and Abuse of Alexander Hamilton," *Presidential Studies Quarterly* 40, no. 3 (September 2010): 531, 536. Adler notes that, throughout his career, "[a]gain and again, Hamilton denied the existence of a presidential power to initiate hostilities." Ibid., 541.

28. Ibid., 540, quoting Hamilton.

29. September 25, 2001, Yoo memo, 7.

30. See Section I for detailed discussion of the problems with the sole organ doctrine.

31. September 25, 2001, Yoo memo, 7.

32. Alexander Hamilton, *Pacificus No. 1,* June 29, 1793, *The Papers of Alexander Hamilton,* Digital Edition, ed. Harold C. Syrett (Charlottesville: University of Virginia Press, Rotunda, 2011), vol. 15 (emphasis in original).

33. Ibid.

34. Ibid.

35. Ibid.

36. If Yoo had considered other writings of Hamilton's, most notably Federalist No. 69, he would have been forced to recognize that Hamilton clearly recognized limits on presidential power over both the military and foreign affairs. However, Yoo's September 25, 2001, memo did not address Federalist No. 69 at all. Law professor Richard Epstein rightly called the Bush administration's failure to consider Federalist No. 69 "scandalous." Charlie Savage, "Recommended Reading," *Boston Globe,* June 11, 2006.

37. In addition to citing Marshall's sole organ reference and Hamilton's *Pacificus* essay, Yoo oddly attempts to enlist Thomas Jefferson as a believer in plenary presidential power. September 25, 2001, Yoo memo. Yoo bases this conclusion on Jefferson's statement that "the transaction of business with foreign nations is executive altogether; it belongs, then, to the head of that department, except as to such portions of it as are specially submitted to the senate. Exceptions are to be construed strictly." Ibid., quoting Thomas Jefferson, *Opinion on the Powers of the Senate* (1790), reprinted in *The Writings of Thomas Jefferson,* ed. Paul L. Ford (New York: G.P. Putnam's Sons, 1895), 5:61. But Jefferson's statement only

makes the point that it falls to the president to represent the nation in interactions with foreign nations. This is similar to Marshall's point in his sole organ speech that it falls to the president to carry out policy as expressed by law. Jefferson was certainly no advocate of unbounded presidential power. Perhaps most famously, he objected to Hamilton's position in *Pacificus* (which, as discussed, did not even go so far as to endorse plenary power) for concentrating too much power in the hands of the president. Jefferson urged Madison to "take up [his] pen" in *Helvidius* in order to expose what Jefferson believed was the danger involved in reading the Constitution to give the president excessive power over foreign affairs. Jefferson letter to Madison, July 7, 1793, *The Papers of Thomas Jefferson*, Digital Edition, ed. Barbara B. Oberg and J. Jefferson Looney (Charlottesville: University of Virginia Press, Rotunda, 2008), vol. 26.

38. Adler, "Presidential Power and Foreign Affairs in the Bush Administration."

39. Authorization for Use of Military Force against Iraq, Pub. L. No. 107–243, 116 Stat. 1498 (2002). After Congress passed the 2002 Iraq AUMF, the Office of Legal Counsel produced another memo that, like Yoo's September 25, 2001, memo, concluded the president had "unilateral power to take military action to protect the national security interests of the United States." Memorandum from Jay S. Bybee, Assistant Attorney General, Office of Legal Counsel, to the Counsel to the President, *Authority of the President under Domestic and International Law to Use Military Force against Iraq* (October 23, 2002) (hereinafter October 23, 2002, Bybee memo), 48. Like Yoo's 2001 memo, Bybee's 2002 memo cited the sole organ doctrine and incorrectly claimed that "[t]he Constitution nowhere requires for the exercise of [military force] the consent of Congress." Ibid., 7–8.

40. Goldsmith, *The Terror Presidency*, 98.

41. October 23, 2002, Bybee memo, 7.

## Chapter 5.
### The Bush Administration and Surveillance

1. Jack Goldsmith, *The Terror Presidency: Law and Judgment inside the Bush Administration* (New York: W. W. Norton, 2007), 182.

2. In the *Terror Presidency*, Goldsmith refers to the program as the "Terrorist Surveillance Program." The Terrorist Surveillance program, we now know, was only part of the larger Presidential Surveillance Program, as discussed in Section III. Office of Director of National Intelligence, "DNI Announces the Declassification of the Existence of Collection Activities Authorized by President George W. Bush Shortly after the Attacks of September 11, 2001," *IC on the Record*, December 21, 2013.

3. Unclassified Report on the President's Surveillance Program, July 10, 2009, 5; Office of Director of National Intelligence, "DNI Announces the Declassification of the Existence of Collection Activities." The PSP was "authorized in a single Presidential Authorization" that was periodically reauthorized every thirty to sixty days. Ibid.

4. Even intelligence analysts who used information gained through the program often did not know where the information came from. Chris Edelson, *Emergency Presidential Power: From the Drafting of the Constitution to the War on Terror* (Madison: University of Wisconsin Press, 2013), 228.

5. James Risen and Eric Lichtblau, "Bush Lets U.S. Spy on Callers without Courts," *New York Times*, December 16, 2005.

6. Unclassified Report on the President's Surveillance Program, July 10, 2009, 4–5. Information about bulk telephony metadata collection during the Obama administration came to light in 2013 after Edward Snowden made key documents available to reporters. Glenn Greenwald, "NSA Collecting Phone Records of Millions of Verizon Customers Daily," *Guardian*, June 5, 2013; Barton Gellman, "U.S. Surveillance Architecture Includes Collection of Revealing Internet, Phone Metadata," *Washington Post*, June 15, 2013. Reporting in 2006 had described bulk telephony metadata collection by the Bush administration. Leslie Cauley, "NSA Has Massive Database of Americans' Phone Calls," *USA Today*, May 10, 2006. The bulk metadata collection of telephone records is discussed in more detail in Section III. Section III also discusses surveillance conducted pursuant to FISA Section 702. These activities are related to the PSP, although Section 702 was not enacted until 2008. Privacy and Civil Liberties Oversight Board, report on the Surveillance Program Operated Pursuant to Section 702 of the Foreign Intelligence Surveillance Act, July 2, 2014, 5: "Section 702 has its roots in the President's Surveillance Program developed in the immediate aftermath of the September 11th attacks."

7. Unclassified Report on the President's Surveillance Program, July 10, 2009, 1, 4–5.

8. Edelson, *Emergency Presidential Power*, 228.

9. Unclassified Report on the President's Surveillance Program, July 10, 2009, 4.

10. Edelson, *Emergency Presidential Power*, 228.

11. 50 U.S.C. §§ 1801 et seq; Unclassified Report on the President's Surveillance Program, July 10, 2009, 21. FISA has since been amended, as discussed in Section III.

12. 50 U.S.C. § 1812.

13. The FISA court, or Foreign Intelligence Surveillance Court (FISC), consists of federal district court judges from around the United States who are named by the U.S. Supreme Court's Chief Justice to serve on the court. FISC judges issue warrants on the basis of a lesser showing of probable cause than is required for ordinary warrants issued in a domestic law enforcement context. The FISC issues warrants if there is "probable cause to believe that the target of the surveillance is a foreign power or an agent of a foreign power . . . and each of the facilities or places at which the electronic surveillance is directed is being used, or is about to be used, by a foreign power or an agent of a foreign power." It is extraordinarily rare for FISC judges to deny warrants; applications have been denied only a handful of times in the more than thirty-five years that the court has been in existence. Edelson, *Emergency Presidential Power*, 26, 322 n. 14. As discussed in Section III, the 2008 FISA amendments now grant the executive branch "authority to engage in broadscale warrantless programmatic surveillance." The Constitution Project's Liberty and Security Committee, "Report on the FISA Amendments Act of 2008," September 6, 2012, 9. The information in this note about the warrant process applies to FISA before the 2008 amendments.

14. 50 U.S.C. §§ 1801(a), 1802, 1805(e)(1)(D), § 1811. FISA has since been amended to permit warrantless surveillance for up to 168 hours in emergencies.

15. 50 U.S.C. § 1801(i).

16. 50 U.S.C. § 1809(c).

17. Goldsmith, *The Terror Presidency*, 181.

18. Memorandum for the Attorney General from John C. Yoo (November 2, 2001) (hereinafter November 2, 2001, Yoo memo); see also Jameel Jaffer, "The Surveillance Memos and a Suggestion for Jack Goldsmith," ACLU Blog of Rights, March 25, 2011: "[Yoo's November 2001 memo] contends that the president has authority as Commander in Chief of the Armed Forces to disregard [FISA]. . . . It also contends that Congress doesn't have the power to regulate the president's authority to gather intelligence for national security purposes."

19. The heavily redacted memo was released in response to a FOIA request made by the ACLU. Jameel Jaffer, "Secrecy and Surveillance," ACLU Blog of Rights, March 24, 2011.

20. November 2, 2001, Yoo memo, 17, 12, 17.

21. I say "apparently" because most of the memo has been redacted, and it is possible that Yoo addressed this question in the redacted portions of the memo.

22. Unclassified Report on the President's Surveillance Program, July 10, 2009, 19–20.

23. Ibid., 20–22. Comey had discussed with Ashcroft his concerns about the program. Ibid., 25.

24. Ibid., 23.

25. Ibid., 23–24. Comey's reference to "my people" is remarkable. It suggests that Comey saw Gonzales and Card—who were executive branch officials acting on behalf of the president—as rivals or even adversaries.

26. Ibid., 25. Part of this account comes from Comey's testimony before the Senate Judiciary Committee.

27. Ibid., 26–27. Goldsmith had prepared a letter of resignation explaining that the "shameful" visit Gonzales and Card had made to Ashcroft in the hospital was one of his reasons for resigning. Ashcroft's chief of staff asked Comey to wait until Ashcroft had recovered so that they could resign together. Ibid., 27.

28. Ibid., 29.

29. The July 10, 2009, Unclassified Report on the PSP states that "on March 17, 2004, the President decided to modify certain PSP intelligence-gathering activities and to discontinue certain Other Intelligence Activities [meaning still-classified activities that were not part of the TSP] that DOJ believed were legally unsupported." Ibid.

30. Jaffer, "The Surveillance Memos and a Suggestion for Jack Goldsmith."

31. Jack L. Goldsmith III, "Memorandum for the Attorney General re: Review of the Legality of the [redacted] Program," May 6, 2004, 37, 51–52.

32. Ibid., 64. Text after "contemplated in" is redacted, but it is clear that the sentence must refer to foreign intelligence surveillance, presumably either some or all of the activities included in the PSP.

33. Ibid., 51–52, 70.

34. Jaffer, "The Surveillance Memos and a Suggestion for Jack Goldsmith."

35. Jack Goldsmith, "DOJ Releases Redacted Version of 2004 Surveillance Opinion," *Lawfare*, March 18, 2011.

36. Department of Justice, "Legal Authorities Supporting the Activities of the National Security Agency Described by the President," January 19, 2006, 1; see also ibid., 5, describing warrantless surveillance of Americans carried out under the TSP.

37. Ibid., 2; see also ibid., 23–28.

38. Ibid., 3. As an aside, describing the warrantless surveillance of Americans' overseas communications as a "narrow context" is perplexing, to put it mildly.

39. Ibid., 7; see also ibid., 30 (invoking unitary executive theory and sole organ doctrine to justify inherent presidential power in the area of foreign intelligence surveillance).

40. Ibid., 10.

41. William E. Moschella, Assistant Attorney General, to Senators Pat Roberts and Jay Rockefeller and Representatives Peter Hoekstra and Jane Harman, December 22, 2005.

42. Prepared Remarks of Attorney General Alberto R. Gonzales, Georgetown University Law Center, January 24, 2006.

43. See Goldsmith, *The Terror Presidency*, 182: "From the beginning the [Bush] administration could have [worked with Congress and the FISA court] to ramp up terrorist surveillance in indisputably lawful ways that would have minimized the likelihood of a devastating national security leak . . . [but] [t]he White House had found it much easier to go it alone, in secret."

44. James P. Pfiffner, *Power Play: The Bush Presidency and the Constitution* (Washington, D.C.: Brookings Institution Press, 2008), 10. The 2007 legislation was the Protect America Act, Pub. L. No. 110-55, 121 Stat. 552. The 2008 legislation was the FISA Amendments Act of 2008, Pub. L. No. 110-261, 122 Stat. 2436 (codified at 50 U.S.C. § 1881a). It has since been reauthorized and extended by the FISA Amendments Act Reauthorization Act of 2012, Pub. L. No. 112-238, 126 Stat. 1631.

45. The Constitution Project's Liberty and Security Committee, "Report on the FISA Amendments Act of 2008.

46. Pfiffner, *Power Play*, 12.


## Chapter 6.
## The Bush Administration and Military Detention

1. The terms "military commissions" and "military tribunals" are used interchangeably.

2. Memorandum from Patrick F. Philbin, Deputy Assistant Attorney General, Office of Legal Counsel, to Counsel to the President, *Legality of the Use of Military Commissions to Try Terrorists* (November 6, 2001), 1 (hereinafter November 6, 2001, Philbin memo). Note that Philbin's memo refers to "terrorists" to be held or tried in the military system. In fact, the prisoners Philbin referred to were mainly suspected terrorists, as their status had generally not been determined at the time they were placed in the military detention system.

3. Ibid., 6–10.

4. Major John Andre was a British officer who plotted with the American general Benedict Arnold to arrange for the American fort at West Point, New York, to be handed over to the British. After meeting with Arnold, Andre was captured behind American lines, tried, and executed as a spy.

5. November 6, 2001, Philbin memo, 7.

6. Scott Horton, "Six Questions for Louis Fisher, Author of *The Constitution and 9/11*," *Harper's Magazine*, January 5, 2009. Philbin attempted to rely on additional historical evidence to support his argument that the president possesses inherent power to convene

military tribunals, pointing to the military trial of the Lincoln assassination conspirators in 1865. November 6, 2001, Philbin memo, 9–10. Fisher's work, again, shows that Philbin's citation to the historical record is misplaced. Critics, including Lincoln's first attorney general, described the 1865 trial as "unlawful" and a "gross blunder" in which the tribunal operated as "a law unto itself . . . [making] its own rules of procedure . . . [and serving] as the sole judge of the law, as well as of the facts." Louis Fisher, *Military Tribunals and Presidential Power: American Revolution to the War on Terrorism* (Lawrence: University Press of Kansas: 2005), 65–69. Citing the Lincoln trial as precedent is similar to citing the flawed proceedings for the German saboteurs during World War II.

7. Philbin suggested that the drafters of the Constitution intended to assign the president, through the Commander in Chief Clause, "the fullest possible range of power available to a military commander." November 6, 2001, Philbin memo, 7, citing John Yoo, "The Continuation of Politics by Other Means: The Original Understanding of War Powers," *California Law Review* 84 (1996): 167, 252–254. But Philbin's (and Yoo's) understanding of the Commander in Chief Clause is obviously incorrect. The Framers clearly did not assign the president under the Constitution the same "range of power" over the military that the British king possessed at the time, as Alexander Hamilton made clear in Federalist No. 69, where he listed specific ways in which the American president had less power than the British king.

8. See Jack Goldsmith, *The Terror Presidency: Law and Judgment inside the Bush Administration* (New York: W. W. Norton, 2007), 109: "Bush's military commission order [of November 13, 2001] was modeled on Roosevelt's order creating the commission that tried eight Nazi saboteurs."

9. Military Order of November 13, 2001: Detention, Treatment, and Trial of Certain Non-Citizens in the War against Terrorism, 66 Fed. Reg. 57, 833, November 16, 2001.

10. Ibid., § 2(a).

11. Ibid., § 4. This was despite the fact that the Uniform Code of Military Justice required military tribunals to follow rules used by courts-martial unless the president determined it was "not practicable" to do so. President Bush's Military Order concluded that it was not practicable for military tribunals to follow rules used by federal district courts but contained no such finding with regard to the impracticability of using court-martial rules. Ibid., § 1(f).

12. Ibid., §§ 3, 7(b); see also Andrei Scheinckman, Margot Williams, Alan McLean, Jeremy Ashkenas, Archie Tise, and Jacob Harris, "The Guantanamo Docket: The Detainees," *New York Times*, accessed online September 23, 2015, at http://projects.nytimes.com /guantanamo/detainees: "Of the roughly 780 people who have been detained at the United States military prison at Guantánamo Bay, Cuba, 657 have been transferred and 114 remain, according to an ongoing analysis by The New York Times and NPR. In addition, nine detainees died while in custody."

13. Richard M. Pious, "Prerogative Power in the Obama Administration: Continuity and Change in the War on Terrorism," *Presidential Studies Quarterly* 41, no. 2 ( June 2011): 272.

14. Chris Edelson, *Emergency Presidential Power: From the Drafting of the Constitution to the War on Terror* (Madison: University of Wisconsin Press, 2013), 156–159.

15. Military Order of November 13, 2001, § 7(a): "Nothing in this order shall be construed to . . . limit the lawful authority of the Secretary of Defense, any military commander, or any other officer or agent of the United States or of any State to detain or try *any* person who is not an individual subject to this order" (emphasis added).

16. Fisher, *The Constitution and 9/11: Recurring Threats to America's Freedoms* (Lawrence: University Press of Kansas, 2008), 190, 197.

17. Edelson, *Emergency Presidential Power*, 158–159.

18. More precisely, relatives filed these petitions on behalf of the prisoners.

19. *Rasul v. Bush*, 542 U.S. 466 (2004), superseded by Detainee Treatment Act of 2005, Pub. L. No. 109-148, div. A, 1001–06, 119 Stat. 2680, 2739, quoting 28 U.S.C. §§ 2241(a), (c)(3); *Hamdi v. Rumsfeld*, 542 U.S. 507 (2004).

20. *Rasul*, 542 U.S. at 475–476. The Court in *Rasul* did not consider the legality of President Bush's military order. It decided only that prisoners at Guantanamo had a statutory right to habeas corpus.

21. *Hamdi*, 542 U.S. at 516–517 (O'Connor, J., plurality opinion).

22. Ibid., at 517. Four justices—Souter, Ginsburg, Scalia, and Stevens—would have held that the AUMF did not provide authority for the president to detain Hamdi, and, absent express congressional authorization (Souter and Ginsburg) or suspension of habeas corpus (Scalia and Stevens), these four justices would have required the executive branch to either indict Hamdi and try him in the criminal justice system or release him. Ibid., at 541 (Souter, J., concurring in part, dissenting in part, and concurring in the judgment); ibid., at 573 (Scalia, J., dissenting). However, Justices Souter and Ginsburg concurred in the judgment reached by the plurality opinion in order "to give practical effect to the conclusions of eight members of the Court rejecting the government's position." Ibid., at 553 (Souter, J., concurring in part, dissenting in part, and concurring in the judgment).

23. Ibid., at 536 (O'Connor, J., plurality opinion).

24. Ibid., at 535 (O'Connor, J., plurality opinion).

25. Ibid., at 536 (O'Connor, J., plurality opinion). However, O'Connor concluded that the limited hearing she and three other justices believed was required could be provided in a military tribunal. Ibid., at 538.

26. Ibid., at 572 (Scalia, J., dissenting).

27. Ibid., at 569 (Scalia, J., dissenting).

28. Ibid., at 545 (Souter, J., concurring in part, dissenting in part, and concurring in the judgment).

29. Charlie Savage, *Takeover: The Return of the Imperial Presidency and the Subversion of American Democracy* (New York: Little, Brown, 2007), 194.

30. *Hamdi*, 542 U.S. at 509 (O'Connor, J., plurality opinion).

31. Deputy Secretary of Defense Paul Wolfowitz, Memorandum for the Secretary of the Navy: Order Establishing Combatant Status Review Tribunal, July 7, 2004 (hereinafter July 7, 2004, CSRT Order).

32. Ibid., ¶¶ a, g(12).

33. Ibid., ¶ a.

34. *Hamdi*, 542 U.S. at 521 (O'Connor, J., plurality opinion).

35. July 7, 2004, CSRT Order, ¶ g(12). The preponderance of the evidence standard

required the government simply to show that it is more likely than not the case that the prisoner could be held as an enemy combatant. This is the standard generally used in civil lawsuits and essentially meant that the government would win if it was more than 50 percent likely that the evidence weighed in its favor.

36. Ibid., ¶ g(12).

37. Ibid., ¶ c.

38. Ibid., ¶ g(9).

39. Edelson, *Emergency Presidential Power*, 199.

40. July 7, 2004, CSRT Order, ¶¶ f, h.

41. Edelson, *Emergency Presidential Power*, 182. The 2005 DTA allowed for judicial review of CSRT decisions by the U.S. Court of Appeals for the District of Columbia Circuit. The Court of Appeals' role on appeal was limited to considering whether the CSRT had followed procedures created by the executive branch and, to the extent the Constitution and statutory law applied, whether those procedures were lawful. The Court of Appeals did not have the ability to overrule CSRT determinations in specific cases.

42. Joseph Margulies, *Guantanamo and the Abuse of Presidential Power* (New York: Simon and Schuster, 2006), 169.

43. Roza Pati, *Due Process and International Terrorism: An International Legal Analysis* (Leiden and Boston: Martinus Nijhoff, 2010), 347, n. 284; see also Celisse Pinkney and Almerindo Ojeda, "The Evanescent Exonerations of Guantanamo Bay," Center for the Study of Human Rights in the Americas, University of California at Davis, undated, http://humanrights.ucdavis.edu/reports/the-evanescent-exonerations-of-guantanamo-bay. Some of the prisoners who were initially found not to be enemy combatants were later found to be enemy combatants by "subsequently formed military panels acting on subsequently found evidence." Ibid.

44. Mark Denbeaux and Joshua Denbeaux, "Report on Guantanamo Detainees: A Profile of 517 Detainees through Analysis of Department of Defense Data," February 8, 2006, 22, 4.

45. Margulies, *Guantanamo*, 162; see also Denbeaux and Denbeaux, "Report on Guantanamo Detainees," 10.

46. Denbeaux and Denbeaux, "Report on Guantanamo Detainees," 9.

47. Margulies, *Guantanamo*, 169.

48. Denbeaux and Denbeaux, "Report on Guantanamo Detainees," 15.

49. Ibid., 21. The Uighurs were released by the Obama administration. Richard A. Serrano, "U.S. Releases Last 3 Uighur Detainees at Guantanamo," *Los Angeles Times*, December 31, 2013. Other prisoners who the government concedes are not enemy combatants continue to be held at Guantanamo by the Obama administration, as discussed in Section III.

50. Chief Justice Roberts recused himself because he had heard the case as a judge on the D.C. Circuit Court of Appeals before he joined the Supreme Court.

51. *Hamdan v. Rumsfeld*, 548 U.S. 557 (2006). Four justices would have also held that conspiracy cannot be charged as a war crime and that the specific procedures created by the Bush administration violated Common Article 3. A fifth justice, Kennedy, did not find it necessary to decide those questions but did agree with the other four—Stevens, Souter,

Ginsburg, and Breyer—that the tribunal's procedures violated the UCMJ and that the tribunal did not comply with Common Article 3 of the Geneva Conventions because it was not a "regularly constituted court." Ibid., at 637 (Kennedy, J., concurring).

52. James P. Pfiffner, *Power Play: The Bush Presidency and the Constitution* (Washington, D.C.: Brookings Institution Press, 2008), 108; see also Goldsmith, *The Terror Presidency*, 208.

53. Though, of course, the Supreme Court had ignored this in the *Quirin* decision, which relied on the fiction that Congress had authorized the tribunal Roosevelt created.

54. Edelson, *Emergency Presidential Power*, 198–200.

55. Pub. L. No. 109–366, 120 Stat. 2601 (2006), § 6(a)(3)(A).

56. Ibid., § 950g(c). The 2006 MCA also provided that the court of appeals could "act only with respect to matters of law." Ibid., §§ 950f(d), 950g(b).

57. Ibid., § 7. The Court struck down this section of the MCA in the 2008 *Boumediene v. Bush* decision. 553 U.S. 723 (2008).

## Chapter 7.
## The Bush Administration and Torture

1. Memorandum from Assistant Attorney General Jay S. Bybee to Acting General Counsel of the CIA John Rizzo, *Interrogation of al Qaeda Operative* (August 1, 2002) (hereinafter Rizzo memo); Memorandum from Assistant Attorney General Jay S. Bybee to Alberto R. Gonzales, Counsel to the President, *Re: Standards of Conduct for Interrogation under 18 U.S.C. §§ 2340–2340A*, August 1, 2002 (hereinafter Yoo-Bybee memo). Although the Yoo-Bybee memo was signed by Jay Bybee, it was drafted by John Yoo. Jack Goldsmith, *The Terror Presidency: Law and Judgment inside the Bush Administration* (New York: W. W. Norton, 2007), 142.

2. Chris Edelson, *Emergency Presidential Power: From the Drafting of the Constitution to the War on Terror* (Madison: University of Wisconsin Press, 2013), 206–211. The CIA wanted to place Zubaydah in a box with an insect because they had learned he feared poisonous insects. Their plan was to tell Zubaydah that the insect could sting him, though it would actually be harmless. Ibid., 207. Although OLC approved the use of this method, along with the other proposed methods, Zubaydah was never placed in a box with an insect. However, he was waterboarded and subjected to sleep deprivation. Ibid., 210–211. It turned out that Zubaydah, though associated with al Qaeda, was not actually a leader in the organization. Ibid., 318 n. 15.

3. 18 U.S.C. § 2441(c), (d)(1); 18 U.S.C. § 2340(1). The anti-torture law, 18 U.S.C. §§ 2340–2340B, provides for statutory enforcement of United States treaty obligations under the United Nations Convention against Torture and Other Cruel, Inhuman, or Degrading Treatment or Punishment (CAT). The CAT requires the United States and other signatories to make all acts of torture a crime. Although existing federal, state, and local laws already applied to acts of torture occurring within the United States, the anti-torture law was enacted in order to ensure that torture occurring outside the United States was also criminalized. Michael John Garcia, "U.N. Convention against Torture (CAT): Overview and Application to Interrogation Methods," Congressional Research Service, January 26, 2009.

4. Goldsmith, *The Terror Presidency*, 97.

5. Yoo-Bybee memo; see also Goldsmith, *The Terror Presidency*, 145. Charles Taylor Jr., a/k/a Roy M. Belfast Jr., a/k/a Charles McArthur Emmanuel, "attached a copy of the [Yoo-Bybee] memo to proposed jury instructions" in his 2008 torture trial in federal court. Johnny Dwyer, "A War Crimes Trial in Florida," *Time*, October 3, 2008. Taylor, the son of the former Liberian dictator Charles Taylor, was unsuccessful in his attempt to use the Yoo-Bybee memo as a defense. He was the first person to be convicted under the U.S. anti-torture statute. *U.S. v. Belfast*, 611 F.3d 783 (11th Cir. 2010), *cert. denied* 131 S. Ct. 1511 (2011).

6. Yoo-Bybee memo.

7. Goldsmith, *The Terror Presidency*, 145.

8. Ibid., 24–25. Then-Attorney General John Ashcroft did not want Yoo heading up OLC.

9. Ibid., 142, 148, 146.

10. Ibid., 146, quoting Yoo-Bybee memo.

11. Ibid., 147, noting the memo "implied that [in addition to the anti-torture statute] many other federal laws that limit interrogation—anti-assault laws, the 1996 War Crimes Act, and the Uniform Code of Military Justice—are also unconstitutional, a conclusion that would have surprised the many prior presidents who signed or ratified those laws, or complied with them during wartime."

12. Ibid., 147, 151. Goldsmith was also concerned that the Yoo-Bybee memo "rested on cursory and one-sided legal arguments that failed to consider Congress's competing wartime constitutional authorities, or the many Supreme Court decisions [most notably *Youngstown Sheet*] potentially in tension with the conclusion [that the president could set aside laws regulating interrogation methods]." Ibid., 149. Overall, Goldsmith described the memo as "legally flawed, tendentious in substance and tone, and overbroad and thus largely unnecessary." Ibid., 151.

13. Ibid., 159. It took Goldsmith six months to do this, in part because he found it very difficult to write a replacement opinion and in part because he had other priorities. Ibid., 155–158.

14. Ibid., 160–161.

15. Memorandum from Daniel Levin, Acting Assistant Attorney General, Office of Legal Counsel, to James B. Comey, Deputy Attorney General, *Legal Standards Applicable under 18 U.S.C. §§ 2340–2340A* (December 30, 2004) (hereinafter Levin memo).

16. Trevor W. Morrison, "Constitutional Alarmism," *Harvard Law Review* 124 (2011): 1688, 1726 n. 144.

17. Jeffrey Rosen, "Conscience of a Conservative," *New York Times Magazine*, September 9, 2007, 40. Rosen refers to more than one withdrawn opinion. The Levin memo purported to supersede only the Yoo-Bybee memo. Rosen may also be referring to a March 2003 OLC opinion from Yoo to the Defense Department, entitled *Military Interrogation of Alien Unlawful Combatants Held outside the United States*. Goldsmith also withdrew that opinion—or, at least, told Jim Haynes, then General Counsel for the Pentagon, not to rely on the March 2003 opinion. Goldsmith, *The Terror Presidency*, 153–155.

18. Levin memo.

19. John Yoo, *War by Other Means: An Insider's Account of the War on Terror* (New York: Atlantic Monthly Press, 2006), 182–183.

20. Andrew Kaufman, "*Lochner* for the Executive Branch: The Torture Memo as Anticanon," *Harvard Law and Policy Review* 7 (2013): 199, 212.

21. Levin memo.

22. Kaufman, "*Lochner* for the Executive Branch," 212–213.

23. Memorandum from Steven G. Bradbury to John A. Rizzo, Senior Deputy General Counsel, Central Intelligence Agency, *Application of 18 U.S.C. §§ 2340–2340A to Certain Techniques That May Be Used in the Interrogation of a High Value al Qaeda Detainee*, May 10, 2005 (hereinafter May 2005 Bradbury memo). The Bradbury memo also authorized other interrogation methods. Bradbury wrote a separate memo to Rizzo, also dated May 10, 2005, entitled *Application of 18 U.S.C. §§ 2340–2340A to the Combined Use of Certain Techniques in the Interrogation of High Value al Qaeda Detainees*. The *Combined Use* memo is not addressed separately, as it addresses the same questions involving the definition of torture that are discussed here in the context of the May 2005 Bradbury memo.

24. 18 U.S.C. §§ 2340(1).

25. Spencer Ackerman, "Former Navy Instructor Offers Another Waterboarding Primer for Mukasey," *TPM Muckraker*, October 31, 2007.

26. Eric Weiner, "Waterboarding: A Tortured History," National Public Radio, November 3, 2007; Evan Wallach, "Waterboarding Used to Be a Crime," *Washington Post*, November 4, 2007; *United States v. Lee*, 744 F.2d 1124 (5th Cir. 1984).

27. Megan Lane and Brian Wheeler, "The Real Victims of Sleep Deprivation," *BBC News Online Magazine*, January 8, 2004.

28. *Ashcraft v. Tennessee*, 322 U.S. 143, 150 (1944), quoting "Report of Committee on Lawless Enforcement of Law made to the Section of Criminal Law and Criminology of the American Bar Association," *American Journal of Police Science* 1 (1930): 575, 579–580.

29. May 2005 Bradbury memo, 6, n. 9.

30. Ibid., 36–45. The Department of Justice's Office of Personal Responsibility later "question[ed] whether it was reasonable . . . to accept such representations [by CIA medical staff] at face value." Department of Justice Office of Personal Responsibility, "Report: Investigation into the Office of Legal Counsel's Memoranda Concerning Issues Relating to the Central Intelligence Agency's Use of 'Enhanced Interrogation Techniques' on Suspected Terrorists," July 29, 2009, 242.

31. May 2005 Bradbury memo, 36–37, 39–40.

32. Michael Scherer, "Scientists Claim CIA Misused Work on Sleep Deprivation," *Time*, April 21, 2009.

33. May 2005 Bradbury memo, 42.

34. U.S. Senate Select Committee on Intelligence, *Committee Study of the CIA's Detention and Interrogation Program*, December 3, 2014 (as revised for declassification), 423.

35. May 2005 Bradbury memo, 42.

36. Scott Horton, "I Challenge Marc Thiessen: Six Questions for Malcolm Nance," *Harper's*, April 30, 2010.

37. Detainee Treatment Act of 2005, Pub. L. No. 109–148, div. A, tit. X, 119 Stat. 2739

(codified at 42 U.S.C. § 2000dd–2000dd-1). The 2005 DTA requires Department of Defense employees to follow U.S. Army Field Manual procedures for interrogating prisoners in their custody.

38. President's Statement on Signing of HR 2683, the Department of Defense, Emergency Supplemental Appropriations to Address Hurricanes in the Gulf of Mexico, and Pandemic Influenza Act, 2006, December 30, 2005.

39. James P. Pfiffner, *Power Play: The Bush Presidency and the Constitution* (Washington, D.C.: Brookings Institution Press, 2008), 160.

40. 18 U.S.C. § 2441; see also Michael John Garcia, "The War Crimes Act: Current Issues," Congressional Research Service, January 22, 2009.

41. George W. Bush, Executive Order 13440, "Interpretation of the Geneva Conventions Common Article 3 as Applied to a Program of Detention and Interrogation Operated by the Central Intelligence Agency," July 20, 2007. President Obama revoked this executive order in January 2009. Executive Order 13491, "Ensuring Lawful Interrogations," January 22, 2009.

42. Mark Mazzetti, "Rules Lay Out CIA's Tactics in Questioning," *New York Times*, July 21, 2007.

43. Memorandum from Stephen G. Bradbury to John A. Rizzo, Acting General Counsel, Central Intelligence Agency, *Re: Application of the War Crimes Act, the Detainee Treatment Act, and Common Article 3 of the Geneva Conventions to Certain Techniques That May Be Used by the CIA in the Interrogation of High Value al Qaeda Detainees*, July 20, 2007 (hereinafter July 2007 Bradbury memo).

44. The July 2007 memo did not address waterboarding.

45. The amendments to the War Crimes Act by the Military Commissions Act of 2006 were made"[i]n response to the Court's ruling in *Hamdan*." Garcia, "The War Crimes Act: Current Issues."

46. U.S. Senate Select Committee on Intelligence, *Committee Study of the CIA's Detention and Interrogation Program*, 434, 415.

47. July 2007 Bradbury memo.

48. U.S. Senate Select Committee on Intelligence, *Committee Study of the CIA's Detention and Interrogation Program*, 435–436.

49. July 2007 Bradbury memo, 47.

50. Ibid. If the prisoner experienced significant physical pain, other methods of keeping him awake could be tried.

51. Seth F. Kreimer, "Too Close to the Rack and Screw: Constitutional Constraints on Torture in the War on Terror," *University of Pennsylvania Journal of Constitutional Law* 6 (2003): 278, 294–295.

52. U.S. Senate Select Committee on Intelligence, *Committee Study of the CIA's Detention and Interrogation Program*, 53, 165.

53. Scott Shane, "Waterboarding Used 266 Times on 2 Suspects," *New York Times*, April 19, 2009.

54. Curtis A. Bradley and Eric A. Posner, "Presidential Signing Statements and Executive Power," *Constitutional Commentary* 23 (2006): 307.

# Chapter 8.
## The Bush Administration and Secrecy

1. David C. Vladeck, "Bush Does It in the Dark," *TomPaine.com*, July 18, 2006.

2. *Reynolds v. United States*, 345 U.S. 1 (1953).

3. Ibid., at 6. An earlier case, the Aaron Burr trial of 1807, also "involved what might have been 'confidential communications' and 'state secrets.'" Louis Fisher, *In the Name of National Security: Unchecked Presidential Power and the Reynolds Case* (Lawrence: University of Kansas Press, 2006), 212–214. However, the Jefferson administration did not seek to prevent Chief Justice John Marshall from seeing documents at issue in this case, and Marshall "did not take at face value the word of the administration, as the Supreme Court did in *Reynolds*." Ibid., at 214. Fisher concludes that "the Burr trial is not a precedent for the state secrets privilege [as later described in *Reynolds*]." Ibid., 218.

4. *Reynolds*, 345 U.S. at 6–11.

5. Alexander Hamilton, Federalist 70, in Alexander Hamilton, John Jay, and James Madison, *The Federalist Papers*, ed. Michael A. Genovese (New York: Palgrave Macmillan, 2009), 200. Chief Justin Vinson did not, however, describe the state secrets privilege as a constitutional doctrine: the Court "ma[de] it perfectly plain that the evidentiary rule it announced in Reynolds was not constitutionally based." David Rudenstine, "The Courts and National Security: The Ordeal of the State Secrets Privilege," *University of Baltimore Law Review* 44(2014): 37, 73.

6. Fisher, *In the Name of National Security*, 98.

7. *Reynolds*, 345 U.S. at 8, 10 (emphasis added).

8. Ibid., at 2.

9. Fisher, *In the Name of National Security*, 3.

10. *Reynolds*, 345 U.S. at 2–5.

11. Fisher, *In the Name of National Security*, 112–113, 253. Fisher notes that "the government misled the Court on the contents of the accident report." Ibid., 98.

12. Ibid., 167–169, 177–179.

13. Ibid., 119, 165, 212.

14. Christina E. Wells, "State Secrets and Executive Accountability," *Constitutional Commentary* 26 (2010): 625, 637. Some argue that dismissing cases under *Reynolds* is made possible only by misusing the 1876 *Totten* case. In *Totten*, the Supreme Court dismissed a case seeking payment allegedly owed to the heir of a Civil War spy for espionage services provided to the U.S. government. *Totten v. U.S.*, 92 U.S. 105 (1876). The Court dismissed the case, concluding that "public policy forbids the maintenance of any [law]suit . . . which would inevitably lead to the disclosure of matters which the law itself regards as confidential." Ibid. The Court would not allow the suit in *Totten* to proceed because it involved allegations of a contract with the government for "secret services," and litigation could force disclosure of a contract that, by its nature, had to be kept secret. Ibid. Although *Totten* was decided in a very specific context and might seem to apply only to similar cases, the Obama administration has relied on it in seeking dismissal of litigation, as discussed in Section III.

15. Holly Wells, "The State Secrets Privilege: Overuse Causing Unintended Consequences," *Arizona Law Review* 50 (2008): 967.

16. *El-Masri v. United States*, 479 F.3d 296 (3rd Cir. 2007), *cert. denied*, 552 U.S. 947 (2007), at 302.

17. Ibid., at 312. The court reviewed only a classified document prepared by the government that claimed to describe "the nature of the information that the Executive seeks to protect and . . . why its disclosure would be detrimental to national security." Ibid.

18. *Arar v. Ashcroft*, 585 F.3d 559, 565–566 (2d Cir. 2009) *en banc, cert. denied*, 130 S. Ct. 3409 (2010).

19. Louis Fisher, "Extraordinary Rendition: The Price of Secrecy," *American University Law Review* 57 (2008): 1405, 1441–1442.

20. Chris Edelson, *Emergency Presidential Power: From the Drafting of the Constitution to the War on Terror* (Madison: University of Wisconsin Press, 2013), 249.

21. 18 U.S.C. § 2340A(c).

22. Michael John Garcia, "Renditions: Constraints Imposed by Laws on Torture," Congressional Research Service, September 8, 2009, 8, citing CAT, Article Three. The Foreign Affairs Reform and Restructuring Act of 1998 (FARRA) "implemented U.S. obligations under CAT Article Three." Ibid.

23. Jay S. Bybee, "Memorandum for William J. Haynes, II, General Counsel, Department of Defense re: The President's Power as Commander in Chief to Transfer Captured Terrorists to the Control and Custody of Foreign Nations" (hereinafter Bybee-to-Haynes memo), Office of Legal Counsel, March 13, 2002, 2. Although the memo was signed by Bybee, "the text of [the memo] is believed to have been written by John Yoo." Jason Leopold, "DOJ Report Likely to Scrutinize Yoo/Bybee Rendition Memo," *The Public Record*, March 15, 2009. In a 2004 law review article that closely tracks the reasoning in the 2002 OLC memo, John Yoo wrote that "statutes and treaties must be interpreted so as to protect the President's constitutional powers [to transfer prisoners held outside the United States] from impermissible encroachment and thereby to avoid any potential constitutional problems." "Transferring Terrorists," *Notre Dame Law Review* 79 (2004): 1183, 1230.

24. Bybee-to-Haynes memo, 34, 19.

25. Fisher, "Extraordinary Rendition," 1451.

26. Leopold, "DOJ Report Likely to Scrutinize Yoo/Bybee Rendition Memo."

27. In the *Arar* case, the courts did not rely on the state secrets privilege to dismiss litigation, but the Bush administration demonstrated it was prepared to use this argument to shield its decisions from outside review.

28. *In re NSA Telecom Litigation*, 671 F.3d 881 (9th Cir. 2012), *cert. denied*, 2012 U.S. LEXIS 25949; see also Wells, "The State Secrets Privilege," 984–989.

## Chapter 9.
### The Barack Obama Administration and National Security Power

1. Harold Koh, "Repairing Our Human Rights Reputation," *Western New England Law Review* 31 (2009): 11, 17.

2. Jack Goldsmith, *Power and Constraint* (New York: W. W. Norton, 2012).

3. Chris Edelson, "In Service to Power: Legal Scholars as Executive Branch Lawyers in the Obama Administration," *Presidential Studies Quarterly* 43, no. 3 (September 2013): 618; Goldsmith, *Power and Constraint*, 3.

4. Barack Obama, Remarks by the President on National Security, May 21, 2009, http://www.whitehouse.gov/the-press-office/remarks-president-national-security-5-21-09.

5. Edelson, "In Service to Power," 618.

6. Glenn Greenwald, "The Impact of Obama's Latest Excellent DOJ Appointments," *Salon*, January 20, 2009. Greenwald later concluded Barron and Lederman had failed to meet his expectations that they would move the Obama administration away from the Bush model. Glenn Greenwald, "The Awlaki Memo and Marty Lederman," *Salon*, October 9, 2011.

7. Bruce Ackerman, "The Demonization of Harold Koh," *Daily Beast*, April 7, 2009.

8. Goldsmith, *Power and Constraint*, 3–4.

9. Ibid., 39. However, it is worth noting that Yoo's successors at OLC often avoided using the language of the unitary executive, as discussed in Section II. Instead they, like executive branch lawyers in the Obama administration, found ways to defang statutory and constitutional limits without expressly claiming presidential power to set aside the law.

10. Ibid., 40, 41.

11. Ibid., 41, 38–39, 48.

12. Ibid., 48.

13. Barack Obama, Executive Order 13491, "Ensuring Lawful Interrogations," January 22, 2009.

## Chapter 10.
## The Obama Administration and the Use of Military Force

1. Charlie Savage, "Barack Obama's Q&A," *Boston Globe*, December 20, 2007.

2. Memorandum for the Attorney General from Caroline Krass, *Authority to Use Military Force in Libya*, April 1, 2011, 4 (hereinafter April 1, 2011, Krass memo).

3. Louis Fisher, "Military Operations in Libya: No War? No Hostilities?," *Presidential Studies Quarterly* 42, no. 1 (March 2012): 179.

4. Louis Fisher, *Presidential War Power*, 3rd ed. (Lawrence: University Press of Kansas, 2013), 90.

5. April 1, 2011, Krass memo.

6. Michael Isikoff, "2001 Memo Reveals Push for Broader Presidential Power," *Newsweek*, December 18, 2004.

7. It is also important to consider what happened *after* Krass wrote her memo—when the Obama administration later sought to continue military operations in Libya beyond the sixty-day War Powers Resolution window considered by Krass. President Obama ultimately rejected OLC's recommendation that operations cease after sixty days absent congressional authorization, relying on advice from Harold Koh, then-legal adviser to the State Department, as discussed later in this chapter.

8. Yoo frequently describes presidential power as "inherent" or plenary. Memorandum opinion from John C. Yoo, Deputy Assistant Attorney General, for Timothy Flanigan,

Deputy Counsel to the President, *The President's Constitutional Authority to Conduct Military Operations against Terrorists and Nations Supporting Them* (September 25, 2001) (hereinafter September 25, 2001, Yoo memo), 1–3, 5 ("the President's independent and plenary constitutional authority over the use of military force"), 7–8 (plenary presidential power over foreign affairs), 22–23. He describes the president as having "complete discretion in exercising the Commander-in-Chief power," 3–4, and refers to "the President's unilateral war powers in an emergency situation like that created by the September 11 incidents."

9.  Ibid., 6, 23, 13–20.

10.  *Zivotofsky v. Kerry*, 576 U.S. ___ (2015).

11.  September 25, 2001, Yoo memo, 8, quoting *U.S. v. Curtiss-Wright Export Corp.*, 299 U.S. 304, 320 (1936).

12.  The problems with the sole organ doctrine are discussed in more detail in Section I.

13.  Yoo's memo suggests that Federalist No. 23 supports his conclusions about broad presidential power: "The President's constitutional power to defend the United States and the lives of its people must be understood in light of the Founders' express intention to create a federal government 'cloathed with all the powers requisite to [the] complete execution of its trust.' . . . As Hamilton explained in arguing for the Constitution's adoption, because 'the circumstances which may affect the public safety are [not] reducible within certain determinate limits . . . it must be admitted as a necessary consequence that there can be no limitation of that authority which is to provide for the defense and protection of the community in any matter essential to its efficiency." September 25, 2001, Yoo memo, 2. In fact (although Yoo does not make this clear), in Federalist No. 23 Hamilton was describing *joint* presidential-congressional authority: "Whether there ought to be a *federal government* intrusted with the care of the common defense, is a question in the first instance, open for discussion; but the moment it is decided in the affirmative, it will follow, that that *government* ought to be clothed with all the powers requisite to complete execution of its trust." Hamilton, Federalist No. 23, in Alexander Hamilton, John Jay, and James Madison, *The Federalist Papers*, ed. Michael A. Genovese (New York: Palgrave Macmillan, 2009), 62 (hereinafter *The Federalist Papers*) (emphasis added). In addition, although Yoo does not explain this, Hamilton acknowledged limits on the power of the federal government as a whole to take action in the name of the common defense. Hamilton's language can be used deceptively, as he speaks about power without limitation (as quoted with approval by Yoo). However, Hamilton made clear that power should exist without limits *only* within the areas of authority specifically assigned to either the president or Congress—that is, the authority "to raise armies; to build and equip fleets; to prescribe rules for the government of both; to direct their operations; to provide for their support." Ibid., 61–64. Hamilton wrote that "*These* powers ought to exist without limitation," meaning that the federal government as a whole ought to have "unlimited power to raise armies, build and equip fleets, prescribe rules for the government of both; to direct their operations; [and] provide for their support," *not* that it ought to have unlimited power over all matters conceivably related to defense of the nation. Ibid., 61 (emphasis added). Hamilton's goal was to explain that the Articles of Confederation had failed because it had given the states too much control over matters of common defense: in other words, he was making an argument over the proper division of power between the national government as a whole and the states. Yoo was taking

Federalist No. 23 out of context by suggesting it supported his argument about broad presidential authority over the use of military force.

14. September 25, 2001, Yoo memo, 5, citing Federalist No. 70.

15. *The Federalist Papers*, Federalist No. 70, 200.

16. September 25, 2001, Yoo memo, 5.

17. *The Federalist Papers*, Federalist No. 70, 200: "That unity is conducive to energy will not be disputed. Decision, activity, secrecy, and despatch will generally characterize the proceedings of *one man* in a much more eminent degree than the proceedings of any greater number; and in proportion as the number is increased, these qualities will be diminished" (emphasis added).

18. *The Federalist Papers*, Federalist No. 69, 193–197.

19. Hamilton also made clear in other writings that he recognized limits on presidential power—for instance, in the *Pacificus* essay (which was also cited by Yoo in his memo, but not for this point).

20. September 25, 2001, Yoo memo, 24.

21. The War Powers Resolution permits the president, in some circumstances, to "introduc[e] . . . U.S. armed forces into hostilities, or into situations where imminent involvement in hostilities is clearly indicated under the circumstances." 50 U.S.C. § 1541(c). However, even when such unilateral presidential action is permitted by the WPR, the president is required to terminate the use of U.S. forces within sixty days after submitting an initial report to Congress (the report must be submitted within forty-eight hours of a decision to begin military operations). 50 U.S.C. § 1544(b). The sixty-day deadline can be extended to ninety days when "the President determines and certifies to the Congress in writing that unavoidable military necessity respecting the safety of United States Armed Forces requires the continued use of such armed forces in the course of bringing about a prompt removal of such forces." 50 U.S.C. § 1544(b)(3).

22. September 25, 2001, Yoo memo, 16.

23. April 1, 2011, Krass memo, 6 (emphasis added, citations omitted).

24. Ibid., 6–7. Yoo's memo also cited Jackson's *Youngstown Sheet* opinion but concluded that it did not present an obstacle because the president could claim "to be operating both under his own Article II authority and with the legislative support of Congress [pursuant to the War Powers Resolution and the AUMF]." September 25, 2001, Yoo memo, 20. Although Yoo did cite Jackson's opinion from *Youngstown Sheet*, much of his memo rejects the logic of Jackson's framework as Yoo expressly endorsed inherent or plenary presidential power, which Jackson rejected. Compare September 25, 2001, Yoo memo, 22–24 ("the President has plenary power to use force even before an attack upon the United States actually occurs, against targets and using methods of his own choosing. . . . Neither statute [the WPR or the AUMF] can place any limits on the President's [decisions to use military force]. . . . These decisions, under our Constitution, are for the President alone to make" with *Youngstown Sheet & Tube Co. v. Sawyer*, 343 U.S. 579, 646–647 (1952) (Jackson, J., concurring) ("Loose and irresponsible use of adjectives colors all nonlegal and much legal discussion of presidential powers. 'Inherent' powers, 'implied' powers, 'incidental' powers, 'plenary' powers, 'war' powers and 'emergency' powers are used, often interchangeably and without fixed or ascertainable meanings.").

25. April 1, 2011, Krass memo, 7: "The President . . . holds 'the implicit advantage . . . over the legislature under our constitutional scheme in situations calling for immediate action,' given that imminent national security threats and rapidly evolving military and diplomatic circumstances may require a swift response by the United States without the opportunity for congressional deliberation and action." I refer to the idea of an energetic executive as "mythic" because it is very difficult to identify specific examples of prompt, unilateral presidential action being necessary to deal with an emergency. The Civil War is the only example that appears as a candidate, and even this example has limited value for the energetic executive school as Lincoln acknowledged the need for retroactive congressional approval. Louis Fisher, "Abraham Lincoln: Preserving the Union and the Constitution," *Albany Government Law Review* 3 (2010); Daniel Farber, *Lincoln's Constitution* (Chicago: University of Chicago Press, 2003). In most cases, Congress has proved capable of acting quickly to respond to an emergency—for example, by declaring war against Japan on December 8, 1941, the day after Pearl Harbor, or passing the Authorization for Use of Military Force on September 14, 2001, three days after the September 11 attacks.

26. April 1, 2011, Krass memo, 7.

27. September 25, 2001, Yoo memo, 13.

28. Ibid., 13–16; April 1, 2011, Krass memo, 7–11.

29. September 25, 2001, Yoo memo, 16–17; April 1, 2011, Krass memo, 7.

30. April 1, 2011, Krass memo, 1, 8.

31. Krass concluded that President Obama could order the use of military force to serve national interests in "preserving regional stability and supporting the [United Nations Security] Council's credibility and effectiveness." Ibid., 10–11.

32. U.S. Constitution, art. I, § 8, cl. 11.

33. Louis Fisher, *Defending Congress and the Constitution* (Lawrence: University Press of Kansas, 2011), 241. See also M. Andrew Campanelli, Kai Draper, and Jack Stucker, "The Original Understanding of the Declare War Clause," *Journal of Law and Politics* 24 (Winter 2008): 49 ("there is compelling evidence that most, if not all [of the Framers and ratifiers of the Constitution] believed that, [by] virtue of its Declare War Clause, the Constitution vests the power to create war in Congress alone"); Nancy Kassop, "Resolved, presidents have usurped the war power that rightfully belongs to Congress," in *Debating the Presidency: Conflicting Perspectives on the American Executive*, ed. Richard J. Ellis and Michael Nelson (Los Angeles: CQ Press, 2015), 163–164 ("The framers could not have been clearer: [t]he decision to go to war belongs to [Congress], because declaring war is a political decision to move the nation from a state of peace to a state of war. Only then [after Congress has declared war] does the president command the troops and conduct military operations.").

34. Max Farrand, ed., *The Records of the Federal Convention of 1787* (New Haven: Yale University Press, 1937), 318–319.

35. Kassop, *Debating the Presidency: Conflicting Perspectives on the American Executive*, 164 (emphasis in original).

36. September 25, 2001, Yoo memo, 5.

37. April 1, 2011, Krass memo, 8–13.

38. Fisher, "Military Operations in Libya: No War? No Hostilities?," 181–182. Fisher's

analysis focused on the meaning of "hostilities" under the War Powers Resolution, but he noted that the same analysis applied to Krass's definition of "war" under the Constitution.

39. September 25, 2001, Yoo memo, 24.

40. April 1, 2011, Krass memo, 10.

41. Krass says that such actions may only be taken to "serve sufficiently important national interests." April 1, 2011, Krass memo, 10. It is hard to distinguish that caveat from Yoo's conclusion that the president can use military force to respond to "any terrorist threat"—surely one could argue that using military force against a possible terrorist threat serves an important national interest. September 25, 2001, Yoo memo, 24.

42. April 1, 2011, Krass memo, 10: "A policy statement in the WPR states that '[t]he constitutional powers of the President as Commander in Chief to introduce United States Armed Forces into hostilities, or into situations where imminent involvement in hostilities is clearly indicated by the circumstances, are exercised only pursuant to (1) a declaration of war, (2) specific statutory authorization, or (3) a national emergency created by attack upon the United States, its territories or possessions, or its armed forces.' 50 U.S.C. § 1541(c). But this policy statement 'is not to be viewed as limiting presidential action in any substantive manner.' . . . The conference committee report accompanying the WPR made clear that 'subsequent sections of the [Resolution] are not dependent on the language of' the policy statement. . . . Moreover, in a later, operative provision, the Resolution makes clear that nothing in it 'is intended to alter the constitutional authority . . . of the President'" (citations omitted). This is similar to Yoo's conclusion that "[t]he executive branch consistently 'has taken the position from the very beginning that section 2(c) of the WPR does not constitute a legally binding definition of Presidential authority to deploy our armed forces." September 25, 2001, Yoo memo, 21.

43. Yoo concluded that "[n]either [the 2001 AUMF nor the WPR] . . . can place any limit on the President's determinations as to any terrorist threat, the amount of military force to be used in response, or the method, timing, and nature of the response. These decisions, under our Constitution, are for the President alone to make." September 25, 2001, Yoo memo, 21. In other words, to the extent that the president concluded the WPR (or any statute) infringes on executive power, the president could simply ignore the statutory limitation.

44. April 1, 2011, Krass memo, 8.

45. Charlie Savage, "2 Top Lawyers Lost to Obama in Libya War Policy Debate," *New York Times*, June 18, 2011. Pentagon general counsel Jeh C. Johnson agreed with Krass's conclusion. Ibid.

46. Chris Edelson, *Emergency Presidential Power: From the Drafting of the Constitution to the War on Terror* (Madison: University of Wisconsin Press, 2013), 268–269.

47. 50 U.S.C. § 1542.

48. Harold Koh, "Testimony on Libya and War Powers before the Senate Foreign Relations Committee," June 28, 2011.

49. *United States Activities in Libya*, June 15, 2011, report submitted by the Obama administration to the House of Representatives, 25. The report to the House of Representatives closely tracks analysis contained in Koh's June 28, 2011, testimony before Congress. Koh, "Testimony on Libya and War Powers before the Senate Foreign Relations Committee."

50. Peter M. Shane, *Madison's Nightmare: How Executive Power Threatens American*

*Democracy* (Chicago: University of Chicago Press, 2009), 132. Shane was not writing about the Obama administration, but his analysis is applicable to its actions.

51. Louis Fisher, "Statement before the Senate Committee on Foreign Relations, 'Libya and War Powers.'" June 28, 2011. See also Robert J. Spitzer, "Comparing the Constitutional Presidencies of George W. Bush and Barack Obama: War Powers, Signing Statements, Vetoes," *White House Studies* 12, no. 2 (October, 2013): 131: "While these attacks [ordered by President Obama in Libya] were relatively brief in duration and arguably did not rise to the definition of 'war,' they undoubtedly are encompassed by the term 'hostilities' found in the [WPR]."

52. Koh agreed with Krass that an important national interest was required in order for the president to authorize the use of military force. Koh, "Testimony on Libya and War Powers before the Senate Foreign Relations Committee."

53. Ibid.; see also April 1, 2011, Krass memo, 10. As we'll see however, the Obama administration later concluded in the context of contemplated military operations in Syria that UN authorization was not necessary to justify unilateral presidential action. Of course, even *with* authorization from the UN Security Council, U.S. constitutional processes must be satisfied. In other words, a UN resolution authorizing member states to use military force cannot take the place of congressional authorization for the use of military force as required by the Constitution. Fisher, "Military Operations in Libya: No War? No Hostilities?," 179.

54. Koh, "Testimony on Libya and War Powers before the Senate Foreign Relations Committee."

55. September 25, 2001, Yoo memo, 5.

56. Spitzer, "Comparing the Constitutional Presidencies of George W. Bush and Barack Obama": "the precedential consequences of Obama's actions—another instance of an intervention without congressional approval, and the first instance of the violation of the 60 day [WPR] limit—are more likely to encourage future presidents tempted to engage in unilateral limited military actions."

57. Jack Goldsmith, *Power and Constraint* (New York: W. W. Norton, 2012), 182, 292 n. 51: "My own view is that the initiation of force in Libya was lawful, but that while the matter is not certain, after sixty days the Obama administration probably violated the War Powers Resolution" (citations omitted). Presumably, that would also mean, in Goldsmith's view, there was no constitutional support for President Obama's actions after the sixty-day WPR window closed.

58. Ibid., 182.

59. James P. Pfiffner, *Power Play: The Bush Presidency and the Constitution* (Washington, D.C.: Brookings Institution Press, 2008), 70.

60. *Youngstown Sheet*, 343 U.S. at 654: "I have no illusion that any decision by this Court can keep power in the hands of Congress if it is not wise and timely in meeting its problems. A crisis that challenges the President equally, or perhaps primarily, challenges Congress. . . . We may say that power to legislate for emergencies belongs in the hands of Congress, but only Congress itself can prevent power from slipping through its fingers."

61. James Ball, "Obama Issues Syria a 'Red Line' Warning on Chemical Weapons," *Washington Post*, August 20, 2012.

62. Reid J. Epstein, "W.H.: 'Very Little Doubt' Syria Used Chemical Weapons," *Politico*, August 25, 2013.

63. Karen DeYoung and Anne Gearan, "After Syria Chemical Allegations, Obama Considering Limited Military Strike," *Washington Post*, August 26, 2013.

64. Charlie Savage, "Obama Tests Limits of Power in Syrian Conflict," *New York Times*, September 8, 2013.

65. Chris Edelson, "Obama and the Power to Go to War," *Los Angeles Times*, August 30, 2013.

66. August 28, 2013, letter from members of Congress to President Obama, http://rigell.house.gov/uploadedfiles/8.28.13_letter_to_potus_with_signatories.pdf; see also Rebecca Shabad, "140 House Members Say Obama Needs Approval from Congress on Syria," *The Hill*, August 29, 2013.

67. David Espo, "Obama to Seek Congressional OK for Syria Action," *Associated Press*, August 31, 2013. Legislation proposed by the administration (but never enacted) would have "authorized [the president] to use the Armed Forces of the United States as he determines to be necessary and appropriate in connection with the use of chemical weapons or other weapons of mass destruction in the conflict in Syria in order to—(1) prevent or deter the use or proliferation (including the transfer to terrorist groups or other state or non-state actors), within, to or from Syria, of any weapons of mass destruction, including chemical or biological weapons or components of or materials used in such weapons; or (2) protect the United States and its allies and partners against the threat posed by such weapons." CNN staff, "Text of Draft Legislation Submitted by Obama to Congress," *CNN.com*, August 31, 2013, http://www.cnn.com/2013/08/31/us/obama-authorization-request-text.

68. Savage, "Obama Tests Limits of Power in Syrian Conflict."

69. Mark Memmott, "'I Always Reserve the Right to Act,' Obama Says of Syria," *NPR.org*, September 4, 2013.

70. Howard Fineman, "John Kerry: Obama Can Bomb Assad Even if Congress Says No," *Huffington Post*, September 6, 2013.

71. Nick Paton Walsh and Elise Labott, "Security Council OKs Syria Resolution, Warns of Consequences," *CNN.com*, September 27, 2013: "The U.N. Security Council, capping a dramatic month of diplomacy, voted unanimously . . . to require Syria to eliminate its arsenal of chemical weapons—or face consequences. . . . The U.N. resolution was based on a deal struck this month between the United States and Russia that averted an American military strike over allegations the Syrian government used sarin nerve gas in an August 21 attack on a Damascus suburb that U.S. officials said left at least 1,400 people dead. The resolution did not authorize the automatic use of force if Syria is said to be in violation, as was previously sought by the United States."

72. Savage, "Obama Tests Limits of Power in Syrian Conflict," quoting University of Colorado law professor Harold H. Bruff.

73. Of course, the line between law and politics is not always clear. If a president (like Obama) decides not to act unilaterally because members of Congress, citing constitutional concerns, object, one could conclude that this is an example of interbranch practice setting constitutional, that is, legal limits on presidential power.

74. *Hamdi v. Rumsfeld*, 542 U.S. 507 (2004).

75. Charlie Savage, *Takeover: The Return of the Imperial Presidency and the Subversion of American Democracy* (New York: Little, Brown, 2007), 194.

76. Also referred to as the Islamic State of Iraq and the Levant (ISIL), Islamic State (IS), or Da'ish. "The Many Names of ISIS (Also Known as IS, ISIL, SIC, and Da'ish)," *The Economist*, September 28, 2014.

77. Arlette Saenz, "President Obama Says ISIS 'Not Religious Leaders, They Are Terrorists,'" *ABC News*, February 18, 2015.

78. Graeme Wood, "What ISIS Really Wants," *Atlantic*, March 2015.

79. Helene Cooper, Mark Landler, and Alissa J. Rubin, "Obama Allows Limited Airstrikes on ISIS," *New York Times*, August 7, 2014.

80. Ibid. To the extent that ISIS posed a threat to Americans in Iraq as of August 2014, that could have initially provided authority for the Obama administration to act unilaterally in their defense. However, the Obama administration has not claimed (as of January 2016) that continued military action against ISIS is justified by self-defense or an imminent threat ISIS poses to Americans.

81. Dan Roberts and Spencer Ackerman, "Barack Obama Authorises Air Strikes against ISIS Militants in Syria," *Guardian*, September 11, 2014.

82. Spencer Ackerman, "Obama's Legal Rationale for ISIS Strikes: Shoot First, Ask Congress Later," *Guardian*, September 10, 2014.

83. Ibid.; see also Barack Obama, "Letter from the President—Authorization for the Use of United States Armed Forces in Connection with the Islamic State of Iraq and the Levant [or ISIS]," February 11, 2015: "existing statutes provide me with the authority I need to take these actions [against ISIS]."

84. Authorization for Use of Military Force, September 18, 2001, Pub. L. No. 107–40, 115 Stat. 224.

85. Ryan Goodman, "Obama Can't Declare a New Iraq War without Approval. Even Bush Knew That," *Guardian*. June 19, 2014.

86. Authorization for Use of Military Force against Iraq, October 16, 2002, Pub. L. No. 107–243, 116 Stat. 1497.

87. Jennifer Daskal, Ryan Goodman, and Steve Vladeck, "The Premature Discussion of ISIS and the 2001/2002 AUMFs," *Just Security*, June 17, 2014.

88. Obama, "Letter from the President—Authorization for the Use of United States Armed Forces in Connection with the Islamic State of Iraq and the Levant [ISIS]."

89. Peter Baker, "Obama's Dual View of War Power Seeks Limits and Leeway," *New York Times*, February 11, 2015.

90. Justin Sink, "Obama Aide: ISIS War Powers Language 'Intentionally' Vague," *The Hill*, February 11, 2015.

91. Peter Baker and Ashley Parker, "Congress Shows a Lack of Enthusiasm for Giving Obama War Powers to Fight ISIS," *New York Times*, February 12, 2015. In December 2015, President Obama again asked Congress to authorize the use of military force against ISIS. Tanya Somander, "President Obama Addresses the Nation on Keeping the American People Safe," White House blog, December 6, 2015. As of this writing, Congress has taken no action.

92. Mark Mazzetti, Eric Schmitt, and Robert F. Worth, "Two-Year Manhunt Led to Killing of Awlaki in Yemen," *New York Times*, September 30, 2011. This section focuses on the Obama administration's use of a drone strike to target a U.S. citizen suspected of being a senior terrorist leader, though this is only a small part of the overall drone program. The Obama administration has used drone strikes more extensively than the Bush administration. For instance, in his first five years in office, President Obama authorized more than 390 drone strikes—"eight times as many as were launched in the entire Bush presidency." Juan Cole, "Death Toll of Obama's Drone Campaign 5 Years Later: 2,400," *Informed Comment*, January 24, 2014; see also Peter Bergen, "Drone Is Obama's Weapon of Choice," *CNN*, September 19, 2012. These drone strikes have reportedly killed hundreds of civilians (drone strikes during the Bush years reportedly killed civilians at a higher rate per strike). Cole, "Death Toll of Obama's Drone Campaign 5 Years Later: 2,400."

93. David J. Barron, Acting Assistant Attorney General, *Memorandum for the Attorney General re: Applicability of Federal Criminal Laws and the Constitution to Contemplated Lethal Actions against Shaykh Anwar Al-Aulaqi*, July 16, 2010 (hereinafter July 16, 2010, Barron memo), published at *New York Times et al. v. United States Dept. of Justice et al.*, 2014 U.S. App. LEXIS 11733, Docket Nos. 13–422 (L), 13–445(Con) (2d Cir., June 23, 2014); see also Charlie Savage, "Secret U.S. Memo Made Legal Case to Kill a Citizen," *New York Times*, October 8, 2011.

94. David Johnston and Scott Shane, "U.S. Knew of Suspect's Tie to Radical Cleric," *New York Times*, November 9, 2009; Peter Finn, "Al-Awlaki Directed Christmas 'Underwear Bomber' Plot, Justice Department Memo Says," *Washington Post*, February 10, 2012.

95. *Nasser al-Aulaqi v. Obama*, 727 F.Supp.2d 1, 11 (D.D.C. 2010).

96. The lawsuit was dismissed on procedural grounds: "Because . . . questions of justiciability require dismissal of this case at the outset, the serious issues regarding the merits of the alleged authorization of the targeted killing of a U.S. citizen overseas must await another day or another (non-judicial) forum." Ibid., at 8.

97. Jeremy Scahill, *Dirty Wars: The World Is a Battlefield* (New York: Nation Books, 2013), 507–508.

98. Complaint, *Nasser Al-Aulaqi and Sarah Khan v. Panetta et al.*, Case No. 1:12-cv-01192-RMC (D.D.C.): "The news media have reported, based on statements attributed to anonymous U.S. government officials, that Samir Khan was not the target of the September 30[, 2011,] strike and that Abdulrahman Al-Aulaqi was not the target of the October 14, 2011, strike." Khan was a member of AQAP "assigned . . . to its media division." Scahill, *Dirty Wars*, 377. Khan worked on propaganda designed "to rally the Western sympathizers and to try and further bolster [AQAP's] roster so they can more easily plan attacks against the West." Ibid., 378. It is not clear why the sixteen-year-old Abdulrahman al-Aulaqi was killed. There is no credible evidence that he was a member of AQAP, let alone a terrorist leader planning attacks against the United States. Scahill, *Dirty Wars*, 507–511.

99. *Nasser al-Aulaqi v. Obama*, 727 F.Supp.2d at 11.

100. Gregory Johnsen, "A False Target in Yemen," *New York Times*, November 19, 2010.

101. Chris Edelson, "In Service to Power: Legal Scholars as Executive Branch Lawyers in the Obama Administration," *Presidential Studies Quarterly* 43, no. 3 (July 2013): 633–634.

102. *New York Times et al. v. United States Dept. of Justice et al.*, 2014 U.S. App. LEXIS 11733, Docket Nos. 13–422 (L), 13–445(Con) (2d Cir., June 23, 2014), Appendix A.

103. Justice News, "Attorney General Eric Holder Speaks at Northwestern University School of Law," March 5, 2012, http://www.justice.gov/iso/opa/ag/speeches/2012/ag-speech-120305ıtml.

104. July 16, 2010, Barron memo, 41.

105. Ibid., 12, 35, 37–38, citing 18 U.S.C. § 1119, 18 U.S.C. § 956(a), and 18 U.S.C. § 2441.

106. Ibid., 30, 35–36.

107. Ibid., 14–15.

108. Ibid., 19–35.

109. Ibid., 20–21.

110. Ibid., 29, n. 39; see also John Yoo, "The Administration's Strange Reasoning on al-Awlaki," *National Review: The Corner*, October 9, 2011.

111. At first glance, the decision to kill Osama Bin Laden would similarly justify the decision to kill al-Aulaqi. Ian Milhiser, "The Uncomfortable Truth Is That Targeted Killings Are Legal Until Congress Says Otherwise," *Think Progress*, May 27, 2014. However, like Yamamoto, Bin Laden is distinguishable from al-Aulaqi (even setting aside the citizenship point): there was no dispute as to Bin Laden's status as a terrorist leader involved in planning attacks against the United States, and, as the head of Al Qaeda, he was clearly within the scope of the 2001 AUMF.

112. July 16, 2010, Barron memo, 21.

113. Gregory Johnsen, "A False Target in Yemen," *New York Times*, November 19, 2010.

114. July 16, 2010, Barron memo, 30 (emphasis added), 21.

115. Ibid., 21, citing *Youngstown Sheet* at 635 (Jackson, J., concurring).

116. Jonathan Masters and Zachary Laub, "Al Qaeda in the Arabian Peninsula (AQAP)," *Council on Foreign Relations: Backgrounders*, August 22, 2013: "The militant Islamist group al-Qaeda in the Arabian Peninsula (AQAP) was formed in January 2009 through a union of the Saudi and Yemeni branches of al-Qaeda." See also Marcy Wheeler, "Obama Doesn't Know Why the F___ He's Entitled to Kill Al-Awlaki, He Just Is, Damnit," *emptywheel*, September 25, 2010; Gregory Johnsen, "How Al Qaeda Grew in Yemen," *Frontline*, May 29, 2012: "The roots of Al Qaeda in the Arabian Peninsula can be traced back to the jailbreak in February 2006 [when] . . . 23 Al Qaeda suspects escaped from a maximum-security prison in Sana'a. . . . In 2009, [Nasir al-] Wuhayshi publicly welcomed several former Guantanamo Bay detainees into the organization and adopted the name Al Qaeda in the Arabian Peninsula (AQAP)."

117. Pub. L. No. 107–40, 115 Stat. 224 (2001) (emphasis added).

118. Oktay F. Tanrisever, ed., *Afghanistan and Central Asia: NATO's Role in Regional Security since 9/11* (Fairfax, VA: IOS Press, 2013), 193.

119. Jennifer Daskal and Stephen I. Vladeck, "After the AUMF," *Harvard National Security Journal* 5 (2014): 115–116: "Although its delegation of power to the President was sweeping, the [2001] AUMF in fact reflected a compromise between Congress and the Bush Administration, which had sought an even broader and more open-ended grant of

authority. Even as fires continued to burn at Ground Zero, Congress pushed back, only authorizing military force against those who could be tied to the groups directly responsible for the September 11 attacks. Thus, despite widespread misrepresentations to the contrary, Congress pointedly refused to declare a 'war on terrorism.' The use of force Congress authorized was instead directed at those who bore responsibility for the 9/11 attacks— namely, al Qaeda and the Taliban." See also Richard F. Grimmett, "Authorization for Use of Force in Response to the 9/11 Attacks (P.L. 107–40): Legislative History," Congressional Research Service Report for Congress, updated January 16, 2007: "The floor debates in the Senate and House on S.J.Res. 23 [the final AUMF bill] make clear that the focus of the military force legislation was on the extent of the authorization that Congress would provide to the President for use of U.S. military force against the international terrorists who attacked the U.S. on September 11, 2001, and those who directly and materially assisted them in carrying out their actions. The language of the enacted legislation, on its face, makes clear—especially in contrast to the White House's draft joint resolution of September 12, 2001—the degree to which Congress limited the scope of the President's authorization to use U.S. military force through P.L. 107–40 [the AUMF] to military actions against only those international terrorists and other parties directly involved in aiding or materially supporting the September 11, 2001, attacks on the United States. The authorization was not framed in terms of use of military action against terrorists generally."

120. July 16, 2010, Barron memo, 38–40.

121. Justice News, "Attorney General Eric Holder Speaks at Northwestern University School of Law," March 5, 2012: "'Due process' and 'judicial process' are not one and the same, particularly when it comes to national security. The Constitution guarantees due process, not judicial process."

122. Noah Feldman, "The Drone Memos Reveal Only Contempt," *Bloomberg News*, June 25, 2014.

123. July 16, 2010, Barron memo, 39, citing *Hamdi v. Rumsfeld*, 542 U.S. 507 (2004).

124. *Hamdi*, 542 U.S. at 532–539; 554–556, 573 (Scalia, J., dissenting); at 545–547, 552–554 (Souter, J., concurring in part and dissenting in part). Justice O'Connor's plurality opinion concluded that due process could be provided by a military tribunal, not only by a civil court, but made clear that *some* court had to be involved. Ibid., at 538.

125. Ibid., at 509, 535, 536.

126. Ibid., at 536–538.

127. Justices Scalia and Stevens dissented because they concluded the plurality opinion was not protective enough of Hamdi's rights. *Hamdi*, 542 U.S. at 554–555 (Scalia, J., dissenting).

128. Ibid., at 555–556, 568, 577.

129. Glenn Greenwald, "Confirmed: Obama Authorizes Assassination of U.S. Citizen," *Salon.com*, April 7, 2010: "The full *Hamdi* Court held that at least some due process was required before Americans could be imprisoned as 'enemy combatants.' Yet now, Barack Obama is claiming the [power] not merely to imprison, but to assassinate far from any battlefield, American citizens with no due process of any kind . . . [as a candidate] Obama said the President lacks the power merely to *detain* U.S. citizens without charges. Now, as President, he claims the power to *assassinate* them without charges" (emphasis in original).

130. *Hamdi*, 542 U.S. at 545 (Souter, J., concurring in part and dissenting in part), quoting Federalist No. 51.

131. John Yoo, "The Real Problem with Obama's Drone Memo," *Wall Street Journal*, February 7, 2013: "The [white paper] shows that for the first time in the history of American arms, presidential advisers will weigh the due-process rights of enemy combatants on the battlefield against the government's interests, judge an individual's 'imminent' threat of violence, and ponder whether capture is feasible before deciding to strike. Under these provisions, the U.S. military's speed and decisiveness will suffer, even as the intelligence needed to identify drone targets dries up with the withdrawals from Iraq and now Afghanistan." Yoo argued that, instead of providing process within the executive branch, the Obama administration "could have simply relied on precedent and stated that under the laws of war U.S. military units can kill any enemy soldiers [even if U.S. citizens] at any time with snipers and artillery, drones and missiles, as well as at closer quarters." Yoo rightly noted that "U.S. citizenship doesn't create a legal force field around Americans who treasonously join the enemy[,]" but he failed to consider the possibility that a U.S. citizen targeted by the administration for killing might not actually be an enemy soldier. Ibid.

## Chapter 11.
## The Obama Administration and Surveillance

1. Glenn Greenwald, "NSA Collecting Phone Records of Millions of Verizon Customers Daily," *Guardian*, June 5, 2013.

2. Glenn Greenwald, *No Place to Hide* (New York: Metropolitan Books, 2014), 27, 40–44.

3. "Telephony" is an unusual and somewhat clunky word. It simply means "the technology associated with the electronic transmission of voice, fax, or other information between distant parties using systems historically associated with the telephone." Search Unified Communications, "Telephony," http://searchunifiedcommunications.techtarget .com/definition/Telephony.

4. Since "bulk telephony metadata collection program" is also somewhat clunky, I will sometimes refer to this program as simply "the metadata program" or "the bulk metadata program." It is important to note, however, that there has been *separate* collection of bulk *Internet* metadata. See e.g. David S. Kris, "On the Bulk Collection of Tangible Things," *LawFare Research Paper Series* 1, no. 4 (September 2013): 5.

5. Greenwald, *No Place to Hide*, 72.

6. Barton Gellman and Laura Poitras, "U.S., British Intelligence Mining Data from Nine U.S. Internet Companies in Broad Secret Program," *Washington Post*, June 6, 2014; Greenwald, *No Place to Hide*, 21, 77. This is the PRISM program, part of the Section 702 FISA program, which is discussed in detail later in this chapter. See also Laura K. Donohue, "Section 702 and the Collection of International Telephone and Internet Content," *Harvard Journal of Law and Public Policy* 38 (2014): 117–265.

7. Privacy and Civil Liberties Oversight Board, "Report on the Telephone Records Program Conducted under Section 215 of the USA PATRIOT Act and on the Operations of the Foreign Intelligence Surveillance Court" (hereinafter "Report on Section 215 Telephone Records Program"), January 23, 2014, 8, 22.

8. Jonathan Stray, "FAQ: What You Need to Know about the NSA's Surveillance Programs," *ProPublica*, June 27, 2013; Kris, "On the Bulk Collection of Tangible Things," 15. NSA officials say they collected records of nearly all U.S. calls in 2006 but as of 2014 collected about 30 percent of U.S. call records. Ellen Nakashima, "NSA Is Collecting Less Than 30% of U.S. Call Data," *Washington Post*, February 7, 2014. Decreased collection may have been related to increased cell phone use by Americans; however, NSA officials were reportedly "taking steps to restore the collection . . . closer to previous levels." Even the reported level of surveillance as of 2014 (about 30 percent) "still probably represents tens of billions of records going back five years." Ibid.

9. Privacy and Civil Liberties Oversight Board, "Report on Section 215 Telephone Records Program," 9.

10. Kris, "On the Bulk Collection of Tangible Things," 5. Mass surveillance of content is discussed in Section II and later in this chapter.

11. Ibid., 5, 6.

12. Barton Gellman, "U.S. Surveillance Architecture Includes Collection of Revealing Internet, Phone Metadata," *Washington Post*, June 15, 2013; Kris, "On the Bulk Collection of Tangible Things," 6; Nakashima, "NSA Is Collecting Less Than 30% of U.S. Call Data" ("The NSA [bulk telephony metadata] collection program began without court or congressional approval after the Sept. 11, 2001, attacks but was placed under court supervision in 2006 when American phone companies balked at providing the data solely at the request of the executive branch").

13. Privacy and Civil Liberties Oversight Board, "Report on Section 215 Telephone Records Program," 8.

14. Codified at 50 U.S.C. § 1861. The application of Section 215 to the metadata program is discussed in more detail later in this chapter.

15. Privacy and Civil Liberties Oversight Board, "Report on Section 215 Telephone Records Program," 22 (citing October 11, 2013, FISC order). The orders are renewed "[a]pproximately every ninety days." Ibid., at 23.

16. Ibid., 24–27. As of December 1, 2015, the bulk metadata collection program was changed, pursuant to legislation passed by Congress, requiring the NSA to get FISC approval before querying records. In addition, bulk metadata records are now maintained by private phone companies, not by the NSA itself, as they were before December 2015. Julian Hatten, "Amid New Battle, NSA to Shut Down Phone Records Program," *The Hill*, November 28, 2015. In January 2014, President Obama had unilaterally decided to require FISC approval for specific queries, as discussed below.

17. The standard the FISC applies in determining whether to issue production orders (under Section 215 of the Patriot Act) is discussed later in this chapter.

18. Before 2006, the FISC had no role in *any* of the process; the NSA both collected and searched phone records on its own, pursuant to presidential authorization and without FISC orders at any stage of the process. Privacy and Civil Liberties Oversight Board, "Report on Section 215 Telephone Records Program," 9. In January 2014, following reporting and debate about the Snowden revelations, President Obama "directed . . . that the Department of Justice . . . seek to modify the [metadata] program to ensure that . . . [a]bsent an emergency situation, the government can query the telephone metadata collected pursuant to the program only after a judge approves the use of specific numbers for such queries

based on national security concerns." The White House, Office of the Press Secretary, "Fact Sheet: The Administration's Proposal for Ending the Section 215 Bulk Telephony Metadata Program," March 27, 2014.

19. Privacy and Civil Liberties Oversight Board, "Report on Section 215 Telephone Records Program," 27. Although the FISC did not give individualized approval for queries of the database on the basis of a suspicious seed number before February 2014, the FISC did have some involvement in the decision to conduct a search of contacts with a specific seed number in the sense that the FISC had designated the terrorist organizations related to the NSA's reasonable and articulable suspicion inquiry. However, the FISC orders in place "do not explain what it means for a selection term, like a telephone number, to be 'associated with' a designated terrorist organization." Before February 2014, this determination was left to the NSA alone, with the one caveat that "the FISA court's orders specify that [a seed number reasonably believed to be used by a U.S. person] may not be regarded as associated with a terrorist organization solely on 'the basis of activities that are protected by the First Amendment to the Constitution." Ibid., at 28.

20. Privacy and Civil Liberties Oversight Board, "Report on Section 215 Telephone Records Program," 28–29.

21. Memorandum opinion in *Klayman v. Obama*, No. 13-0851 (D.D.C. December 16, 2013), 19 n. 21.

22. Ibid., 18. Therefore, even though the NSA reported using fewer than three hundred seeds to query its databases in 2012, those three hundred queries could have easily involved the searches of tens of millions of phone records. Ibid., 18–19; see also Privacy and Civil Liberties Oversight Board, "Report on Section 215 Telephone Records Program," 30–31: "[i]f the NSA queries around 300 seed numbers a year, as it did in 2012, then based on the estimates . . . about the number of records produced in response to a single query, the [NSA could ultimately search] records containing over 120 million telephone numbers."

23. Privacy and Civil Liberties Oversight Board, "Report on Section 215 Telephone Records Program," 31. Before sharing information gained from searches of call records with other federal agencies, the NSA must follow minimization procedures designed "to ensure that the NSA's activities are conducted consistent with [statutory] law and the Fourth Amendment to the Constitution." Ibid., at 31–32. The NSA has had "a series of compliance issues" where it violated FISC orders designed to limit the scope of the metadata program. Ibid., 46–54.

24. That may not be the only question, though. The fact that something is legally justified does not always mean it should be done.

25. Privacy and Civil Liberties Oversight Board, "Report on Section 215 Telephone Records Program," 41–42.

26. Note, however, that the NSA, not the FBI, received metadata records from the FISA court pursuant to the bulk metadata program.

27. Privacy and Civil Liberties Oversight Board, "Report on Section 215 Telephone Records Program," 40 (citing superseded section of FISA).

28. Ibid., 40–41 (citing superseded section of FISA). The terms "foreign power" and "agent of a foreign power" are defined at 50 U.S.C. § 1801(a) and (b).

29. Ibid., 40 (citing superseded section of FISA).

30. Ibid., 41; see also Greenwald, *No Place to Hide*, 28.

31. 50 U.S.C. § 1861(a)(1).

32. Privacy and Civil Liberties Oversight Board, "Report on Section 215 Telephone Records Program," 41.

33. 50 U.S.C. § 1861(b)(2)A). Section 215 included a sunset provision, but it has been renewed several times, most recently in 2011. Memorandum opinion in *ACLU v. Clapper*, No. 13-3994 (SDNY December 27, 2013), 28–31 (overruled by 2nd Circuit in May 2015). The current version of Section 215, as discussed here, expired on May 31, 2015. Privacy and Civil Liberties Oversight Board, "Report on Section 215 Telephone Records Program," 97. Congress enacted the USA Freedom Act, which President Obama signed into law on June 2, 2015, as discussed later in this chapter.

34. Privacy and Civil Liberties Oversight Board, "Report on Section 215 Telephone Records Program," 41 (citing superseded section of FISA).

35. Ibid., quoting 50 U.S.C. § 1861(b)(2)(A). When the amended version of Section 215 was enacted, in 2006, some legislators argued that the relevance standard would be a way to limit executive branch access to records. However, Senator Russ Feingold prophetically observed that "[r]elevance is a very broad standard that could arguably justify the collection of all kinds of information about law-abiding Americans." Jennifer Valentino-DeVries and Siobhan Gorman, "Secret Court's Redefinition of 'Relevant' Empowered Vast NSA Data-Gathering," *Wall Street Journal*, July 8, 2013.

36. Greenwald, *No Place to Hide*, 28.

37. As discussed, bulk metadata collection had been carried out before 2006 pursuant to the PSP, without FISC approval.

38. Privacy and Civil Liberties Oversight Board, "Report on Section 215 Telephone Records Program," 43 (citation omitted), 60.

39. Kris, "On the Bulk Collection of Tangible Things," 27; Privacy and Civil Liberties Oversight Board, "Report on Section 215 Telephone Records Program," 139.

40. Privacy and Civil Liberties Oversight Board, "Report on Section 215 Telephone Records Program," 42–46, 60. The executive branch's position with regard to the meaning of the word "relevant" under Section 215 is set forth in two documents: (1) an August 9, 2013, administration white paper and (2) an August 29, 2013, FISC opinion. Privacy and Civil Liberties Oversight Board, "Report on Section 215 Telephone Records Program," 60–61, citing Administration White Paper, "Bulk Collection of Telephony Metadata under Section 215 of the USA PATRIOT Act" (August 9, 2013), and *In re Application of the Federal Bureau of Investigation for an Order Requiring the Production of Tangible Things*, No. BR 13-109 (FISA Court August 29, 2013). Each of those documents is addressed in this chapter.

41. Privacy and Civil Liberties Oversight Board, "Report on Section 215 Telephone Records Program," 54.

42. Administration White Paper, "Bulk Collection of Telephony Metadata," 8–10. The administration cited an example here from other contexts where different records were sought but argued that the same principle applies to the telephony metadata program. Ibid.; see also Privacy and Civil Liberties Oversight Board, "Report on Section 215 Telephone Records Program," 64.

43. Privacy and Civil Liberties Oversight Board, "Report on Section 215 Telephone Records Program," 61.

44. Administration White Paper, "Bulk Collection of Telephony Metadata," 13–14; Amended Memorandum Opinion, *In re Application of the Federal Bureau of Investigation for an Order Requiring the Production of Tangible Things*, No. BR 13–109, 18–23 (concluding at 20 that "bulk collections such as these are 'necessary to identify the much smaller number of [international terrorist] communications." Citation omitted.).

45. *In re Application of the Federal Bureau of Investigation for an Order Requiring the Production of Tangible Things*, 22.

46. Privacy and Civil Liberties Oversight Board, "Report on Section 215 Telephone Records Program," 60. The Privacy and Civil Liberties Oversight Board (hereinafter PCLOB) "is an independent bipartisan agency within the executive branch established by the Implementing Recommendations of the 9/11 Commission Act of 2007. The PCLOB is composed of four part-time members and a full-time chairman, all appointed by the president and confirmed by the Senate." Privacy and Civil Liberties Oversight Board, "Report on Section 215 Telephone Records Program," 2. The PCLOB has two main responsibilities: (1) to review executive branch actions taken in the name of defending the United States against terrorism, making sure that such actions are balanced against "the need to protect privacy and civil liberties"; and (2) making sure "that liberty concerns are appropriately considered in the development and implementation of laws, regulations, and policies related to efforts to protect the nation against terrorism." Ibid. The PCLOB issued a January 23, 2014, document titled "Report on the Telephone Records Program Conducted under Section 215 of the USA PATRIOT Act and on the Operations of the Foreign Intelligence Surveillance Court," which has been cited extensively here. In that report, the PCLOB concluded by a 3–2 margin that the metadata program could not be justified by Section 215 of the Patriot Act. Ibid., 10. Two Board members disagreed with this conclusion. Ibid., 208–218.

47. Ibid., 62.

48. Administration White Paper, "Bulk Collection of Telephony Metadata," 2 (emphasis added).

49. Privacy and Civil Liberties Oversight Board, "Report on Section 215 Telephone Records Program," 62 (emphasis in original).

50. Jim Sensenbrenner, "This Abuse of the Patriot Act Must End," *Guardian*, June 9, 2013.

51. Valentino-DeVries and Gorman, "Secret Court's Redefinition of 'Relevant' Empowered Vast NSA Data-Gathering."

52. At the time Goitein wrote, it was not yet clear how the administration believed the metadata program was legally justified. However, she correctly identified this definition of Section 215 as one possible approach the Obama administration might take (and in fact did take).

53. Elizabeth (Liza) Goitein, "Who Says the NSA's Metadata Collection Is Legal?," Brennan Center for Justice at New York University School of Law blog, June 18, 2013.

54. Adina Schwartz, "The NSA's Surveillance of Metadata," John Jay College of Criminal Justice, Center for Cybercrime Studies, June 28, 2013.

55. Mike Lillis, "Hoyer: No Comparison between Obama, Bush on Secret NSA Surveillance," *The Hill*, June 11, 2013. In the wake of the Snowden revelations, Senator Dianne Feinstein similarly declared, "As far as I know, this [metadata collection] is the exact three-month renewal of what has been in place for the past seven years. This renewal has been carried out by the [FISC] under the business records section of the Patriot Act. Therefore it is lawful." Tom Mak and Burgess Everett, "Dianne Feinstein on NSA: 'It's Called Protecting America,'" *Politico*, June 6, 2013.

56. Privacy and Civil Liberties Oversight Board, "Report on Section 215 Telephone Records Program," 37–38.

57. Ibid., 42–56.

58. Peter M. Shane, *Madison's Nightmare: How Executive Power Threatens American Democracy* (Chicago: University of Chicago Press, 2009), 141. The Obama administration white paper claiming legal authority under Section 215 for the metadata program can also be described as an example of faux law. Administration White Paper, "Bulk Collection of Telephony Metadata."

59. Glenn Greenwald and other critics of the FISC describe the court as a rubber stamp. Greenwald, *No Place to Hide*, 128; Dina Temple-Raston, "FISA Court Appears to Be Rubber Stamp for Government Requests," *NPR.org*, June 13, 2013; Marcy Wheeler, "Former Presiding Judge, John Bates, Makes Compelling Case to Eliminate FISA Court," *emptywheel.net*, January 15, 2014.

60. The metadata program may also violate the Constitution. Memorandum opinion in *Klayman v. Obama*, 42–64. However, on the constitutional question, the Obama administration (and the FISC) can plausibly argue that it relied on Supreme Court precedent and/or that precedent is not clear in concluding the metadata program was constitutional. Privacy and Civil Liberties Oversight Board, "Report on Section 215 Telephone Records Program," 103–136. Since the Obama administration's argument on the constitutional points is not implausible, it does not represent a rejection of meaningful limits on presidential power. The same cannot be said of the statutory argument, as discussed here.

61. Ibid., 102; see also Marcy Wheeler, "Dictionary Arbitrage and Section 215: 'Relevant,'" *emptywheel.net*, August 10, 2013 (arguing that an Obama administration white paper presenting the claimed legal justification for the metadata program relied on an esoteric definition of the word "relevant," rather than the standard definition: "[h]aving significant and demonstrable bearing on the matter and hand" or "closely connected with the subject you are discussing or the situation you are thinking about." The white paper is discussed elsewhere in this chapter. Administration White Paper, "Bulk Collection of Telephony Metadata").

62. Privacy and Civil Liberties Oversight Board, "Report on Section 215 Telephone Records Program," 81.

63. Ibid., 65: "Regardless of the broad scope courts have afforded the relevance standard with respect to discovery and government subpoenas, there is always a qualitative limiting principle that connects the range of documents sought to the facts of the investigation at hand, thus placing a check on the power to acquire information. Relevance limitations are a shield that protects against overreaching, not a sword that enables it."

64. Ibid., 61, 62.

65. Chris Edelson, *Emergency Presidential Power: From the Drafting of the Constitution to the War on Terror* (Madison: University of Wisconsin Press, 2013), 225–234.

66. Jack Goldsmith, *Power and Constraint* (New York: W. W. Norton, 2012), 16–17. Goldsmith did not address the Obama administration's continued use of the metadata program, as that program had not been disclosed to the public at the time Goldsmith wrote his book.

67. Privacy and Civil Liberties Oversight Board, "Report on Section 215 Telephone Records Program," 46.

68. *ACLU v. Clapper*, Docket No. 14–42-cv (2d Cir., May 7, 2015), 2, 54–59.

69. Ibid., 90–92. The court also noted that any statutory changes would have to pass constitutional muster. Ibid.

70. HR 2048; see also Dan Froomkin, "USA Freedom Act: Small Step for Post-Snowden Reform, Giant Leap for Congress," *Intercept*, June 2, 2015.

71. Jennifer Steinhauer and Jonathan Weisman, "U.S. Surveillance in Place since 9/11 Is Sharply Limited," *New York Times*, June 2, 2015.

72. Spencer Ackerman, "Obama Lawyers Asked Secret Court to Ignore Public Court's Decision on Spying," *Guardian*, June 9, 2015.

73. A "United States person" under FISA is defined as "a citizen of the United States, an alien lawfully admitted for permanent residence . . . an unincorporated association a substantial number of members of which are citizens of the United States or aliens lawfully admitted for permanent residence, or a corporation which is incorporated in the United States, but does not include a corporation or an association which is a foreign power." 50 U.S.C. § 1801(i). Individuals who are non-U.S. persons under FISA are neither citizens nor lawful permanent residents of the United States. Privacy and Civil Liberties Oversight Board, Report on the Surveillance Program Operated Pursuant to Section 702 of the Foreign Intelligence Surveillance Act (hereinafter "Report on Section 702"), July 2, 2014, 81. A non-U.S. person can also include "groups, entities, associations, corporations or foreign powers." Privacy and Civil Liberties Oversight Board, "Report on Section 702," 21.

74. 50 U.S.C. § 1881a(a), (b). Foreign intelligence information is defined by FISA (with regard to non-U.S. persons) as (1) "information that relates to . . . the ability of the United States to protect against (A) actual or potential attack or other grave hostile acts of a foreign power or an agent of a foreign power; (B) sabotage, international terrorism, or the international proliferation of weapons of mass destruction by a foreign power or an agent of a foreign power; or (C) clandestine intelligence activities by an intelligence service or network of a foreign power or by an agent of a foreign power; or (2) information with respect to a foreign power or foreign territory that relates to . . . (A) the national defense or the security of the United States; or (B) the conduct of the foreign affairs of the United States." 50 U.S.C. § 1801(e).

75. 50 U.S.C. § 1881a(b).

76. 50 U.S.C. § 1881a(b)(2).

77. 50 U.S.C. § 1881a(g). The PCLOB report explains that "[m]inimization procedures are best understood as a set of controls on data to balance privacy and national security interests. Specifically, under FISA, minimization procedures must be 'specific procedures . . .

that are reasonably designed in light of the purpose and technique of the particular surveillance to minimize the acquisition and retention, and prohibit the dissemination, of non-publicly available information concerning unconsenting United States persons consistent with the need of the United States to obtain, produce, and disseminate foreign intelligence information." Privacy and Civil Liberties Oversight Board, "Report on Section 702," 50, quoting 50 U.S.C. § 1801(h)(1). The goal of these minimization procedures is to limit the acquisition of information that is not permitted by Section 702—in other words, to avoid unnecessarily acquiring information about U.S. persons. Ibid., 52. There is a tension or paradox here, however, as some of the information collected will necessarily include Americans' international communications. In fact, the ACLU argues that Section 702 "is *designed* to allow the government to conduct large-scale warrantless surveillance of [Americans' international] communications." Jameel Jaffer, submission at Privacy and Civil Liberties Oversight Board public hearing on Section 702 of the FISA Amendments Act (hereinafter PCLOB submission), March 19, 2014, 13 (emphasis in original).

78. Privacy and Civil Liberties Oversight Board, "Report on Section 702," 28.

79. Ibid., 8–9.

80. Katherine Hawkins, "ODNI's Transparency Report: What It Tells Us, and What It Doesn't," *OpentheGovernment.org*, Classified Section, June 30, 2014; see also Privacy and Civil Liberties Oversight Board, "Report on Section 702," 25–26: "while only non-U.S. persons may be intentionally targeted . . . information of or concerning U.S. persons may be acquired through Section 702 targeting in a variety of ways, such as when a U.S. person is in communication with a non-U.S. person [who is a] Section 702 target, [or] because two non-U.S. persons are discussing a U.S. person."

81. Hawkins, "ODNI's Transparency Report"; see also Privacy and Civil Liberties Oversight Board, "Report on Section 702," 33: "[t]he government estimates that 89,138 persons were targeted under Section 702 during 2013."

82. Jaffer, "PCLOB submission," 1.

83. Privacy and Civil Liberties Oversight Board, "Report on Section 702," 112.

84. Jaffer, "PCLOB submission," 1.

85. 50 U.S.C. § 1881a.

86. 50 U.S.C. § 1881a(a). The 2008 FAA replaced a temporary statute, the Protect America Act of 2007 (PAA). Section 702 of FISA continues to provide surveillance authority previously authorized under the PAA. Donohue, "Section 702 and the Collection of International Telephone and Internet Content," 135–142. The 2008 FAA, including Section 702, was renewed in December 2012 and is scheduled to expire in December 2017 (unless it is renewed again or modified). FISA Amendments Reauthorization Act of 2012, Pub. L. No. 112–238, 126 Stat. 1631 (2012).

87. 50 U.S.C. § 1881a(g)(2)(A)(i) (emphasis added).

88. 50 U.S.C. § 1881a(g)(2)(A)(v).

89. Edward C. Liu, "Reauthorization of the FISA Amendments Act," Congressional Research Service, April 8, 2013.

90. Privacy and Civil Liberties Oversight Board, "Report on Section 702," 21, 33.

91. 50 U.S.C. § 1881a(i)(2).

92. Jaffer, "PCLOB submission," 5.

93. Privacy and Civil Liberties Oversight Board, "Report on Section 702," 42. Some information is available about the executive branch's targeting procedures, but "neither the NSA nor the FBI targeting procedures have been declassified in full." Ibid. The NSA "initiate[s] Section 702 collection[,]" but the FBI can create its own targeting procedures after the NSA makes initial determinations about the procedures, and both "the CIA and FBI [can] 'nominate' targets to the NSA for Section 702 targeting." Ibid. While the FISC does not typically review individual targeting decisions, "the NSA is required . . . to document every targeting decision made under its targeting procedures." Ibid., 70. The Department of Justice conducts a review of these decisions (after the fact) to determine whether individual targeting decisions "complied with the targeting procedures." Ibid. If the Department of Justice finds evidence of noncompliance, it forwards that information to the FISC. Ibid., 75. The FISC "has required the government to make changes to its collection under Section 702 in the past [when it has reviewed evidence of noncompliance]." Ibid., 81. The attorney general is also required by the FAA "to report every incident of noncompliance to the [Senate Select Committee on Intelligence, Senate Committee on the Judiciary, House Permanent Select Committee on Intelligence, and House Judiciary Committee] in a semiannual report." Ibid., 74, 76.

94. U.S. Constitution, Amendment 4; The Constitution Project's Liberty and Security Committee, "Report on the FISA Amendments Act of 2008," September 6, 2012, 7. As the Constitution Project's report aptly puts it, "the [2008] FAA stipulates that surveillance 'shall be conducted in a manner consistent with the Fourth Amendment . . .' but this statutory declaration does not assure that surveillance authorized by the FAA *in fact* complies with the Fourth Amendment." Ibid., emphasis in original, internal citation omitted.

95. Privacy and Civil Liberties Oversight Board, "Report on Section 702," 7. This is the PRISM portion of the program; the separate "upstream" portion of the program is described later. Service providers that receive orders through PRISM can challenge those directives before the FISC, and providers can appeal FISC decisions to the FISC review court and ultimately to the U.S. Supreme Court. 50 U.S.C. § 1881a(h)(4), (6).

96. Privacy and Civil Liberties Oversight Board, "Report on Section 702," 42, 43. The PCLOB concluded that this determination "is not a 51% to 49% test." Ibid., 44. In other words, it is not enough to determine that it is more likely than not that the target is a non-U.S. person. However, the standard used by NSA for determining that the target is a non-U.S. person "is not a probable cause standard." Ibid. As noted, there is no judicial review of specific targeting decision themselves—only of the general procedures used.

97. Ibid., 45–46.

98. Greenwald, *No Place to Hide*, 108, 116; see also Privacy and Civil Liberties Oversight Board, "Report on Section 702," 81: "the government utilizes two collection methods under Section 702—PRISM collection and upstream collection (which includes acquiring 'about' communications)."

99. Privacy and Civil Liberties Oversight Board, "Report on Section 702," 33, 82, 7.

100. Ibid., 33–34: "As of mid-2011, 91 percent of the Internet communications that the NSA acquired each year were obtained through PRISM collection."

101. Ibid., 35 (emphasis added). This can be useful to the NSA when a targeted person interacts with a "foreign telephone or Internet compan[y], which the government cannot

compel to comply with a Section 702 directive." Ibid. This is particularly useful to the NSA because many of the companies operating the "backbone" that makes the Internet function are based in the United States. Jonathan Strickland, "Who Owns the Internet?," *HowStuffWorks.com*, March 3, 2008.

102. Privacy and Civil Liberties Oversight Board, "Report on Section 702," 7, 37, 39, 85–86.

103. The CIA and FBI are also able to run searches or "queries" of information collected pursuant to Section 702 surveillance. Ibid., 55.

104. Ibid., 8.

105. Jaffer, "PCLOB submission," 6, 16.

106. Ibid., 17.

107. The Constitution Project's Liberty and Security Committee, "Report on the FISA Amendments Act of 2008," 7.

108. Ibid., 6; Privacy and Civil Liberties Oversight Board, "Report on Section 702," 6.

109. Jaffer, "PCLOB submission," 13.

110. The Constitution Project's Liberty and Security Committee, "Report on the FISA Amendments Act of 2008," 7.

111. Privacy and Civil Liberties Oversight Board, "Report on Section 702," 6.

112. Jaffer, "PCLOB submission," 3.

113. Privacy and Civil Liberties Oversight Board, "Report on Section 702," 24–25.

114. Unclassified Report on the President's Surveillance Program, July 10, 2009, 1.

115. *ACLU v. NSA*, 438 F.Supp.2d 754 (E.D. Mich. 2006), vacated on jurisdictional grounds, 493 F.3d 644 (6th Cir. 2007). The district court also found that the TSP violated the Constitution.

116. Privacy and Civil Liberties Oversight Board, "Report on Section 702," 18; see also ibid., 5: "Section 702 [surveillance] has its roots in the President's Surveillance Program [more specifically, in the TSP] developed in the immediate aftermath of the September 11th attacks."

117. Jaffer, "PCLOB submission," 4.

118. Privacy and Civil Liberties Oversight Board, "Report on Section 702," 18–19, 80.

119. Jaffer, "PCLOB submission," 5 (emphasis in original); see also Privacy and Civil Liberties Oversight Board, "Report on Section 702," 82: "The collection of communications [under PRISM] to and from a target inevitably returns communications in which non-targets are on the other end, some of whom will be U.S. persons. Such 'incidental' collection of communications is not accidental, nor is it inadvertent."

120. Jaffer, "PCLOB submission," 13.

121. 50 U.S.C. § 1881a(b)(2).

122. Jaffer, "PCLOB submission," 13, quoting 50 U.S.C. § 1881a(b)(2) (emphasis in original).

123. Ibid., 13, 14–15.

124. Ibid., 6–20.

125. Privacy and Civil Liberties Oversight Board, "Report on Section 702," 86: "foreigners located outside of the United States . . . lack Fourth Amendment rights."

126. Under "about" surveillance, discussed later. Ibid., 82, 85.

127. Jaffer, "PCLOB submission," 6, 17, 10 (emphasis in original).

128. Indeed, the PCLOB concedes that "certain aspects of the Section 702 program [including searches for information contained in the communications of U.S. persons and 'about' surveillance] *push the entire program close to the line of constitutional reasonableness.*" Privacy and Civil Liberties Oversight Board, "Report on Section 702," 88 (emphasis added). The PCLOB offered a set of recommended changes "designed to push the program more comfortably into the sphere of [constitutional] reasonableness." Ibid., 97. However, it described these suggestions as "policy recommendations" rather than constitutionally required changes. Ibid. The ACLU points out that Section 702 surveillance also raises First Amendment concerns because it may have a chilling effect on protected speech. Jaffer, "PCLOB submission," 17–20.

129. Ibid., 20, 21. "About" surveillance is conducted as part of upstream collection. Privacy and Civil Liberties Oversight Board, "Report on Section 702," 37.

130. Hawkins, "ODNI's Transparency Report."

131. Privacy and Civil Liberties Oversight Board, "Report on Section 702," 81.

132. Charlie Savage, "NSA Said to Search Content of Messages to and from U.S.," *New York Times*, August 8, 2013.

133. Privacy and Civil Liberties Oversight Board, "Report on Section 702," 85 (emphasis added).

134. The PCLOB is critical of reporting on "about" collection, claiming suggestions that the NSA is broadly searching essentially all international communications by Americans for information referring to targeted foreigners "represents a misunderstanding of a more complex reality." Ibid., 119, 123–124. However, the PCLOB report fails to make clear why reporting on "about" surveillance is based on a misunderstanding. The PCLOB report explains that "'about' collection takes place exclusively in the NSA's acquisition of Internet communications through [the] upstream collection process . . . as distinguished from the NSA's PRISM collection, in which U.S.-based Internet service providers transmit communications to the government directly." Ibid. But, as Katherine Hawkins observed after the PCLOB's report was released, "it's [still] unclear exactly what ['about'] collection does involve." Hawkins, "PCLOB Report: We Don't Know How Many Americans' Emails the NSA Collects under Section 702—But We Don't Need to Know," *OpentheGovernment .org*, Classified Section, July 3, 2014. Cindy Cohn argues that the PCLOB is "[h]iding behind the 'complexity' of the technology." Cohn, "Flawed Oversight Board Report Endorses General Warrants," Electronic Frontier Foundation, July 1, 2014. Cohn argues that the PCLOB's discussion of "about" collection "skips over the essential privacy problem with the 702 'upstream' program: that the government has access to or is acquiring nearly all communications that travel over the Internet. The board focuses only on the government's methods for searching and filtering out unwanted information. This ignores the fact that the government is collecting and searching through the content of millions of emails, social networking posts, and other Internet communications, steps that occur before the PCLOB analysis starts." Ibid. It is also worth noting that part of the reason why the PCLOB report accepted "about" collection is "the inextricability of the practice from a broader form of collection that has unique value." Privacy and Civil Liberties Oversight Board, "Report on Section 702," 124. In other words, the PCLOB suggested that "about" collection should be

continued because "ending all 'about' collection would require ending even those forms of 'about' collection that the Board regards as appropriate and valuable, and that have very little chance of impacting the privacy of people in the United States." Ibid., 123. The implication (though it is only that—an implication) is that the Board may believe that *some* "about" collection is legally problematic but that it cannot be stopped without endangering other valuable and legitimate forms of "about" collection. The PCLOB recommended that "the NSA work to develop technology that would enable it to identify and distinguish among the types of 'about' collection at the acquisition stage, and then selectively limit or modify its 'about' collection, as may later be deemed appropriate." Ibid., 145.

135.　Privacy and Civil Liberties Oversight Board, "Report on Section 702," 81.

136.　Ibid., 83.

137.　50 U.S.C. § 1881a(b).

138.　Privacy and Civil Liberties Oversight Board, "Report on Section 702," 70.

139.　Jaffer, "PCLOB submission," 21, 22, 24.

140.　50 U.S.C. § 1881a(b)(2).

141.　Jaffer, "PCLOB submission," 25.

142.　Minimization procedures in place before the 2011 changes prohibited backdoor searches. Jaffer, "PCLOB submission," 25.

143.　Elizabeth Goitein, "The NSA's Backdoor Search Loophole," *Boston Review*, November 14, 2013; James Ball and Spencer Ackerman, "NSA Loophole Allows Warrantless Search for U.S. Citizens' Emails and Phone Calls," *Guardian*, August 9, 2013.

144.　Jaffer, "PCLOB submission," 25. In February 2015, the Obama administration announced new rules designed to limit the use of backdoor searches. Under the new procedures, "the NSA and CIA will be permitted to query the database with US person identifiers (a unique identifier associated such as a name, phone number, email address, etc.) only after developing a written statement of facts showing that a query is reasonably likely to return foreign intelligence information, as recommended by the Privacy and Civil Liberties Oversight Board in its report on Section 702." Jake Laperruque, "Updates to Section 702 Minimization Rules Still Leave Loopholes," Center for Democracy and Technology, February 9, 2015. However, as Laperruque observes, this step, while a useful start, "is a far cry from requiring a judicial finding of probable cause that the person whose communications are sought is an agent of a foreign power" and leaves the administration a great deal of room to search its database to review the contents of Americans' communications without a judicial warrant. Ibid.

145.　Privacy and Civil Liberties Oversight Board, "Report on Section 702," 104.

146.　Jaffer, "PCLOB submission," 21.

147.　Steven Levy, "How the NSA Almost Killed the Internet," *Wired.com*, January 7, 2014.

148.　Section 702 has been challenged in court on constitutional grounds, but the Supreme Court ruled in 2013 that plaintiffs (attorneys, journalists, human rights workers, and others involved in international phone and e-mail communications as part of their work) lacked standing to challenge the law because they could not demonstrate that their communications were actually subject to surveillance. *Clapper v. Amnesty Int'l USA*, 133 S. Ct. 1138 (2013).

# Chapter 12.
## The Obama Administration and Military Detention

1. Executive Order 13492, "Review and Disposition of Individuals Detained at the Guantanamo Bay Naval Base and Closure of Detention Facility," January 22, 2009.

2. Barack Obama, "Remarks by the President on National Security," National Archives, May 21, 2009.

3. Chris Edelson, *Emergency Presidential Power: From the Drafting of the Constitution to the War on Terror* (Madison: University of Wisconsin Press, 2013), 158.

4. Hanna F. Madbak, "Is Bagram President Obama's Guantanamo?," *Civil Rights Committee Blog, New York State Bar Association*, June 10, 2010: "[In 2008] presidential candidate Barack Obama . . . hailed the *Boumediene* decision as 'a rejection of the Bush Administration's attempt to create a legal black hole at Guantánamo,' and praised the Supreme Court for 'rejecting a false choice between fighting terrorism and respecting *habeas corpus*.'" However, the Obama administration itself rejected the idea that habeas rights applied to prisoners held by the United States in Afghanistan. Ibid.; see also Glenn Greenwald, "Obama Wins the Right to Detain People with No Habeas Review," *Salon*, May 21, 2010.

5. Michael John Garcia, Jennifer K. Elsea, R. Chuck Mason, and Edward C. Liu, "Closing the Guantanamo Detention Center: Legal Issues," Congressional Research Service, May 30, 2013, 3–4.

6. As Jonathan Hafetz notes, indefinite detention after 9/11 has not been limited to Guantanamo: "[it] includes individuals held by the United States at Bagram Air Base in Afghanistan as well as prisoners previously detained in secret CIA 'black sites.'" Jonathan Hafetz, "Military Detention in the 'War on Terrorism': Normalizing the Exceptional after 9/11" (sidebar), *Columbia Law Review* 112 (2012): 31, 32. President Obama ended the black site interrogation program in 2009. Adam Goldman, "The Hidden History of the CIA's Prison in Poland," *Washington Post*, January 23, 2014. The Bagram prison is now controlled by the Afghan government. Alex Rodriguez, "U.S. Hands over Control of Bagram Prison to Afghan Government," *Los Angeles Times*, March 25, 2013. Accordingly, this chapter focuses on detention at Guantanamo.

7. Louis Fisher, "Closing Guantanamo: A Presidential Commitment Unfulfilled," in *Congress and Civil-Military Relations*, ed. Colton C. Campbell and David P. Auerswald (Washington, D.C.: Georgetown University Press, 2015), 148–165.

8. Obama, "Remarks by the President on National Security."

9. Ibid. The executive order was 13492, "Review and Disposition of Individuals Detained at the Guantanamo Bay Naval Base and Closure of Detention Facility," January 22, 2009.

10. Obama, "Remarks by the President on National Security."

11. Ibid.

12. Ibid.

13. Memorandum from Patrick F. Philbin, Deputy Assistant Attorney General, Office of Legal Counsel, to Counsel to the President, *Legality of the Use of Military Commissions to Try Terrorists*, November 6, 2001 (hereinafter November 6, 2001, Philbin memo); see also

Military Order of November 13, 2001: Detention, Treatment, and Trial of Certain Non-Citizens in the War against Terrorism, 66 Fed. Reg. 57,833, November 16, 2001.

14. Missy Ryan and Adam Goldman, "U.S. Prepares to Accelerate Detainee Transfers from Guantanamo Bay Prison," *Washington Post*, December 24, 2014.

15. Fisher, "Closing Guantanamo: A Presidential Commitment Unfulfilled."

16. Natsu Taylor Saito, "Internments, Then and Now: Constitutional Accountability in Post-9/11 America," *Duke Forum for Law and Social Change* 2 (2010): 71, 93.

17. Nancy Kassop, "Rivals for Influence on Counterterrorism Policy: White House Political Staff versus Executive Branch Legal Advisors," *Presidential Studies Quarterly* 43, no. 2 ( June 2013): 253.

18. Glenn Greenwald, "Welcome to Gitmo North," *Salon*, December 15, 2009; Eric Posner, "President Obama Can Shut Guantanamo Whenever He Wants," *Slate*, May 2, 2013.

19. Sam Kleiner, "Sorry, Lindsey Graham: Obama's Trials for Terror Suspects Have Been a Tremendous Success," *New Republic*, June 18, 2014: "the Obama administration has created a careful model of allowing for interrogation of a suspected terrorist under military custody and then transferring him over for prosecution in a federal court."

20. Fisher, "Closing Guantanamo: A Presidential Commitment Unfulfilled": "The [Obama] administration was determined not to add other individuals to Guantánamo." See also Robert Chesney, "Postwar," *Harvard National Security Journal* 5 (2014): 305, 313: "the Obama Administration has made clear since 2009 that it will not bring new detainees to Guantánamo."

21. *Hamdan v. Rumsfeld*, 548 U.S. 557 (2006).

22. November 6, 2001, Philbin memo.

23. The Military Commissions Act of 2009 was enacted as part of the National Defense Authorization Act for Fiscal Year 2010, Pub. L. No. 111–84.

24. *Hamdan v. U.S.*, 696 F.3d 1238 (D.C. Cir. 2012), overruled in part on statutory grounds by *Al-Bahlul v. U.S.*, 767 F.3d 1 (D.C. Cir. 2014). This case is referred to as "*Hamdan II*" to distinguish it from the Supreme Court decision in 2006.

25. *Hamdan II*, at 1241.

26. Although *Hamdan II* was overruled in part in a later case by the D.C. Circuit (*en banc*) on statutory grounds, the D.C. Circuit continues to endorse the conclusion that, regardless of statutory intent, it would be an ex post facto violation to enter convictions for material support for terrorism based on pre-2006 conduct. *Al-Bahlul v. U.S.*, 767 F.3d 1, 29 (2014).

27. Andrew Cohen, "This Month in Terror Law: Hamdan Wins Again!," *Atlantic*, October 16, 2012: "we'll know in the coming months about the scope of the impact this *Hamdan* decision will have on other detainee cases. Does the precedent immediately strike out other uses of 'material support provisions' for conduct before 2006, which would mean virtually every such charge at Gitmo?" In fact, the D.C. Circuit, sitting *en banc*, vacated another material support conviction in 2014. *Al-Bahlul v. U.S.*, 767 F.3d 1 (2014). *Al-Bahlul* overruled *Hamdan II* on statutory grounds, finding that Congress in the 2006 MCA had intended to retroactively make material support for terrorism a war crime. However, the D.C. Circuit in *al-Bahlul* ruled that, even though Congress intended to make material support for terrorism a war crime for offenses committed before 2006, there was no

sufficient basis for concluding that material support for terrorism was triable by a military tribunal prior to 2006. 767 F.3d at 29. In other words, it remained an ex post facto violation to convict Bahlul for material support for terrorism based on pre-2006 conduct because it had not previously been recognized as a war crime. Ibid.

28. David Glazier, "Destined for an Epic Fail: The Problematic Guantanamo Military Commissions," *Ohio State Law Journal* 75 (2014): 903, 951, citing *al-Bahlul*, 767 F.3d 1.

29. Ibid., at 924.

30. Ibid., at 920–924. The Supreme Court held in *Hamdan* that Common Article 3 applies to military trials of suspected members of al Qaeda. 548 U.S. at 629–632.

31. Glazier also raises substantive concerns, discussed later.

32. Although the 2009 MCA bars the use of such evidence, Glazier writes that, "[d]espite these clear rules, commission prosecutors have rationalized that it is the judge's responsibility, not theirs, to act as the admissibility gatekeeper. Successful efforts to get [Omar] Khadr's statements admitted in the summer of 2010 show that this effort continued even under the Obama Administration. This might be justified if commission judges were in a position to objectively weigh the relevant factors necessary to determine a statement's pedigree, but they are not. In an adversarial system, the judge must rely on the parties to present the information necessary to reach their decisions. But the government holds all the cards with respect to how these detainee statements were obtained. Through control of the classification system, restrictions on the identification of, and access to, potential witnesses, and limitations on what discovery is provided, it effectively restricts the defense's access to the information needed to credibly challenge the admission of statements obtained through coercion. 'Letting the judge decide' is thus tantamount to allowing coerced statements to be used in contravention of the clear statutory prohibitions against doing so." Glazier, "Destined for an Epic Fail," 990.

33. Ibid., at 924–942.

34. Ibid., at 966.

35. Ibid., at 960.

36. Ibid., at 964–965.

37. Ibid., at 963.

38. Sari Horwitz, "Holder Says His Plan to Try 9/11 Suspects in Civilian Court in New York Was Right One," *Washington Post*, November 4, 2013.

39. David Welna, "'No End in Sight' for Sept. 11 Proceedings at Guantanamo Bay," National Public Radio, February 26, 2015; see also David Glovin and David Lerman, "Khalid Sheikh Mohammed's 9/11 Trial Tests Military Courts," *Bloomberg*, May 4, 2012.

40. Welna, "'No End in Sight' for Sept. 11 Proceedings at Guantanamo Bay."

41. Carol J. Williams, "Obama's Renewed Push to Close Guantanamo Prison Is Seen as Promising," *Los Angeles Times*, January 24, 2015.

42. It is worth noting that critics argue even trial in federal civilian court would not have been legitimate since the Obama administration had suggested prisoners would not be released if they were acquitted at trial. Michael Isikoff, "'Heads I Win, Tails You Lose': In 9/11 Case, KSM Won't Walk Free Even If Found Not Guilty," *Newsweek*, November 18, 2009.

43. Fisher, "Closing Guantanamo: A Presidential Commitment Unfulfilled."

44. Nicolas L. Martinez, "Pinching the President's Prosecutorial Prerogative: Can Congress Use Its Purse Power to Block Khalid Sheikh Mohammed's Transfer to the United States?," *Stanford Law Review* 64 (2012): 1469, 1475–1476; see also Ike Skelton National Defense Authorization Act for Fiscal Year 2011, Pub. L. No. 111-383, § 1032, 124 Stat. 4137, 4351 (2010).

45. Eric Holder, "Statement of the Attorney General on the Prosecution of the 9/11 Conspirators," Department of Justice, Washington, D.C., April 4, 2011.

46. It is possible that Congress's action raises constitutional concerns. Todd Garvey, "The Take Care Clause and Executive Discretion in the Enforcement of Law," Congressional Research Service, September 4, 2014: "legislation that can be characterized as significantly restricting the exercise of executive branch enforcement decisions, in either the criminal, civil, or administrative context, could raise questions under the separation of powers." However, it is more likely that the administration's objection was based on policy considerations, not a constitutional argument. David J.R. Frakt, "Prisoners of Congress: The Constitutional and Political Clash over Detainees and the Closure of Guantanamo," *University of Pittsburgh Law Review* 74 (2012): 179, 251.

47. Barack Obama, "Remarks by the President on National Security."

48. Eric Holder, "Attorney General Announces Forum Decisions for Guantanamo Detainees," Department of Justice, Washington, D.C., November 13, 2009; see also Jennifer K. Elsea, "The Military Commissions Act of 2009 (MCA of 2009): Overview and Legal Issues," Congressional Research Service, August 4, 2014, 3–4. David Glazier raised significant legal concerns about military tribunals the Obama administration convened for Khadr and Al-Nashiri. Glazier, "Destined for an Epic Fail," 942–960.

49. U.S. district judge William G. Young suggested the possibility of jurors participating by video connection. Nicolas Martinez objected that "trying a criminal defendant in an Article III court outside the physical presence of a jury would raise significant Fifth and Sixth Amendment concerns" but praised Judge Young for "think[ing] imaginatively about ways to preserve our rule of law tradition." Nicolas L. Martinez, "Pulling the Plug on the Virtual Jury: Why Khalid Sheikh Mohammed Should Not Be Tried at Guantanamo Bay by Jurors Sitting in New York City," *Stanford Law Review Online* 65 (2012): 47.

50. *Hamdi v. Rumsfeld*, 542 U.S. 507, 516 (O'Connor, J., plurality opinion).

51. Ibid., at 535–536. Although Justice O'Connor wrote a plurality opinion, eight justices fundamentally agreed with her conclusions with regard to separation of powers and the rule of law, as discussed in Section II.

52. Barack Obama, "Remarks by the President on National Security."

53. Hafetz, "Military Detention in the 'War on Terrorism,'" 41.

54. *Hamdi*, 542 U.S. at 509 (O'Connor, J., plurality opinion). Justices Souter and Ginsburg joined the plurality on this point, saying that Hamdi was "entitled at a minimum" to such a hearing. 542 U.S. at 553 (Souter, J., concurring in part, dissenting in part, and concurring in the judgment).

55. *Boumediene v. Bush*, 553 U.S. 723, 765 (2008); Jennifer K. Elsea, "Substantive Due Process and U.S. Jurisdiction over Foreign Nationals," *Fordham Law Review* 82 (2014):

2077, 2080: "the Supreme Court has in fact found that the Due Process Clause extends to all aliens within the United States, even those whose presence is 'unlawful, involuntary, or transitory'" (citation omitted).

56. Joseph Margulies, *Guantanamo and the Abuse of Presidential Power* (New York: Simon and Schuster, 2006), 169.

57. Mark Denbeaux, Joshua Denbeaux, David Gratz, John Gregorek, Matthew Darby, Shana Edwards, Daniel Mann, Megan Sassaman, and Helen Skinner, "No-Hearing Hearings: An Analysis of the Government's Combatant Status Review Tribunals at Guantanamo," *Seton Hall Law Review* 41 (2011): 1231, 1232–1233.

58. Ibid., at 1233–1236.

59. Barack Obama, "Remarks by the President on National Security."

60. Heather Brandon, "Four Years and 14 Hearings—the PRB Limps Along," Human Rights First, March 3, 2015.

61. Barack Obama, "Periodic Review of Individuals Detained at Guantanamo Bay Naval Station Pursuant to Authorization to Use Military Force," Executive Order 13567, 76 Fed. Reg. 13275, March 10, 2011. PRBs were later endorsed by Congress in legislation.

62. Fisher, "Closing Guantanamo: A Presidential Commitment Unfulfilled."

63. Executive Order 13567, preamble. The preamble does also refer to "authority vested in [President Obama] by the Constitution" but does not contain any reference to plenary or inherent power. The order refers to "detention authorized by Congress under the [2001] AUMF" rather than claiming any unilateral presidential detention authority. Of course, President Bush's November 2001 military order similarly referred to statutory authority—but the Bush administration also claimed plenary power to detain in argument before the Supreme Court. *Hamdi*, 542 U.S. at 507.

64. Executive Order 13567 § 3. The order provided that more limited "file" reviews would also be conducted every six months to check for new information that might justify a full hearing in "the intervening years between full reviews." Ibid., § 3(c).

65. Carol Rosenberg, "71 Guantanamo Prisoners Will Get Parole-Style Hearings, Pentagon Says," *Washington Post*, July 21, 2013. Six prisoners who had been convicted or were awaiting trial and eighty-six prisoners already cleared for release would not get PRB hearings. Ibid.

66. Edelson, *Emergency Presidential Power*, 237, quoting Executive Order 13567.

67. Human Rights First, "Fact Sheet: Guantanamo Periodic Review Boards," updated as of December 2015.

68. Brandon, "Four Years and 14 Hearings—the PRB Limps Along."

69. Jacob Sullum, "Periodic Detention Reviews—Now with More Reviewers!," *Reason.com*, March 9, 2011.

70. Zak Newman, "Guantanamo's New Purgatory," *Defense One*, July 25, 2014. Many prisoners who have been cleared for transfer (including by the PRBs) are still held. Editorial Board, "Perpetuating Guantanamo's Travesty," *New York Times*, January 17, 2015; Cora Currier and Margot Williams, "Thirteen Years On, Yemeni Prisoners Await Release from Guantanamo," *Intercept*, January 12, 2015. The Bush administration released 532 prisoners from Guantanamo by January 2009. Editorial Board, "Perpetuating Guantanamo's Travesty." The Obama administration has released or transferred more than one hundred

prisoners. Human Rights First, "Fact Sheet: Guantanamo by the Numbers," September 2015.

71. Andy Worthington, "As Last Egyptian Is Cleared for Release from Guantánamo, Another Yemeni Faces Periodic Review Board," *andyworthington.com/uk*, February 26, 2015.

72. Newman, "Guantanamo's New Purgatory."

73. *Boumediene*, 553 U.S. 723.

74. Stephen I. Vladeck, "The D.C. Circuit after *Boumediene*," *Seton Hall Law Review* 41 (2011): 1451. The Supreme Court held that habeas entitles prisoners to a "meaningful review of both the cause for detention and the Executive's power to detain." *Boumediene*, 553 U.S. at 783. However, the Court "left entirely open the question of what exactly would constitute "meaningful review" of the legal basis for their detention." Adam R. Pearlman, "Meaningful Review and Process Due: How Guantanamo Detention is Changing the Battlefield," *Harvard National Security Journal* 6 (2015): 255, 269.

75. Hafetz, "Military Detention in the 'War on Terrorism,'" 39–40.

76. *Al-Bihani v. Obama*, 590 F.3d 866, 872 (D.C. Cir. 2010), at 869.

77. Ibid., at 872–873. The court concluded that his unit was affiliated with al Qaeda because al Qaeda members "participated in its command structure" and because his unit "fought alongside the Taliban while the Taliban was harboring al Qaeda." Ibid., at 872.

78. Unclassified Summary of Final PRB Determination for Ghaled Nassar Al Bihani, May 15, 2014.

79. Hafetz, "Military Detention in the 'War on Terrorism,'" 40. The case Hafetz referred to is *Latif v. Obama*, 677 F.3d 1175 (D.C. Cir. 2012).

80. Mark Denbeaux, Jonathan Hafetz, Sara Ben-David, Nicholas Stratton, and Lauren Winchester, "No Hearing Habeas: D.C. Circuit Restricts Meaningful Review," Seton Hall University School of Law, Center for Policy and Research, May 1, 2012.

81. Clive Stafford Smith, "Federal Courts Reject Virtually All Habeas Petitions from Gitmo: Study," *Daily Beast*, May 13, 2012.

82. Some members of Congress think Guantanamo should not be closed and are not concerned about the possibility that innocent prisoners may be held there. Senator Tom Cotton declared that "the only problem with Guantanamo Bay is there are too many empty beds and cells there right now. . . . We should be sending more terrorists there for further interrogation to keep this country safe. As far as I'm concerned, every last one of them can rot in hell. But as long as they can't do that, they can rot in Guantanamo Bay." Sarah D. Wire, "Cotton, 3 Other Senators, Touring Cuba Base," *Northwest Arkansas Democrat Gazette*, March 13, 2015. In January 2015, Senator Kelly Ayotte said that "now is not the time to be emptying Guantanamo with no plan for . . . where these individuals are going to go, no assurances of security for those who have been released." Jeremy Herb, "GOP Senators Move to Keep Gitmo Open," *Politico*, January 13, 2015.

83. Miranda Green, "His Name Is Clifford Sloan, and He Could Be the Guy to Finally Close Guantanamo," *Daily Beast*, June 19, 2013; Cliff Sloan, "The Path to Closing Guantanamo," *New York Times*, January 5, 2015; Ryan and Goldman, "U.S. Prepares to Accelerate Detainee Transfers from Guantanamo Bay Prison." More than forty prisoners were transferred in 2009 and 2010. Guantanamo Review Task Force, Final Report, Department of Justice, Department of Defense, Department of State, Department of Homeland

Security, Office of the Director of National Intelligence, Joint Chiefs of Staff, January 22, 2010. In all, the Obama administration has "transferred, repatriated, or resettled" more than one hundred prisoners from Guantanamo. Human Rights First, "Fact Sheet: Guantanamo by the Numbers," September 2015, citing "The Guantanamo Docket: Timeline," *New York Times*. The Bush administration released more than five hundred prisoners from Guantanamo (of course, it also imprisoned far more than have been held during the Obama years). Human Rights First, "Fact Sheet: Guantanamo by the Numbers."

84. Human Rights First, "Fact Sheet: Guantanamo by the Numbers," September 2015.

85. Guantanamo Review Task Force, Final Report.

86. "Former Guantanamo Envoy Says Prison Undermines National Security," National Public Radio transcript, December 27, 2014.

87. Guantanamo Review Task Force, Final Report.

88. Ike Skelton National Defense Authorization Act for Fiscal Year 2011, Pub. L. No. 111–383, 124 Stat. 4351 (2011), § 1033(b).

89. Statement by the President on HR 6523, January 7, 2011.

90. Jennifer K. Elsea and Michael John Garcia, "Wartime Detention Provisions in Recent Defense Authorization Legislation," Congressional Research Service, January 23, 2015, 29–32, 38–39, 42–44.

91. National Defense Authorization Act for Fiscal Year 2014, Pub. L. No. 113–66, 127 Stat. 671, § 1035 (2013). Transfer was also permitted "to effectuate an order affecting disposition of the individual by a court or competent tribunal of the United States having jurisdiction." Ibid., § 1035(a) (2).

92. Ibid., § 1035(d).

93. Elsea and Garcia, "Wartime Detention Provisions in Recent Defense Authorization Legislation," 42, 44.

94. Statement by the President on HR 3304, December 26, 2013.

95. Fisher, "Closing Guantanamo: A Presidential Commitment Unfulfilled."

96. Charlie Savage, "Obama Lifts Moratorium on Transfer of Detainees," *New York Times*, May 13, 2013; Sloan, "The Path to Closing Guantanamo."

97. "Envoy Says Administration Moving Aggressively to Transfer Guantanamo Detainees," *PBS Newshour* transcript, January 2, 2014.

98. Sloan, "The Path to Closing Guantanamo."

99. Helene Cooper, "Obama Nears Goal for Guantanamo with Faster Pace of Releases," *New York Times*, January 5, 2015.

100. Helene Cooper, "Cliff Sloan, Guantanamo Envoy, Quits Amid Delays in Prisoner Releases," *New York Times*, December 22, 2014.

101. Human Rights First, "Fact Sheet: Guantanamo by the Numbers," January 2016.

102. Statement by the President on the Release of Sergeant Bowe Bergdahl, May 31, 2014; Anne Gearan, "Sources Outline Conditions on Taliban Leaders' Release in Exchange for Bergdahl," *Washington Post*, June 5, 2014.

103. Emily Bazelon, "Gitmo Fail," *Slate*, June 4, 2014; Gearan, "Sources Outline Conditions on Taliban Leaders' Release in Exchange for Bergdahl."

104. Peter Baker, "Obama Defends Swap of Taliban for American P.O.W.," *New York Times*, June 3, 2014.

105. Gearan, "Sources Outline Conditions on Taliban Leaders' Release in Exchange for Bergdahl."

106. Baker, "Obama Defends Swap of Taliban for American P.O.W."

107. Statement by NSC Spokesperson Caitlin Hayden on the NDAA and the Transfer of Taliban Detainees from Guantanamo, June 3, 2014, National Security Council Press Office.

108. Louis Fisher, "Abraham Lincoln: Preserving the Union and the Constitution," *Albany Government Law Review* 3 (2010): 503, 522–528; David Gray Adler, "The Framers and Executive Prerogative: A Constitutional and Historical Rebuke," *Presidential Studies Quarterly* 42, no. 2 (June 2012): 378, 379.

109. Statement by NSC Spokesperson Caitlin Hayden on the NDAA and the Transfer of Taliban Detainees from Guantanamo.

110. Christopher S. Kelley, "Rethinking Presidential Power: The Unitary Executive and the George W. Bush Presidency," paper presented at Midwest Political Science Association Annual Meeting, Chicago, April 7–10, 2005.

111. Charlie Savage, "Barack Obama's Q&A," *Boston Globe*, December 20, 2007.

112. Chris Edelson, "Obama's Swap for Bergdahl: A Presidential Power Play?," *Los Angeles Times*, June 6, 2014.

113. Barton Gellman, *Angler: The Cheney Vice Presidency* (New York: Penguin Press, 2008), 171.

## Chapter 13.
## The Obama Administration and Torture

1. See chapter 7.

2. Asa Hutchinson, James R. Jones, Talbot "Sandy" D'Alemberte, Richard A. Epstein, David P. Gushee, Azizah Y. al-Hibri, David R. Irvine, Claudia Kennedy, Thomas R. Pickering, William S. Sessions, and Gerald E. Thomson, "The Report of the Constitution Project's Task Force on Detainee Treatment" (Washington, D.C.: The Constitution Project, 2013), 311.

3. Barack Obama, Executive Order 13491, "Ensuring Lawful Interrogations," January 22, 2009.

4. Later in 2009, the Obama administration also publicly released four Bush-era OLC memos on interrogation, including one of the August 1, 2002, Jay Bybee memos and three May 2005 memos written by Steven Bradbury. Mark Mazzetti and Scott Shane, "Interrogation Methods Detail Harsh Tactics by the CIA," *New York Times*, April 16, 2009.

5. Obama, Executive Order 13491.

6. Army Field Manual, Human Intelligence Collector Operations, FM 2–22.3, 5–75.

7. Matthew Alexander, "Torture's Loopholes," *New York Times*, January 20, 2010. Appendix M of the Army Field Manual does not expressly address this kind of sleep deprivation. Beth Van Schaack, "The Torture Convention and Appendix M of the Army Field Manual on Interrogations," *Just Security*, December 5, 2014. Van Schaack notes that Appendix M does not expressly prohibit sleep deprivation of "4 hours [per] day of sleep for a prolonged period of time."

8. Alexander, "Torture's Loopholes."

9. Task Force Report, "Ethics Abandoned: Medical Professionalism and Detainee Abuse in the 'War on Terror,'" Institute on Medicine as a Profession and the Open Society Foundations, November 2013, xxxii.

10. Alexander, "Torture's Loopholes."

11. Foreword by Chairman Dianne Feinstein to U.S. Senate Select Committee on Intelligence, Committee Study of the Central Intelligence Agency's Detention and Interrogation Program, December 3, 2014, declassification release, 4.

12. Hutchinson et al., "The Constitution Project's Task Force on Detainee Treatment," 334.

13. David Johnston and Charlie Savage, "Obama Reluctant to Look into Bush Programs," *New York Times*, January 11, 2009.

14. Josh Meyer and Greg Miller, "Holder Opens Investigations into CIA Interrogations," *Los Angeles Times*, August 25, 2009.

15. Statement of Attorney General Eric Holder on Closure of Investigation into the Interrogation of Certain Detainees, August 30, 2012; see also Glenn Greenwald, "Obama's Justice Department Grants Final Immunity to Bush's CIA Torturers," *Guardian*, August 31, 2012.

16. Marjorie Cohn, "A Legal Duty to Prosecute Torturers," *Jurist*, October 1, 2012.

17. Roger Alford suggests that the U.S. Senate Intelligence Committee's report on detention and interrogation, a redacted version of which was made public in December 2014, marked "a transition point for the United States" in terms of "moving in the direction of truth-telling [about torture]." Roger Alford, "The Senate Torture Report as a Truth Commission," *Opinio Juris*, December 10, 2014. However, even assuming Alford is correct, that report was published by a Senate committee, not by the Obama administration.

18. Christopher H. Pyle, "Barack Obama and Civil Liberties," *Presidential Studies Quarterly* 42, no. 4 (December 2012): 868, 869.

19. Mark Mazzetti, "Obama Releases Interrogation Methods, Says C.I.A. Operatives Won't Be Prosecuted," *New York Times* (*The Caucus* blog), April 9, 2009.

20. Pyle, "Barack Obama and Civil Liberties," 869.

21. Hutchinson et al., "Constitution Project's Task Force on Detainee Treatment," 334.

22. Charlie Savage, "Election to Decide Future Interrogation Methods in Terrorism Cases," *New York Times*, September 27, 2012. Some Republican candidates for the 2016 presidential nomination, including Carly Fiorina and Donald Trump, have indicated their support for waterboarding. Other candidates for the 2016 nomination have refused to say whether they would rule out waterboarding. Emily Atkin, "Carly Fiorina: Waterboarding Helped 'Keep Our Nation Safe,'" *Think Progress*, September 28, 2015.

23. Ed Pilkington, "Guantanamo Inmate Makes New Force-Feeding Complaint after Judge's Ruling," *Guardian*, June 3, 2014; Rebecca Gordon, "U.S. Torture Didn't End When Bush Left Office," *Nation*, December 15, 2014; see also Krysta Contino, Kevin Capuzzi, and Peter A. Clark, "Force-Feeding at Guantanamo: Medical, Ethical, and Legal Analysis," *Internet Journal of Law, Healthcare, and Ethics* 10, no. 1 (2014). Force-feeding of Guantanamo prisoners during hunger strikes began under the Bush administration. Andy

Worthington, "Torture in Guantanamo: The Force-Feeding of Hunger Strikers," *ACLU*, June 26, 2009, citing Clive Stafford Smith, "Gitmo: America's Black Hole," *Los Angeles Times*, October 5, 2007.

24. Agence France-Presse, "UN Officials: Force-Feeding Guantanamo Protesters Violates International Law," May 1, 2013.

25. Human Rights Watch, Submission to the United Nations Commission against Torture, October 20, 2014.

26. Julian Ku, "Is Force Feeding Always Illegal?," *Opinio Juris*, May 1, 2013.

27. The Bush administration itself claims to have waterboarded three prisoners in all and to have stopped waterboarding entirely after 2003. Those claims, however, have been disputed by Human Rights Watch, which claims that the Bush administration waterboarded additional prisoners after 2003. The prisoners were allegedly waterboarded by U.S. officials before being transferred to Libya for additional torture. "Delivered into Enemy Hands: U.S.-Led Abuse and Rendition of Opponents to Gaddafi's Libya," Human Rights Watch (2012).

28. Lauren Fox and Dustin Voltz, "Sen. Mark Udall, Discussing Secret CIA Report, Calls for Director's Resignation," *National Journal*, December 10, 2014.

29. Eric Posner, "Why Obama Won't Prosecute Torturers," *Slate.com*, December 9, 2014. Posner concludes, however, that prosecutions for torture during the Bush years would not have been successful in court and that "[t]he only way to ensure that U.S. officials will not use torture in the next national-security emergency is to elect presidents who won't authorize it."

## Chapter 14.
## The Obama Administration and Secrecy

1. Huma Khan, "On 'State Secrets,' Meet Barack W. Obama," *ABC News (Political Punch)*, April 10, 2009.

2. Christina E. Wells, "State Secrets and Executive Accountability," *Constitutional Commentary* 26, no. 3 (Summer 2010): 627.

3. Bruce Fein, "Czar Obama," *Slate.com*, April 9, 2009.

4. John Schwartz, "Obama Backs Off a Reversal on Secrets," *New York Times*, February 9, 2009; see also Marc Ambinder, "Obama Holds on to State Secrets Privilege in Jeppesen Case," *Atlantic*, June 12, 2009.

5. *Jewel v. NSA*, "Government Defendants' Memorandum in Support of Motion to Dismiss and for Summary Judgment," filed April 3, 2009.

6. Glenn Greenwald, "New and Worse Secrecy and Immunity Claims from the Obama DOJ," *Salon.com*, April 6, 2009.

7. Memorandum from Attorney General Eric Holder to Heads of Executive Departments and Agencies and Heads of Department Components, September 23, 2009.

8. Ibid.

9. Ibid.

10. Chris Edelson, *Emergency Presidential Power: From the Drafting of the Constitution to the War on Terror* (Madison: University of Wisconsin Press, 2013), 250.

11.  Wells, "State Secrets and Executive Accountability," 646 (emphasis in original), 650. When Wells wrote in 2010, she also hoped that the policy might turn out to be "a positive first step." However, developments since 2010 show that her concern that the Holder policy might turn out to be only symbolic was prescient.

12.  *Mohamed v. Jeppesen Dataplan, Inc.*, 614 F.3d 1070 (9th Cir. 2010) (*en banc*), *cert. denied*, 131 S. Ct. 2442 (2011).

13.  Ibid., at 1076.

14.  Ibid., at 1095 (Hawkins, J., dissenting).

15.  Ibid., at 1070.

16.  Ibid., at 1087, citing *El-Masri v. United States*, 479 F.3d 296 (3rd Cir. 2007), at 312 (emphasis omitted).

17.  *Jeppesen Dataplan Inc.*, at 1080.

18.  Ibid., at 1095 n. 1 (Hawkins, J., dissenting).

19.  *Jewel v. NSA*, Government's Motion to Dismiss and for Summary Judgment.

20.  *Jewel v. NSA*, 2013 U.S. Dist. LEXIS 94967 (N.D. Cal. July 8, 2013). The case had previously been dismissed by the district court on standing grounds, but that decision was overruled by the Ninth Circuit on appeal.

21.  *Jewel v. NSA*, 2015 U.S. Dist. LEXIS 16200 (N.D. Cal. Feb. 10, 2015), *19.

22.  Ibid., at *20.

23.  Louis Fisher, "Government Errors Are Shrouded in Secrecy," *National Law Journal*, March 10, 2014.

24.  Murtaza Hussain, "Obama DOJ's New Abuse of State Secrets Privilege Revealed," *Intercept*, February 14, 2014.

25.  *Mohamed v. Holder*, 995 F.Supp.2d 520 (E.D. Va. 2014), at 523–524.

26.  Ibid., at 524–525.

27.  *Mohamed v. Holder*, Plaintiff's Opposition to Defendant's Motion to Dismiss as a Result of Assertion of the State Secrets Privilege, July 7, 2014; see also Nick Baumann, "2008 Obama Would Have Slammed 2014 Obama for This Government Secrecy Case," *Mother Jones*, July 14, 2014.

28.  Michael J. Glennon, *National Security and Double Government* (New York: Oxford University Press, 2015), 2–3.

29.  Mary-Rose Papandrea, "Leaker Traitor Whistleblower Spy: National Security Leaks and the First Amendment," *Boston University Law Review* 94 (March 2014): 449, 451.

30.  Glenn Greenwald, "On the Espionage Act Charges against Edward Snowden," *Guardian*, June 22, 2013. It is worth noting that Greenwald is one of the journalists who made Snowden's revelations public, although that does not detract from the merits of Greenwald's observations here.

31.  See chapter 11.

32.  Greenwald, "On the Espionage Act Charges against Edward Snowden."

33.  Mike Masnick, "Obama Administration Has Declared War on Whistleblowers, Describes Leaks as 'Aiding the Enemy,'" *Techdirt.com*, June 21, 2013, quoting 2008 Obama campaign document.

34. Greenwald, "On the Espionage Act Charges against Edward Snowden."

35. Conor Friedersdorf, "Daniel Ellsberg: Snowden Kept His Oath Better Than Anyone in the NSA," *Atlantic*, July 25, 2014.

36. Steve Coll, "The Spy Who Said Too Much: Why the Administration Targeted a C.I.A. Officer," *The New Yorker*, April 1, 2013. The information Kiriakou gave to reporters about Abu Zubaydah providing useful information after being waterboarded was incorrect. Kiriakou later explained that his colleagues "told me it worked. . . . And that was a lie."

37. Ibid.

38. David Wise, "Leaks and the Law: The Story of Thomas Drake," *Smithsonian*, August 2011. Drake's prosecution began during the Bush administration. Emily Bazelon, "Obama's War on Journalists," *Slate.com*, May 14, 2013.

39. Ellen Nakashima, "Ex-NSA Manager Accepts Plea Bargains in Espionage Act Case," *Washington Post*, June 9, 2011.

40. Scott Shane, "No Jail Time in Trial over NSA Leak," *New York Times*, July 15, 2011.

41. Papandrea, "Leaker Traitor Whistleblower Spy: National Security Leaks and the First Amendment," 451–452.

42. Wise, "Leaks and the Law: The Story of Thomas Drake."

43. Ibid.

44. Ann E. Marimow, "Justice Department's Scrutiny of Fox News Reporter in Leak Case Draws Fire," *Washington Post*, May 20, 2013.

45. Glenn Greenwald, "Obama DOJ Formally Accuses Journalist in Leak Case of Committing Crimes," *Guardian*, May 20, 2013. There was speculation that Greenwald himself might face prosecution for his role in reporting on Snowden's NSA revelations, but the Department of Justice announced it would not prosecute Greenwald. Noam Cohen and Leslie Kaufman, "Blogger, with Focus on Surveillance, Is at Center of a Debate," *New York Times*, June 6, 2013; Mike Masnick, "Eric Holder Doesn't See Any Basis to Prosecute Glenn Greenwald . . . For Now," *Wired.com*, November 15, 2013.

46. The discussion here of those who have been prosecuted or threatened with prosecution is not an exhaustive account. See also Cora Currier, "Charting Obama's Crackdown on National Security Leaks," *ProPublica*, July 30, 2013; Kevin Poulsen, "Feds Drop Probe of NSA Wiretapping Whistleblower," *Wired*, April 26, 2011; Marisa Taylor and Jonathan S. Landay, "Obama's Crackdown Views Leaks as Aiding Enemies of U.S.," *McClatchy*, June 20, 2013.

47. Wells, "State Secrets and Executive Accountability," 650.

### Conclusion

1. Jack Goldsmith, *Power and Constraint* (New York: W. W. Norton, 2012), 24–26.

2. Nancy Kassop, "Rivals for Influence on Counterterrorism Policy: White House Political Staff versus Executive Branch Legal Advisors," *Presidential Studies Quarterly* 43, no. 2 ( June 2013). Kassop's conclusions may overlap with Glennon's (below) if the political and policy advisors she describes were part of or deferential to the national security bureaucracy Glennon describes as making most national security policy decisions.

3. Michael J. Glennon, *National Security and Double Government* (New York: Oxford University Press, 2015).

4. James Madison, Federalist No. 54, in Alexander Hamilton, John Jay, and James Madison, *The Federalist Papers*, ed. Michael A. Genovese (New York: Palgrave Macmillan, 2009) (hereinafter *The Federalist Papers*), 120.

5. Christopher Pyle, "Barack Obama and Civil Liberties," *Presidential Studies Quarterly* 42, no. 4 (December 2012): 877.

6. Madison would list the people first as "the primary control on the government." *The Federalist Papers*, Federalist No. 51, 120.

7. Glennon, *Double Government*, 39–49.

8. Louis Fisher, *Defending Congress and the Constitution* (Lawrence: University Press of Kansas, 2011).

9. Glennon, *Double Government*, 112.

10. David Gray Adler, "Presidential Powers Are Widely Misunderstood," *Idaho Statesman*, August 14, 2014. Adler argues that the press has undermined public understanding of the way the U.S. Constitution assigns power to the different branches of government.

11. Peter Shane, "Executive Branch Self-Policing in Times of Crisis: The Challenges for Conscientious Legal Analysis," *Journal of National Security Law and Policy* 5, no. 2 (July 2012): 507, 511, 512, 515.

# INDEX

Bush, George W., administration (*continued*) and, 3–5, 43–46, 84; NSA and, 52–53, 57–58; plenary power and, 18, 43–44, 47–51, 54, 56–59, 62–63, 65–66, 69, 85; PSP and, 44, 52–59, 109, 114; rule of law and, 7, 43–44, 76, 84–85, 91–92, 149–50, 161; sole organ doctrine and, 18, 50, 56–57, 90–92; state secrets privilege and, 7, 76–79, 152–54, 161; surveillance and, 44, 52–59, 109, 111–12, 114–15, 117–18, 121–22, 161; torture and, 7, 67–75, 78–79, 86, 147–51, 158, 161; TSP and, 52–53, 57–59, 109, 122, 155; unitary executive theory and, 4, 14, 43–44, 51, 68, 70, 72, 84–86, 88–89, 91–92, 115, 136, 144–45, 147, 161, 163. *See also under* OLC (Office of Legal Counsel)

Bybee, Jay S., 67–71, 74–75, 147, 163

Campanelli, M. Andrew, 49

Card, Andrew, 55–56

CAT (United Nations Convention against Torture and Other Cruel, Inhuman, or Degrading Treatment or Punishment), 78, 147

Central Intelligence Agency (CIA), 67, 69, 71–74, 78, 103–4, 148–50, 158

checks and balances (separation of powers): courts and, 20, 62–63, 98–99, 106; Madison and, 6, 48, 63, 107, 162; national security power and, 11–12; pre-9/11 national security power and, 22–23, 36–37; rule of law and, 19–20, 45, 84, 136; unitary executive theory and, 15–16, 105–6

Cheney, Dick, 6, 38–39, 43–44, 53, 55, 85

CIA (Central Intelligence Agency), 67, 69, 71–74, 78, 103–4, 148–50, 158

citizens, United States: military detention and, 61–63, 98–99, 136; no-fly list and, 156–57; surveillance and, 53, 156, 158; targeted killing of, 22, 86, 101–7

Clinton, Bill, administration, 92, 98

Combatant Status Review Tribunals (CSRTs), 63–65, 132, 137–38

Comey, James, 44, 55–56, 109

Common Article 3 of Geneva Conventions, 66, 73, 134, 147

Congress, United States: acquiescence of, 4, 22, 43–46, 59, 66, 83, 85, 92, 162; Article I

Declare War Clause and, 13–14, 28, 48–50, 93; Bush administration and, 43–51, 53–59, 66, 68, 84–85, 89–91; Constitution and, 13–14, 20, 24, 28, 48–50, 63, 93; extraordinary rendition, 84; foreign affairs and, 17–18; future changes and, 163; habeas corpus petitions and, 24, 35; military detention and, 61, 64, 143–44, 146; national security and, 13–15, 19; Obama administration and, 4, 7, 59, 84–85, 89, 95–101, 104, 143–44, 146, 162; plenary power and, 4, 11, 13, 85; Reagan administration and, 38; retroactive approval from, 19, 22, 28, 44–45, 79, 144; Roosevelt administration and, 24–27; surveillance and, 53–59; Truman administration and, 28–36, 92; unitary executive theory and, 17–19. *See also specific laws*

Constitution, United States: Article I Declare War Clause and, 13–14, 28, 48–50, 93; Article II Take Care Clause and, 30, 32, 34–35; Article II Vesting Clause and, 12–13, 24, 30, 32, 34, 48, 50, 68; Bush administration and, 12–13, 47–50, 54, 68, 90–93; Fifth Amendment and, 136–37; First Amendment and, 111, 123, 159; foreign affairs and, 38–39; Fourth Amendment and, 117, 119; military detention and, 61; national security power and, 7, 162; Obama administration and, 89, 92–93, 96–97, 103, 117; plenary power and, 12–14, 16–18, 21; rule of law and, 12, 14–15, 18–21, 45, 84, 136; sole organ doctrine and, 16–18; unitary executive theory and, 12–16, 19, 48; Yoo memos and, 47–50. *See also* Article II Commander in Chief Clause; checks and balances (separation of powers)

Convention against Torture and Other Cruel, Inhuman, or Degrading Treatment or Punishment (CAT), United Nations, 78, 147

courts: acquiescence of, 4, 162; Bush administration and, 14, 44, 60–62; checks and balances and, 20, 62–63, 98–99, 105–6; FISC and, 52–53, 59, 109–23, 125–26, 162; future changes and, 163; Nixon administration and, 37; Obama administration and, 109–12, 115–16, 157; plenary power and, 4, 11, 17–18; Roosevelt administration and, 24–27; Truman administration and, 29–34. *See also specific cases and judges*

Obama, Barack, administration: AUMF and, 100–102, 104–5, 136–37; Congress and, 4, 7, 59, 84–85, 89, 95–101, 143–44, 146, 162; Constitution and, 89, 92–93, 96–97, 103, 117; courts and, 4, 7, 85, 109–12, 115–16, 157; DOJ and, 117–18, 147–49, 152–56, 159; Executive Order 13567 and, 138; extraordinary rendition, 84, 152, 154–55; "faux law" and, 7, 45, 83, 95, 114, 126; national security power and, 3–6, 83–87, 161–62; plenary power and, 85; rule of law and, 7, 84–86, 88, 92–96, 99–101, 103, 126, 128, 149–50, 161, 163; sole organ doctrine and, 3–4, 6, 91–92, 94–95; state secrets privilege and, 7, 78–79, 83–84, 86, 152–60, 161; torture and, 7, 86, 147–51, 154–55, 158, 161–62; unitary executive theory and, 3–4, 6–7, 85–86, 92, 97, 115, 132, 136, 141, 143–45, 161, 163. *See also under* OLC (Office of Legal Counsel)

Obama administration, and military detention: overview of, 7, 127–32, 145–46, 161–62; force-feeding during hunger strikes and, 150; habeas corpus petitions and, 128, 139–40; military tribunals and, 7, 83, 86, 106, 128–30, 133–36, 161; prisoner transfer and release and, 128, 130, 135, 138, 140–45; without prosecution, 136–40

Obama administration, and military force: overview of, 7, 88–89, 161–62; ISIS and, 86, 99–101; Libya and, 4–5, 86, 89, 92–97, 102–3, 127; OLC memos and, 89, 91–96, 102–5; Syria and, 97–99, 162; targeted killing of U.S. citizens and, 22, 86, 101–7

Obama administration, and surveillance: overview of, 7, 108, 152, 161; bulk metadata collection and, 86, 108–16, 157; courts and, 109–12, 115–16; DOJ and, 117–18, 152–53; FAA and, 110, 121–22; "faux law" and, 114; FISA and, 109–11, 114, 116, 118, 121–22, 125, 156; FISC and, 109–23, 125–26, 162; NSA and, 108–11, 114–21, 124–26, 152, 155–58; PCLOB and, 112–13, 115, 118–19, 123–26; PRISM program and, 59, 119–20, 123–24; Section 702 program and, 86, 116–26

O'Connor, Sandra Day, 62, 98–99, 105–7

Office of Legal Counsel (OLC). *See* OLC (Office of Legal Counsel)

OLC (Office of Legal Counsel): extraordinary

rendition during Bush administration and, 79; future changes and, 163; military force during Bush administration and, 12–13, 43, 47–51, 89–94, 96, 102–3, 107; military force during Obama administration and, 43, 89–96, 102–5; rule of law and, 163; surveillance during Bush administration and, 53–57; targeted killing of U.S. citizens and, 102–3; torture during Bush administration and, 67–71, 67–75, 147–49

Papandrea, Mary-Rose, 158

Patriot Act of 2001, 109–11, 113–16, 125

PCLOB (Privacy and Civil Liberties Oversight Board), 112–13, 115, 117–19, 123–26

Periodic Review Board (PRB) hearings, 137–40

Pevehouse, Jon C., 14–15

Pfiffner, James P., 19–20, 44, 49, 59, 73

Philbin, Patrick, 54–55, 60

Pine, David A., 30–31

Pious, Dick, 4–5

plenary power: Bush administration and, 18, 43–44, 47–51, 54, 56–59, 62–63, 65–66, 69, 85; Congress and, 4, 11, 13, 85; Constitution and, 12–14, 16–18, 21; courts and, 4, 11, 17–18; FISA and, 38; Obama administration and, 85; Roosevelt administration and, 23–27, 32–33; Truman administration and, 28–33

Posner, Eric, 4, 14, 18–19

PRB (Periodic Review Board) hearings, 137–40

pre-9/11 national security power: overview of, 22–23; checks and balances and, 22–23, 36–37; Nixon administration and, 15, 36–38; Reagan administration and, 14, 22, 38–39, 92, 98; Roosevelt administration and, 15, 23–27, 32–33; Truman administration and, 15, 27–36, 39, 92; unitary executive theory and, 14, 19, 25–26, 28–30, 45. *See also* national security power

Presidential Surveillance Program (PSP), 44, 52–59, 109, 114

presidents. *See* checks and balances (separation of powers); plenary power; unitary executive theory; *and specific individuals*

PRISM program, 59, 119–20, 123–24

prisoner transfer and release, 128, 130, 135, 138, 140–45